CITIESPEOPLE**PLANET**

Herbert Girardet

For my grandchildren
Hallam, Milo, Fleur and Daisy

CITIESPEOPLEPLANET

Liveable Cities for a Sustainable World

Herbert Girardet

Published in Great Britain in 2004 by Wiley-Academy, a division of John Wiley & Sons Ltd

Copyright © 2004   John Wiley & Sons Ltd,
The Atrium, Southern Gate,
Chichester, West Sussex PO19 8SQ,
England
Telephone (+44) 1243 779777

Email (for orders and customer service enquiries): cs-books@wiley.co.uk
Visit our Home Page on www.wileyeurope.com or www.wiley.com

Other Wiley Editorial Offices

John Wiley & Sons Inc., 111 River Street, Hoboken, NJ 07030, USA

Jossey-Bass, 989 Market Street, San Francisco, CA 94103–1741, USA

Wiley-VCH Verlag GmbH, Boschstr. 12, D-69469 Weinheim, Germany

John Wiley & Sons Australia Ltd, 33 Park Road, Milton, Queensland 4064, Australia

John Wiley & Sons (Asia) Pte Ltd, 2 Clementi Loop #02–01, Jin Xing Distripark, Singapore 129809

John Wiley & Sons Canada Ltd, 22 Worcester Road, Etobicoke, Ontario, Canada M9W 1L1

Wiley also publishes its books in a variety of electronic formats. Some content that appears in print may not be available in electronic books.

British Library Cataloguing in Publication Data

A catalogue record for this book is available from the British Library

Hardback ISBN 0-470-86575-X

Paperback ISBN 0-470-85284-4

Typeset by Florence Production Ltd, Stoodleigh, Devon, UK

Printed and bound in Italy by Conti Tipocolor

This book is printed on acid-free paper responsibly manufactured from sustainable forestry in which at least two trees are planted for each one used for paper production.

Contents

Preface

Cities People Planet by Herbert Girardet is an impassioned plea for a different approach to cities. He argues that unless we change the way we live and use the resources within them, we may not survive. This powerful challenge should make us all think long and hard about our human dependence on the natural environment.

**Anne Power, Professor of Social Policy,
London School of Economics and Political Science**

Over the past decade I have been trying to fathom what sustainability means in a world of cities. I have been working as a consultant, filmmaker, academic and speaking at conferences in many parts of the world. The various documentaries I have produced allowed me to make connections between cities and their increasingly global hinterland, whilst also exploring environmental and social conditions within cities themselves.

Apart from using my own extensive library, I have also greatly benefited from the vast range of material on urban history and planning at the British Library. In addition I have also utilised a lot of material on the World Wide Web. Whilst I am aware that some of the websites that are listed in the endnotes could be redundant at some point in the future, I have tried my best to draw on websites that are likely to be there for some time to come.

I wish to thank Mick Csaky of Antelope Productions for allowing me to draw on the work we did together on the TV series *The People's Planet* for NHK TV, Tokyo, CNN and the Discovery Channel just before the start of the new millennium. I have also used material from other documentaries such as *Halting the Fires and Deadline 2000*, which I produced for Channel 4, London. In addition, I have drawn on three of my previous books, *Far From Paradise*, *The Gaia Atlas of Cities* and *Creating Sustainable Cities*.

I have also utilised my nine-week stint as Thinker in Residence in Adelaide in 2003 in writing this book. Compiling my report *Creating a Sustainable Adelaide*, www.planning.sa.gov.au/csa/report.pdf, made me aware of how working towards environmental sustainability can also have tremendous social and economic benefits. Many recommendations in my report are now being implemented. I wish to think South Australia premier Mike Rann, and my colleagues in Adelaide, particularly Trixie Mead, Margie Caust and Ann Clancy, for supporting and coordinating my work. Also a big thanks to David Lloyd for providing pictures for the book.

The text of the book also draws on my consultancy work for UN Habitat, the City of Vienna, the Greater London Authority, the Corporation of London and the London Development Agency. I particularly wish to thank John Joplin, a co-trustee of the Sustainable London Trust, who initiated our joint report *Creating a Sustainable London*.

When John Wiley & Sons commissioned me to write *Cities People Planet*, I was both elated and somewhat daunted, because this meant a year or more without a significant income stream. I was therefore delighted and very grateful when James and Margaret Sainsbury came to my aid to substantially support the book, allowing me to work on it without feeling pressured. So a big thanks to both of you.

I wish to thank Maggie Toy for commissioning this book and to Helen Castle, Famida Rasheed and Vivienne Wickham for seeing it through to publication. I am grateful to Sally Lansdell for copy editing the book and to Sarah Moore and Kelly Gray for meticulously proof reading and typesetting the book.

I particularly wish to thank my wife Barbara for her love and support, and for putting up with me sitting at the dinner table and mumbling unintelligibly about the ecological footprints of cities. I know of people whose obsessive writing of a new book has fatally damaged their marriage. I am pleased to say that we have come out of this experience unscathed.

Herbert Girardet
October, 2004

CHAPTER 1

Big Feet, Small Planet

This book is about novel ways of looking at urban living. In the last 100 years we have acquired the capacity to see the earth from above—first looking down from airplanes, then taking pictures with cameras mounted on satellites. These views have revealed vast land areas across the world punctuated by dense urban clusters. The growth of large cities and their transport systems—connecting urban districts, and linking cities to each other and to the remotest regions of the planet—is a novel development that has enormous consequences for humanity, and for all life on earth.

As we take off or land in a plane, we can observe the awesome urban structures we have created—clusters of tall buildings in city centres; roads full of motor vehicles; factories and warehouses; high-rise apartment buildings and suburban sprawl; and farms and forests beyond the edge of the city, intersected by railway lines and motorways. The crucial dependence of cities on the land beyond their periphery seems obvious when seen from above, yet it gets barely a mention in the literature. An urbanising humanity has come to dominate much of the surface of the earth.

The job of urban planners and managers is to create spatial structures that satisfy the needs of city people. We want them to provide a secure habitat for us, to allow us to move about our cities efficiently, and to provide pleasant spaces for work, for recreation and for meeting people. We want urban environments that are free from pollution and in which wastes don't accumulate.

But it is time that we also got to grips with our impacts beyond the boundaries of our cities.

Humans have always affected the environment from which they draw their sustenance. Hunting and the use of fire by our ancestors had significant impacts on living creatures and their habitats. Farmers throughout history have significantly modified the landscapes they work and inhabit. But urban society, with its fossil fuel-powered industrial, farming and transport systems, has had unprecedented impacts on nature. Our numbers are larger than ever before, and our power to affect the global environment, has reached a critical stage. We need to reverse the collision course between humans and nature on which we now find ourselves, and this book suggests that this is, above all else, a challenge for city people.

Hong Kong
This urban landscape could not have existed 100 years ago. It is entirely dependent on vast inputs from elsewhere — food, energy, timber and other resources.

Urban consumption and waste disposal are threatening both nature and human existence. In the last 30 years a third of the natural world has been obliterated.[1] But as a consequence, we are also starting to learn an important lesson—that we damage the world's life-support system at our peril. We are faced with a new imperative: modern living needs to be in harmony with the planet—and this is a challenge to individuals, business and government, and also to urban planners. Science, technology, individual action and government policies can be harnessed for restoring the health of our planet. Today, millions of people across the world are working to try to improve the condition of the global environment.

These are the main themes that this book is seeking to explore: can a world of ever-larger cities be sustainable—environmentally, socially and economically? Can cities continue to prosper if they significantly increase their resource productivity? Can they mimic natural ecosystems and transform themselves into circular, not linear, systems? How can we create cities of physical beauty, social diversity and cultural vigour that are also sustainable economically and environmentally? How can we put the pulsing heart of conviviality back into our cities?

Across the world, we need a revolution in urban problem solving, finding ways of making cities 'future proof'. The director general of the 1992 Rio Earth Summit, Maurice Strong, sums these issues up well: 'The battle to ensure that our planet remains a hospitable and sustainable home for the human species will be won or lost in the major urban areas.'[2]

AN URBAN PLANET

In the last 100 years, an extraordinary change has occurred on the face of the earth: cities are becoming our primary habitat. In 1900, 15 per cent of a global population of 1.5 billion people lived in cities. By 2000, 47 per cent of a global population of 6 billion lived in cities. In 1900, four cities of around one million—Beijing, Tokyo, Delhi and London—were the largest cities on earth. By 2000, there were 200 cities of one million, 100 between one and ten million, and some 20 megacities of more than ten million people. By 2030, 60 per cent of the world population, or 4.9 billion people, are expected to live in urban areas.[3]

All-out urbanisation is fundamentally changing the condition of humanity and our relationship to the earth. We have been undergoing a staggering transformation: from living in a world of farms, villages and small towns, we are transforming ourselves into an urban species. From relying primarily on nature's local annual harvest, more and more of us are drawing on global food and timber supplies. From drawing on local energy sources, we have switched to tapping into stores of non-renewable energy resources across the world. From leading locally self-sufficient lives, more and more of us are becoming citizens of a human-centred planet.

Megacities of 10 million people or more are by far the largest structures ever to appear on the face of the earth. They reach deep underground, rise hundreds of metres into the air and stretch out horizontally over several hundred thousand hectares, with transport routes linking them to each other and to a global hinterland. With millions of citizens pursuing a vast diversity of activities—in commercial enterprises, markets, service industries and cultural endeavours—large modern cities are the most complex manifestation of human activity ever to emerge.

For simplicity's sake I use the word *city* to encompass both towns and cities. The definition of the word city varies greatly, depending on how much surrounding countryside is included within urban boundaries.

> *For instance, the current population of most of the world's largest areas including London, Los Angeles, Shanghai, Beijing, Jakarta, Dhaka and Bombay can vary by many millions of inhabitants in any year, depending on which boundaries are used to define their populations.*[4]

The main task of this book is to outline imaginative and realistic options for change. More often than not, the tools, techniques and partnerships that can help us create liveable cities can also be central to creating a sustainable relationship between people and planet. Urban growth has been well documented, but less so the growth of urban ecological impacts. My primary concern is not with urban growth per se, but rather with its implications both in terms of global use of resources and human living conditions. To make current urban lifestyles possible, cities are sucking in resources from all over the world. Located on just 2 per cent of the world's land surface, they use 75 per cent of its resources.[5] If the energy use of urban food supply systems was included, this figure would be even higher. In the USA, the number of people fed per farm worker has grown more than sixfold, from 15 in 1950 to 96 in 1998, by a massive scaling up of the use of farming technology.[6] In an urbanising world, the combined ecological footprints of cities extend to much of the earth's productive land.

São Paulo panorama
Never have urban landscapes, such as São Paulo with 18 million people, and sprawling over hundreds of thousands of square kilometres, been possible before.

Large modern cities, as centres of human endeavour, tend to regard themselves as centres of the universe and have effectively declared their independence from nature. And yet, they are vitally dependent on its integrity. American economist Robert Constanza has valued the world's 'ecosystem services' at $33 trillion per year—almost twice the combined global GNP of $18 trillion, which is primarily generated by urban-based economic activity.[7] Ecosystem services include absolute necessities such as water supply, climate regulation, nutrient cycling, soil formation and pollination, as well as recreational services, all of which city people ultimately require for their existence.

As the urban visionary Patrick Geddes insisted half a century ago, it is crucial to understand cities as being embedded in their rural hinterland. Today, on a globalising planet, cities need to see themselves as part of a worldwide hinterland on whose ecosystem services they ultimately depend.

Can we lead enjoyable urban lives while minimising our impact on the local and global environment? City officials are usually preoccupied with pressing issues such as housing provision, public works, policing, transport, education and health care. Yet it is vital not to lose sight of wider and longer-term perspectives that underpin the viability of their cities. Ecology is the science of 'home making'. In a world of large cities, we urgently need to learn to create sustainable urban habitats. It is therefore very important to understand our cities as complex systems that coexist in a dynamic relationship with the world's ecosystems. This approach adds a new dimension to urban planning and management, and requires us to address local and global issues at the same time. These are new challenges for city authorities as well as citizens. For this purpose we need vibrant new partnerships between governments, local authorities, urban communities, NGOs and the private sector.

CREATING SUSTAINABLE CITIES

What, then, is a sustainable city? Here is my attempt at a definition:

> A 'sustainable city' enables all its citizens to meet their own needs and to enhance their well-being, without degrading the natural world or the lives of other people, now or in the future.

We have to ask ourselves what specific measures need to be taken to create sustainable urban habitats, and how environmental and social concerns can be brought together into one compelling win–win scenario. The world community has vigorously addressed these issues since the early 1990s, starting with Agenda 21, the primary outcome of the 1992 Rio Earth Summit.[8] The Aalborg Charter, which was produced by the cities and towns of Europe in 1994, states this:

> We understand that our present urban lifestyle, in particular our patterns of division of labour and functions, land-use, transport, industrial production, agriculture, consumption, and leisure activities, and hence our standard of living, make us essentially responsible for many environmental problems humankind is facing. This is particularly relevant as 80 per cent of Europe's population live in urban areas.[9]

It further states that environmental sustainability means maintaining rather than depleting the world's natural capital, and that actions should urgently be taken to assure that the consumption of renewable material, water and energy resources does not exceed the rate at which natural systems can replenish themselves. Many new jobs can be created that contribute to both the environmental and economic sustainability of communities.

The Istanbul Declaration on Human Settlements, arising out of the Istanbul UN City Summit of 1996, endorses the universal goals of ensuring adequate shelter for all and making human settlements more liveable, equitable and sustainable.

> *In order to sustain our global environment and improve the quality of living in our human settlements, we commit ourselves to sustainable patterns of production, consumption, transportation and settlements development; pollution prevention; respect for the carrying capacity of ecosystems; and the preservation of opportunities for future generations. In this connection, we shall cooperate in a spirit of global partnership to conserve, protect and restore the health and integrity of the Earth's ecosystem.*[10]

In the Local Government Declaration to the 2002 UN Johannesburg Earth Summit, representatives from cities around the world issued expressed similar ideas:

> *With half of the world's population now living in urban settlements, and with the world's population due to grow to 8 billion by 2025 . . . sustainable urban management and development is one of the critical issues for the 21st century. National states cannot, on their own, centrally manage and control the complex, fast-moving, cities and towns of today and tomorrow—only strong decentralised local governments, in touch with and involving their citizens, and working in partnership with national governments, are in a position to do so.*[11]

CITIES AND NATIONAL ECONOMIES

An important issue for conceptualising sustainable urban development is to understand that cities are engines of economic power. They are the places where production is concentrated, where great wealth is generated and where most consumption takes place. They are the control centres of economic, political and media activity. National economies are embedded in and controlled from cities: 'the steady increase in the level or urbanisation since 1950 reflects the fact that the size of the world's economy has grown many times since then'.[12] In fact, the world economy has grown no less than fifteenfold since 1950 and this has certainly helped to improve people's standard of living. But there is a price to pay: for instance, in many parts of the world forests are shrinking as the value of global trade in forest products has climbed, from $29 billion in 1961 to $139 billion in 1998. And fisheries are collapsing as fish exports rise, growing nearly fivefold in value since 1970 to reach $52 billion in 1997.[13]

With half of humanity living and working in cities, the other half increasingly depends on them for their economic survival. They profoundly affect rural economies far beyond urban boundaries. As better roads are built and access to urban products and information systems is assured, rural people aspire to urban standards of living, and the mindset to go with them. Cities have come to define the state of human consciousness. It is therefore vital for city people to understand more clearly that the deteriorating condition of the global environment is primarily due to urban resource use.

The concentration of intense economic processes and high levels of consumption in cities stimulate their demands for resources. Urban agglomerations and their consumption patterns have become the dominant feature of the human presence on earth, fundamentally changing humanity's relationship to its host planet and ecosystems. Since most population and economic growth in the coming decades will continue to occur in urban areas, the overexploitation of natural resources could become even more acute, unless we find different ways of managing them.

In developing countries people migrating from rural to urban areas usually expect substantial increases in living standards, which also means per capita increases in resource consumption. A critical issue for the coming years is that the two most populous and traditionally rural countries, China and India, are urbanising rapidly. In China in particular, economic growth has been hovering between 7 and 9 per cent a year since the 1980s, with industrialisation and urbanisation closely linked. In the last ten years, some 400 new urban centres have been created. In the next two decades, about 12 million people are expected to relocate from rural to urban areas every year and China is planning to build another 400 new cities with populations averaging 600,000 people.[14]

India too, with economic growth of 6 to 8 per cent a year, is engaged in a rapid process of industrialisation and urbanisation. In both countries, as disposable incomes grow, substantial increases in energy consumption are occurring as people switch from using firewood and charcoal to electricity and kerosene and to utilising energy-intensive products and services.[15] Major changes in diet towards greater meat consumption and increases in per capita demand for timber and paper also have major environmental implications, with impacts often occurring far away.

CITIES, ENERGY AND CLIMATE

The foundations for the world's unprecedented urban growth were laid in the 19th and early 20th centuries. It was occurring mainly in the north, as a result of the spread of industrialisation and the rapid increase in the use of fossil fuel-based technologies. Today, the world's largest and fastest-growing cities are emerging in the south, because of urban-industrial development, mechanisation of agriculture and also, in some places, as a result of dramatic rural decline.

Large modern cities are, first and foremost, products of the development of fossil fuel technologies. The cover image of this book shows how, looking down from space at night, astronauts can see a 'new Milky Way', our brilliantly illuminated planet—vast city clusters lit up by millions of light bulbs and by the flares of oil wells and refineries. While our ancestors sought to assure steady supplies of firewood and charcoal, we turn on electric or gas appliances with the flick of a switch, hardly aware of the power station, refinery or gas field that we tap into.

Today's cities are gas guzzlers par excellence. They use energy very differently from those in the past. Most of the world's energy is used in cities and for their benefit—by cities themselves and by the farming, industrial production and transport systems that supply them. Historically there has never been a city of more than a couple of million people that was not running on fossil fuels. Without routine use of coal, oil and gas, the growth of megacities would not have occurred. All their internal activities—local transport, electricity supply, home living, services provision and manufacturing—crucially depend on using fossil fuels.

In 1992, seven million Londoners used around 20 million tonnes of oil equivalent per year, or two supertankers a week, and discharged some 60 million tonnes of carbon dioxide into the atmosphere. But at least the same amount of fuel again is required to bring in goods and products from outside, with more and more being flown in halfway around the world.[16]

Moving people and goods across vast distances is becoming the norm. Low transport costs have rendered distances irrelevant, plugging cities into an increasingly global hinterland. The actual location of settlements is becoming less important as cities are connected together in a global transport web based on cheap fossil fuels. This process is often facilitated by substantial government subsidies on transport infrastructure.[17]

Today we don't really live in a *civilisation* but in a *mobilisation*—of natural resources, people and products. The world's major transport systems start and end in cities. They are the nodes from which mobility emanates, along roads, railway lines, aircraft routes and telephone lines. Cities in the rich countries also sprawl ever outwards along urban motorways and railway lines to their suburbs and shopping malls and beyond, while their centre is often devoid of life outside business hours. They are both the origin and the destination of this mobilisation that has come to define our new existence as *amplified humans*—people amplified by the power of modern technology. We have changed profoundly as a result, with technologies now merged into our very being and the experience of nature becoming ever more distant.

We rarely have cause to reflect on the environmental impacts of our daily energy use, unless we choke on exhaust fumes on a busy local street. But again, there is a price to pay: waste gases, such as nitrogen dioxide and sulphur dioxide, discharged by chimneys and exhaust pipes, affect the health of city people themselves and, beyond urban boundaries, that of forests and farmland downwind. And most of the increase of carbon dioxide in the atmosphere is attributable to combustion in the world's cities. Concern about climate change is now shared by virtually all the world's climatologists. The earth's atmosphere has become the sink for billions of tonnes of urban waste gases every year.

Since the beginning of the industrial revolution, carbon dioxide in the atmosphere has increased by some 30 per cent, from 280 to 370 parts per million, and average temperatures on earth have risen by 0.6 degrees centigrade. According to the Intergovernmental Panel on Climate Change (IPPC), by the year 2100 average temperatures are expected to rise by up to 5.8 degrees centigrade. And the climate boomerang could hit cities especially severely: rising sea levels in particular will take a heavy toll on cities because many are located on low ground close to the sea. Already the sea level has risen by around 20 centimetres and could rise by up to 90 centimetres by 2100.[18] Robert Watson, former head of the IPCC, says:

> *The 1990s was the hottest decade of the last century and the*
> *warming in the 20th century was warmer than anything in the last*

Flyover in Tokyo
Today we don't really live in a 'civilisation', but in a 'mobilisation', of resources, products and people.

1,000 years in the Northern Hemisphere. We will see a drier summer in arid and semi-arid areas which will make water management much more difficult in the future. Major ecosystems such as coral reefs and forests will suffer from the rising temperatures as never before.[19]

Global climate change is becoming an irrefutable reality and energy consumption by cities is directly implicated. All over the world glaciers are melting. Billions of people are experiencing the ever-growing incidence of storms, floods, forest fires and irregular weather patterns. In December 2003 Munich Reinsurance, the world's biggest reinsurance company, expressed alarm about a sharp increase in weather-related disasters. Some 20,000 people were killed by that year's summer heat wave in Europe, which is widely attributed to global warming.[20]

CITIES AS ECO-TECHNICAL SYSTEMS

Much effort has been taken to define the identity of modern cities. In Chapter 6, I describe them as 'eco-technical systems'. Biology still characterises cities in many ways: in gardens, ponds and urban forests, they invariably contain the remnants of a great variety of ecosystems; they rely on farming for a steady supply of food; and their human inhabitants continue to reproduce and have children. But modern cities have increasingly become a new fusion of ecology and technology. In the last 100 years, they have come to be defined ever more by fossil fuel-based energy and transportation systems, technical infrastructure, industrial production and global communications.

Worldwide, urbanisation is closely associated with increased production and consumption. Compared with rural dwellers, city people in developing countries have much higher levels of consumption, with massively increased throughput of fossil fuels, metals, timber, meat and manufactured products. On the one hand this means significantly increased standards of living, on the other hand there is the need to deal with much larger amounts of solid, liquid and gaseous wastes. With determination, modern cities *can* make efficient use of resources. How can we assure that appropriate policies to achieve this potential will be implemented?

Recent proposals for improving the resource productivity of modern production and consumption by a factor of four, or even ten, apply directly

The return of the tram
In the French city of Montpellier a new, state-of-the-art tram system has persuaded many drivers to leave their cars at home and to go to work by public transport instead.

to managing our urban systems.[21] Cities are centres of human knowledge and today, more than ever before, this must also mean knowledge of the world and how we can reduce our impact on it. This is as much about education, information dissemination and participation as about better uses of technology. The critical issue for a sustainable future is: can cities function as sustainable, self-regulating systems *internally*, as well as in their relationship to the *outside* world?

Optimising the urban use of resources is a global challenge. Says American author Paul Hawken:

> *We're in a world in which everybody cannot have what the average*
> *Japanese or United States citizen has. And the point is that the*
> *rest of the world is aiming for that and wants it desperately. And*
> *to a certain extent they deserve it just as much as you and I.*
> *And so the question is, how can we reconfigure the world in*
> *such a way that we dramatically reduce our impact upon the*

environment, and at the same time really improve the quality of
life for people both in the southern developing countries as well as
industrialised countries?

A wide range of new technical options is becoming available to us. Wind and solar power, fuel cell technology, novel solid waste and sewage recycling systems are all on the way to becoming cost competitive with older urban technologies. New insulation materials can make buildings highly energy efficient, minimising the need for heating and cooling. Buildings can become net producers rather than consumers of energy. The market for these technologies is booming worldwide, driven by increased international and national legislation and regulation. In 1999, the OECD estimated that it was worth $300 billion and predicted a doubling by 2009. A wide range of new local jobs is associated with this market, in many disciplines from research, manufacturing and installation to marketing and consultancy. These new options will be discussed in much more detail in the following chapters.

CREATING LIVEABLE CITIES

In a world in which most people spend most of their time in cities, people need to be able to enjoy stimulating, diverse, clean, safe and healthy urban environments. Innovative planners, architects and civil engineers all over the world are working to make liveable cities a tangible reality, but much more still needs to be done. The key features of liveable cities are the widespread presence of nature; clean, attractive public spaces and buildings; walkable city centres and neighbourhoods; and a vibrant and diverse street culture.

Great cities such as London, New York or Paris are widely celebrated as the epitome of cultural development. But in these cities many people can't afford to go to concerts, the theatre or the opera. A liveable city makes sure that these issues are addressed and that the participation of all people in a diverse variety of cultural activities is assured. We also need to remember that cities aren't only places for people, but that trees, plants and animals also need their own distinct urban habitats.

Liveability and sustainability are intimately connected, but they are not always the same thing. Here are three examples from London.

When Joseph Bazalgette created London's sewage system in the 19th century, his brief was to stop people's exposure to human wastes. By building a complex web of sewers, London's rivers were cleaned up and the city's sewage was disposed of into the Thames estuary, out of harm's way. But most of it was not recycled and returned to the land that fed Londoners. London became more liveable, but not more sustainable.

After smog blanketed the city and killed 4,000 people in December 1952, Britain's Clean Air Act of 1956 was introduced as a result. Burning smoke-less coal was made mandatory and London's power generation was moved to locations outside the city. As a result, the air quality was greatly improved, making it a much more liveable city. However, the carbon dioxide produced by London's energy system was, if anything, increased due to longer power lines. London became more liveable, but less sustainable.

On the other hand, the London congestion charge, introduced in February 2003, reduced traffic in the inner city by some 18 per cent and substantially increased the use of public transport. This has improved London's air quality and reduced its discharge of carbon monoxide, making it both more liveable and more sustainable.

Creating more liveable urban environments increases people's sense of well-being. After the destruction of cities in the Second World War, planners welcomed the opportunities for rebuilding Europe's cities. In many places they replaced old narrow urban streets with a brave new world of tower blocks and wide thoroughfares for car traffic. But the construction of vast new concrete buildings and the triumph of the motor car combined to create increasingly inhospitable cities. Negative reactions to high-rise living caused a loss of confidence among planners. Cars were a great symbol of individual freedom, but they also became a menace in the urban environment. Many cities made brave attempts to reduce people's dependence on private motor cars and to assure integration of public transport into daily urban life.

Planners have increasingly used public consultation exercises to reach a consensus on liveable and people-sensitive urban design. Allowing people's creativity to become an important input into planning has become a key chal-lenge in the new quest to bring 'conviviality' back into our cities. How can we create cities of cultural vigour, physical beauty, thriving natural habitats and opportunities for lively social encounters that are also economically and environmentally sustainable at the same time?

Liveability is just as important for developed as for developing countries. In the rapidly growing cities of developing countries, poverty and environ-mental pollution are commonplace. The most urgent issue here is to create acceptable living conditions, rather than reducing urban impacts on the regional and global environment. As many as 50 per cent of people live in squatter camps without adequate water supplies, sewage systems or any other services. Never before have so many people faced such appalling environmental conditions. Diseases such as cholera, typhoid and TB, well known in Europe 150 years ago, are now occurring in many developing cities, with epidemics threatening particularly the poorest communities.

Urbanist Jane Jacobs says:

> The pseudo science of planning seems almost neurotic in its determination to imitate empiric failure and ignore empiric success. To create better cities all over the world, both active public participation and innovative design are essential. Much work has been done to collect examples of best urban practices and policies around the world, featuring novel approaches to architecture, public space design, energy systems, urban infrastructure and waste management. It is critical for these to be disseminated as widely as possible.[22]

WHAT FUTURE FOR VILLAGES?

The world's two million villages are losing out to cities.[23] Their economic dependence on urban centres is growing all the time and rural–urban migration is continuing to sap their energy. Mechanisation of agriculture is reducing rural job opportunities and is causing the amalgamation of farms. In some parts of the world, major environmental changes such as soil erosion, salinisation and loss of forest cover have been contributing to the decline of rural economies. Villages are being swamped increasingly by the manifestations of urban culture, partly as a result of rural electrification, which has thus become a mixed blessing.

In Europe and North America, there has been some reversal of the outflow of people from villages to cities as a result of the ubiquitous use of the motor car and the desire of city people to own second homes, but this, too, is often being experienced as detrimental by village communities that cannot compete with the prices that city people can pay for village houses and cottages. As a result, villages near cities are often becoming dormitories, and in remoter but picturesque locations, village houses used as second homes stand empty for much of the year.

However, in many parts of the world, village life is by no means dead. Many villages maintain their vibrant, traditional cultures, with tourism sometimes being a significant element within this trend. Ecotourism can make a substantial contribution to village economies. Another feature of the resurgence of village life in some parts of the world is the desire of people from the city to set up their full-time homes in villages and to try to participate actively in local life. New communication technologies such as broadband have substantially contributed to this trend, allowing people in villages to do work that could only be done in cities until recently.

MAKING IT HAPPEN

Cities cannot exist indefinitely by routinely using non-renewable resources from ever more distant hinterlands, and using the biosphere, the oceans and the atmosphere as a sink for their wastes. In a world of cities, sustainable development must be sustainable *urban* development. There will be no sustainable world without sustainable cities. The challenge is to create a new relationship between cities and nature, while also creating a more equitable relationship between people.

Solar building, Gelsenkirchen
This solar powered building in Germany, gives a vivid impression of the new solar architecture that will transform our cities.

Europe, America, Japan and Australia, with their unprecedented dependence on fossil fuel-based technologies and processes, their complex technical infrastructure and their ever-growing consumerism, are currently the most unsustainable regions of the planet. But as developing countries pursue economic and urban growth, they also have to confront the same problems.

In recent years the social agenda has dominated discussions on the future of cities. In many areas of the world, riots have become part of the vocabulary of people who feel alienated and abandoned. A great deal of effort has gone into addressing unemployment, deprivation, apathy, crime and social discontent.

The convergence of *economic* and *environmental* sustainability offers tremendous new opportunities. In the age of globalisation, local jobs are becoming a rare commodity. In many towns and cities, the commercial priorities of companies, rather than democratic decision making, have come to determine people's well-being. This needs to be challenged. Municipal authorities, as the elected representatives of local people, should seek to play an active role in ensuring a sense of continuity for their populace, and this should certainly include economic stability.

It is beginning to dawn on decision makers that regeneration and environmentally sustainable development offer tremendous new opportunities for creating local jobs, shifting employment from extractive and polluting industries towards resource conservation—enhancing recycling and the energy efficiency of cities and individual buildings. Seeing the potential of their cities as environmentally, socially and economically sustainable systems offers city authorities an exciting range of new policy options.

In recent years, cities all over the world have been wrestling with the implementation of sustainable development. It would be an illusion to think that the necessary changes can be achieved only by top-down public policy. Sustainability can only work with strong popular involvement and participation. In fact, the most successful examples of policy development and implementation are driven by strong public demand and the active collaboration of municipal authorities, NGOs and neighbourhood groups.

LESSONS OF HISTORY

All over the world tourists flock to old cities that excel because of their beautiful buildings and design, such as Prague, Salzburg, Burgos, Kyoto, Udaipur, Taroudant, Xian or Timbuktu. People love visiting cities with an ancient history because they provide a sense of continuity that is often lacking in modern cities. For creating great cities in the 21st century, it is useful for us to learn from history in the awareness that settlements, at best, are magnificent manifestations of human creativity. From their very origins people have planned their settlements and there is much that we can learn from the ideas and design concepts that have been adopted throughout history. Most cities in the past were small and human-scale places created for walking and this has defined their essence. Can we create convivial, charismatic cities today?

Many old cities are manifestations of a *culture* of sustainability, passing on the baton of urban stewardship from generation to generation. Historically, many traditional cities grew and prospered by assuring sustainable supplies of food and forest products from the surrounding countryside. This is true of medieval European cities such as Siena or Dinkelsbuehl, with their concentric rings of market gardens, forests, orchards, farm and grazing land, as well as of many cities in Asia, where this practice continues today. Future cities can learn a great deal from this model, even if we cannot simply import traditional practices into the 21st century unchanged.

The history of human settlements is full of magnificent achievement as well as misery, decline and despair. While many have existed continuously for hundreds or even thousands of years, others have dissolved into heaps of dust surrounded by desert. They imploded after devastating the local environments from which they drew their resources, or as a result of social cataclysm and war. Such examples show that there are limits to the growth of cities, in the past, as well as today.

The next three chapters try to develop a historical perspective on the rise and, sometimes, the fall of cities, starting with the very earliest human settlements.

CHAPTER 2

In the Beginning

The eminent author Louis Mumford said 50 years ago: 'If we would lay a new foundation for urban life, we must understand the historic nature of the city.'[1]

This statement is highly significant, particularly at a time when many cities across the world are growing at an unprecedented scale. Many historic cities continue to thrive after thousands of years. But many others have dissolved into heaps of rubble and dust. In this urban age, it is important to know what is likely to assure the long-term existence of cities and what contributes to their decline.

This chapter starts by looking at the very first human settlements and ends in Athens 2,300 years ago. I believe that early history has much to teach us about creating liveable and sustainable cities today.

The history of human settlements starts with hunter-gatherer bands setting up temporary camps or occupying caves in areas where fruits, nuts, fish and game were plentiful. For hundreds of thousands of years, our ancestors roamed the forests, savannahs, river valleys and coastal landscapes of the world. Marshall Sahlin's seminal book *Stone Age Economics* strongly emphasised that stone-age hunter-gatherers often led lives of considerable material security and even affluence. Theirs was a low-density lifestyle, requiring them to have access to large areas of land on which they shared food resources with other living species.[2]

Today, no more than minimal traces of the camps and settlements of our hunter-gatherer ancestors remain. They only left behind their own fossilised bones and the animal bone and stone tools they used. Initially, they lived in Africa and then, as they migrated outwards and onwards, they became a global species, setting up camp in suitable environments all over the world.

Hunter-gatherers also left their traces in the form of charcoal deposits—at their campsites and in their surrounding landscapes. They are now known to have significantly modified their living environment through the large-scale, deliberate use of fire. In Australia, for instance, the appearance of aboriginals some 60,000 years ago resulted in significant changes in the composition of the indigenous fauna and flora, with fire-loving eucalypts and open grasslands favourable for kangaroos and other grazers spreading across the continent.[3]

The enigmatic rock paintings of hunter-gatherers in Australia and also in Africa, dating back tens of thousands of years, are another important legacy. They graphically demonstrate the ancient origins of conscious cultural expression. Caves offered a secure home to our ancestors and painting and decorating go back a long time. Some of the magnificent stone-age cave paintings found in France, Spain and other parts of the world date to tens of

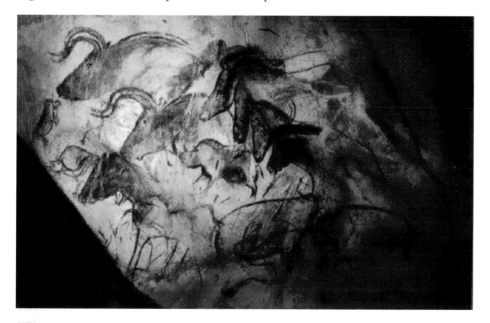

Cave painting, Chauvet, France
The history of human artistic creativity dates back tens of thousands of years. Human consciousness is not only a feature of modern society.

thousands of years ago. They offer tantalising glimpses of the sophisticated psychology and artistic skills of our forebears. The oldest and largest found so far, the Cave de Chauvet-Pont-d'Arc, in the Ardèche, is dated at least 30,000 BC. Its red and black drawings and engravings portray a wide range of animals—bears, horses, mammoths, bisons, lions, panthers and rhinoceroses. Its 300 paintings are as vivid and skilful as any found at the famous cave of Lascaux, dated at around 13,000 BC. Some 350 caves with paintings and engravings have been found in Europe so far, half of these in France. Many are located in river valleys or in coastal locations. Today, some are deep underwater and may never be fully explored, since sea levels during the last ice age were 115 metres lower than today.[4]

The beginnings of farming go back to around 10,000 BC. The emergence of settled living, with tens or even hundreds of people inhabiting one shared space, was only possible through the deliberate concentration of food production on clearly defined areas of land. This was a dramatic departure from nomadic hunting and gathering. The compelling logic of agriculture is that it yields more food per unit area of land, allowing more people to live in a given area, enabling them to lead a sedentary lifestyle. But it also introduces new challenges: keeping land used for growing crops productive on a continuous basis, through manipulation and enhancement of soil fertility, and the protection and storage of crops between growing seasons.[5]

By 9,000 BC there is evidence of farming in places as far apart as the Near and Middle East, India, the Far East and Mesoamerica. Many of today's staple crops—wheat, barley, oats, millet, rice, pulses, potatoes and maize—were cultivated and cattle, pigs, sheep, donkeys, camels and llamas were domesticated in different regions of the world. Farm implements such as hoes, sickles, ploughs and threshing devices came into widespread use. Fish were caught with harpoons, nets and fish poison. Trade spread ever wider as travel by land, rivers and the sea advanced.

Hunting and gathering gave way not only to sedentary farming, but also to cattle herding, particularly in places such as East Africa. These herding cultures are now known to date back some 9,000 years. Some African tribes have practised cattle herding sustainably for millennia and have never adopted agriculture at all. Tribes such as the Tutsi, Dinka, Nuer and Masai of eastern Africa live off the milk of their cattle which they mix with blood, only rarely slaughtering their animals. Belgian geneticist Olivier Hanotte, in a recent pioneering study, found that African cattle domestication is indigenous and that crossbreeding with cattle from the Near East was a much later development.[6]

52. Plan of Massa homestead. Yagoua, Cameroon, Africa.

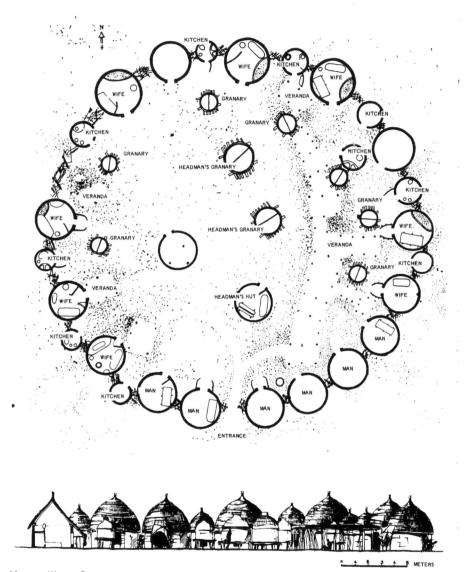

Massa village, Cameroon
Settlement planning goes back to the beginnings of civilisation. The settlements of many African tribes are a sophisticated reflection of their cosmology whilst also protecting the village from the outside world.

Herding cultures live in well-planned semi-permanent settlements, using circular layouts and circular buildings. They include houses as well as the kraals used to milk and shelter their animals. Mothers and young children normally lead quite sedentary lives while the men are more mobile, moving their herds around in well-established annual migration patterns in search of grazing and water. Much ritual and a great variety of annual festivals are associated with these ancient lifestyles.

THE FIRST VILLAGES

The first sedentary farming villages emerged after wheat and barley had been domesticated in the Levant around 8,500 BC. This had the most profound effect on humanity, making bread into a staple part of the diet for the first time. Grain was stored and then ground by hand. Bread was leavened and baked in small brick ovens. Thousands of people lived in one space by growing crops on clearly defined areas of land and fishing the fertile waters of rivers, lakes or the sea. Early settlements spawned new levels in the human control of nature through technological innovation, with hoes, ploughs and sickles used to farm the land and pottery jars made to store the harvest. The emergence of towns and cities is also the story of complex forms of social organisation, with the appearance of formalised political and spiritual hierarchies, administrations, writing and military power.

The last ice age lasted from 23,000 to 12,000 BC. After this date the ice started to melt. It seems as though the ice age ended relatively rapidly, in 100 years or so, coinciding with stories of catastrophic floods that may have occurred around 10,500 BC.

A still unanswered question is whether early towns were built in coastal locations during the last ice age that were subsequently inundated by rising sea levels. Tantalising glimpses of submerged cities are being brought to our attention by divers exploring coastal waters as far apart as the Gulf of Cambay off Gujarat, the coastal waters off Morocco, the Bay of Bengal, around Malta and off the Azores, in the Caribbean and off the coast of Britain, echoing the story of the lost city of Atlantis.

The author Peter Russell wrote:

If we ask, 'Where was Atlantis located?' the answer may be 'Everywhere.' We should be looking . . . on continental shelves all around the world, or rather in all those regions that were far enough from the poles that human communities could thrive.[7]

IT STARTED AT JERICHO

The earliest town to have been excavated so far was not built on a sea coast but in the Jordan Valley in the Middle East. Jericho, located 17 miles north-east of Jerusalem, was founded around 8,000 BC.

Excavations have been conducted here since the middle of the 19th century. Like all early settlements, its favourable setting assured an ample supply of food and water. Jericho benefited from irrigation afforded by the nearby Jordan river, which rises in the Central Mountains. Its underground tributaries fed the town's famous oasis. Recent excavations have uncovered 23 layers of civilizations.

Jericho's massive defence tower dates back to around 7,000 BC. It has the world's earliest surviving city walls and stone staircase. Its fortifications enclosed ten acres of land with space for a permanent population of some 1,200 people. Others would have lived outside Jericho and sought protection within its walls in times of siege. There was sufficient water, and enough storage capacity for grain for months or even years. Jericho was certainly a tough place for outsiders to conquer.[8]

In the book of Joshua in the Old Testament, one can read perhaps the earliest written description of a common feature of urban life until recent times—the sacking of a walled town. The Israelites led by Joshua, after their exodus from Egypt and after several bad years in Sinai, sacked Jericho as they entered the Promised Land. Excavations undertaken from AD 1,900 onwards date the destruction of the city at around 1,400 BC. Whether the sounds of trumpets, as described in the Bible, caused the collapse of the walls is another matter.

The text suggests that the Israelites had laid siege to Jericho for about a week. Then:

> at the sound of the trumpet, when the people gave a loud shout,
> the wall collapsed; so every man charged straight in, and they
> took the city. They . . . destroyed with the sword every living thing
> in it—men and women, young and old, cattle, sheep and donkeys
> . . . They burned the whole city and everything in it, but they put
> the silver and gold and the articles of bronze and iron into the
> treasury of the Lord's house.[9]

Jericho was not actually taken over by the Israelites and remained in a dilapidated condition until it was repaired during the reign of Ahab, a king of Israel from 874 to 852 BC. Hiel then fortified and repaired it some 400 years after its destruction. The ruins of the ancient town are located some two miles from contemporary Jericho.

CATAL HUYUK, ANATOLIAN SUPERNOVA

Catal Huyuk, located on a fertile, well-watered plateau in Anatolia 1,000 metres above sea level, must have looked like a futuristic man-made mountain when it first appeared in the landscape. It seems to have been the world's first substantial town, dating back to 7,100 BC, and existed for some 1,500 years. The 32 acre site is thought to have had a population of some 6,000 people. Excavations by James Mellaart and other archaeologists have revealed a thriving market and spiritual centre that was the central hub of a thriving farming region with a substantial obsidian industry. Catal Huyuk was laid out according to a 'beehive' pattern. Mud-brick houses surrounding a shared courtyard were tightly joined together and connected by narrow lanes. These houses had no outward openings, such as doors or windows, and access was only by ladders through openings in their flat roofs. Clustered together they formed a defensible town that is thought to be have surrounded by tent camps, craft workshops, stock corrals and farms.

'Catal Huyuk shines like a supernova among the rather dim galaxy of contemporary peasant cultures', says Mellaart.[10] Excavations have revealed beautiful murals in red, brown, yellow, blue, green, mauve, grey and black, the leopard's spots being a favourite motif. There are traces of woven fabric. By 6,000 BC high-temperature kilns were used to make pottery. At that time traces of metal working also appeared. Much evidence of long-distance trade has been found: cowrie shells from the Mediterranean, manganese copper and turquoise from eastern Anatolia and the Sinai, mercury ore from Sizmar and tabular flint from the Taurus Mountains.

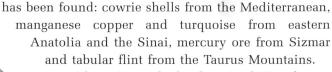

There is no doubt that Catal Huyuk was also a spiritual centre. Many clay statuettes of a goddess have been found, often with her hands resting on the heads of leopards.

Catal Huyuk Goddess
Catal Huyuk in Anatolia, one of the earliest towns in human history, had a guardian goddess of whom hundreds of statuettes were found in the ruins.

There are remnants of many shrines and temples, mostly dedicated to a mother goddess religion that dominated much of Europe and the Near East before the rise of the great cities of Mesopotamia and Egypt.

Did the builders of Catal Huyuk believe they were creating a city that would last forever? Well, certainly little remains of it today. Twelve successive layers of building have been found with the top, most recent layer dating to 5,600 BC. After 4,900 BC occupation of the site appears to have ceased, but there are as yet no clear indications why. All that is left is a mound of rubble, set in a rolling landscape still farmed today. Much more excavation work needs to be done before it will become clear why and how Catal Huyuk came to a seemingly abrupt end.[11]

Towns like Catal Huyuk set a new trend in human endeavour. In Iraq, Greece and Italy fully developed agricultural and trading settlements started

The Cheops Pyramid, Cairo
While the cities of ancient Egypt are in ruins today, the pyramids have endured. They are a lasting expression of human will-power, technical and organisational ingenuity, and a legacy of primary importance to modern Egypt's tourist economy.

to appear between 6,400 and 5,800 BC. By 4,500 BC they were emerging in many places, particularly in fertile river valleys—such as the Nile, the Euphrates and the Tigris. The Harappans occupied the Indus Valley from 3,500 BC building cities such as Mohenjo-daro and Harappa, which had populations of tens of thousands of people. The Canaanites—later known as the Phoenicians—settled in what is now the Lebanon in 3,000 BC and spread their culture throughout the Mediterranean. The great period of pyramid building in Egypt took place between 2,680 and 2,565 BC. Settlements based on rice farming emerged in an area that ranged from Taiwan to Central India. In Britain, settlements linked to Silbury Hill date back to 2,700 BC and those connected to Stonehenge to 2,000 BC.

THE RISE AND FALL OF SUMERIA'S CITIES

Sumeria was a region in southern Mesopotamia, between the Lower Tigris and Euphrates rivers in today's southern Iraq. European visitors in the 19th century were intrigued to encounter what appeared to be many man-made mounds surrounded by infertile, salt-encrusted land. They started to excavate and found the remnants of dozens of ancient cities. Archaeological research indicates that the Sumerians created the world's first complex urban societies around 3,500 BC. In the last 100 years, the ruins of cities such as Uruk and Ur have revealed their astonishing secrets.

Some very significant cultural advances occurred in these pioneering cities: the invention of writing, the development of bronze, gold and silver metallurgy, and the first use of the wheel. The Sumerians made use of gold, ivory, jewels, lapis lazuli, leather, clay, stone, wood and paint in their art. Many examples of exquisite jewellery have been excavated. Instruments such as the lyre were played like a harp. Woven clothes were made from wool or flax. Men wore skirt-like garments tied at the waist and women wore long gowns. Boats were made from inflated animal skins.

Intriguingly, the Sumerian's unique cultural legacy was saved from oblivion by the excavation of large, pioneering libraries of 'cuneiform' clay tablets that were buried under their ruins when they were damaged by earthquakes or burned to the ground. These tablets were of no value to robbers and raiders.

In the space of a few hundred years, dozens of cities emerged in Sumeria. They owed their sustenance to another new invention—irrigation-based farming systems, whose origins date back to about 6,000 BC. Using complex systems of dykes, dams and canals, the Sumerians utilised the rains that fed the Euphrates and Tigris in the mountains of Turkey for their farming activities hundreds of miles south. This 'hydraulic society' required much organization and collective effort to create its complex irrigation system.

Agriculture was highly developed. Wheat, barley, leeks, onions, lentils, sesame, vegetable dyes, herbs and spices were grown, and dates, figs and grapes were cultivated, the latter being used for making wine. Olive oil was used for cooking as well as medicine, a perfume base, lamp fuel and soap.

> *Each city housed a temple that was the seat of a major god in the Sumerian pantheon . . . The city leaders had a duty to please the town's patron deity, not only for the good will of that god or goddess, but also for the good will of the other deities in the council of gods. The priesthood initially held this role, and even after secular kings ascended to power, the clergy still held great authority through the interpretation of omens and dreams.*[12]

The Sumerians believed that human beings were created to serve their many gods. They formed highly stratified societies with kings and priests representing the divine powers. They sculpted stone statues and built great temples for them in the form of ziggurats. The wealthy and powerful upper class consisted of kings, priests and nobles. The middle class was made up of artisans, craftsmen, businessmen, teachers and scribes. The lowest class were slaves who had to perform a wide variety of physical tasks.

URUK AND THE STORY OF GILGAMESH

Archaeologists in the 19th century were spurred on by biblical accounts to dig into Sumeria's city mounds. When Uruk was excavated, it turned out to be the ancient city called Erech in the Old Testament (Genesis 10). The excavations revealed monumental ziggurats topped with temple complexes and adorned with colourful mosaics, as well as schools, family houses and a cemetery full of sarcophagi. Recent studies, utilising magnetometers, have revealed that the city was criss-crossed with navigable canals, like an ancient Venice.[13]

In Uruk, archaeologists dug up the remains of the earliest wheels ever recorded. They also found clay tablets inscribed in an early wedge-shaped script, the world's earliest recorded writing. Pictograms from around 3,300 BC depict the names of people, places, crop records and matters of governance and commerce.

On the northwest side of the city, a large mound still rises from the desert landscape. This ziggurat was dedicated to Anu, Lord of Creation, and Inanna, the Goddess of Love. Archaeologists have found the traces of a wide range of different buildings including other temples and houses of varying sizes. At its peak, at around 3,000 BC, Uruk was probably the world's largest city, with some 50,000 inhabitants on some 550 hectares. Its influence can be detected as far away as eastern Iran and the Nile and Indus Valleys. It remained important until about 2,000 BC, when it gradually declined into a minor urban centre.

Uruk is perhaps the first city to have been ruled by a powerful king, a man who claimed superhuman qualities for himself and had the burning ambition to build a magnificent city. On clay tablets, Enmerkar is named as 'the man who build Uruk'. His grandson Gilgamesh, who was responsible for building its defensive wall, which was 11 kilometres long and up to 10 metres thick, is thought to have lived around 2,700 BC. Stories about his exploits were written down in the Sumerian language on clay tablets that still survive. However, the most comprehensive version of the Gilgamesh epic is derived from 12 stone tablets written in the Akkadian language and found in the ruined library of another Mesopotamian city, Nineveh.[14]

In the epic, Gilgamesh is described as two-thirds god and one-third human, as the greatest king on earth and the strongest superhuman ever to have lived. However, he harshly oppresses his people and they call out to the sky-god Anu to help them. In response, in the great Cedar forest near the city Anu creates a wild man, Enkidu, whose strength of a dozen wild animals is meant to rival Gilgamesh. Shamhat, a temple harlot, is brought to meet Enkidu in the forest and offers herself to him. He succumbs and after days of monumental love-making he loses his wildness, but gains knowledge and understanding instead. Enkidu laments his lost power. After living for a time with a group of shepherds, who teach him how to tend flocks, to eat and speak properly and to wear clothes, Shamhat takes him to meet Gilgamesh in his magnificent city. Soon they become inseparable friends.

Enkidu gradually becomes lazy from living in the opulent city. Then one day, Gilgamesh proposes a great expedition: the two of them are to travel to a large cedar forest on the banks of the Tigris, to cut it down and make a great new gate for Uruk. Enkidu tries to convince Gilgamesh of the folly of this undertaking, but to no avail. As they arrive at the forest, Gilgamesh starts chopping down the trees with his axe, but soon the forest's guardian, the demon Humbaba appears. The epic says:

Gilgamesh gripped the axe
And with it felled the cedar.
Humbaba, hearing the sound of this,
Fell into a fury and raged:
'Who is it who has come—
Come and interfered with my trees?
My trees which have grown on my own mountains?
And has also felled the cedars? . . .'

Enkidu said to his friend, said to Gilgamesh:
'My friend, Humbaba the guardian of the Cedar Forest . . .

Mud-brick city, Morocco
The ancient mud-brick cities of Morocco give a glimpse of what cities such as Ur and Uruk may have looked like some 4,500 years ago.

Strike him to maim him.
Kill him! Crush him! And quickly . . .
Before God Enlil, the Foremost hears his cries.
The gods will be filled with wrath against us for our deed.'[15]

In an epic battle, Gilgamesh eventually cuts off Humbaba's head with a mighty blow of his sword. At this point, the cedars start trembling in fear at having lost their protector. He and Enkidu carry on cutting the trees regardless of the consequences and tie them together to float them down the Euphrates back to Uruk. But the gods are angry and decide that Enkidu should be punished for betraying his former friend Umbaba. Enkidu falls ill and finds out from the priests that he has been singled out for vengeance by the gods. Enraged at the injustice of this decision, Enkidu curses the great cedar gate and those who introduced him to civilization. He dies and a demon drags him down to hell. Gilgamesh is devastated by the death of his friend. He then goes on a quest to find the secret of eternal life, but in the end he learns that death is inevitable and all human effort is only a temporary thing.[16]

Why is all this of relevance here? Because throughout history urbanisation has also been the story of deforestation: forests are cut down for urban construction and for clearing farmland. And even the grandest city is vulnerable to decline and decay and even the mightiest ruler will die. In the Gilgamesh epic, we have an archetypal story whose relevance continues to this very day.

OF SILT AND SALT

Another Sumerian city, Ur, grew even larger than Uruk. From the Bible, Ur is known as the temporary home of Abraham and the Israelites. During the third millennium BC, it became a city of up to 360,000 people, the capital of a mighty empire. Ur had three dynasties of rulers who at various times controlled all of Sumeria. In 2,100 BC, king Ur-Nammu built Ur's ziggurat as the earthly home of the city's chief god, Nanna.

Ur appears to have developed apace after cuneiform writing was invented there around 1,700 BC. Clay tablets were used to keep records of events, register annual harvests, and write down stories and poetry, even favourite recipes. (Meat in a sauce eaten with bread seems to have been very popular, with side dishes of vegetables such watercress and mustard leaves.)

One author conjures up life in Ur:

Most of the people we pass in the streets would be farmers, market gardeners, herdsmen and fishermen and correspondingly many of the goods transported in carts would be food products. However, some of the farmers could have had other roles as well: carpenters, smiths, potters, stone-cutters, basket-makers, leatherworkers, wool-spinners, baker and brewers are all recorded, as are merchants and what we might call the 'civil service' of the temple community—the priests and the scribes.[17]

Ur was excavated by the British archaeologist Sir Leonard Woolley. In his book *Excavations at Ur*, he describes an astonishing find:

Starting then below the level at which the graves had been found we sank a little shaft . . . into the underlying soil and went down through the mixed rubbish that is characteristic of old inhabited sites . . . This went on for about three feet and then, suddenly, it all stopped; there were no more potsherds, no ashes, only clean water-laid mud, and the Arab workmen . . . told me that he had reached virgin soil . . . I told the man to get back and go on digging . . . he dug through eight feet of it in all and then, suddenly, there appeared flint implements and fragments of painted al'Ubaid pottery vessels. I . . . was quite convinced of what it all meant; but I wanted to see whether others would come to the same conclusion. So I brought up two of my staff and, after pointing out the facts, asked for their interpretation. They did not know what to say. My wife came along and looked and asked the same question, and she turned away remarking casually, 'Well, of course, it's the Flood.' That was the right answer.[18]

The three-foot layer of mud that had inundated Ur has been dated to 2,500 BC. There is much evidence of floods and mudslides inundating all the cities of Mesopotamia, from both excavations and ancient texts. Some of the earliest clay tablets found there anticipate the story of Noah's flood. This story, Athrahasis, features Enki, a predecessor to Noah, and is dated 1,640 BC:

Enki made his voice heard . . .
Dismantle the house, build a boat
Reject possessions, and save living things.
The boat that you build . . .

Make upper and lower decks.
The tackle must be very strong,
The bitumen strong, to give it strength

I shall make rain fall on you here.
The Flood roared like a bull,
Like a wild ass screaming the winds
The darkness was total, there was no sun . . .
For seven days and seven nights
The torrent, storm and flood came on.[19]

Early cities such as Ur had a substantial environmental impact. As they grew, they came to depend on ever more resources from an ever larger hinterland. Trees were not only used for building timber but also for baking clay bricks for urban construction. Deforestation certainly occurred on a massive scale in the hills around Mesopotamia and the headwaters of the Euphrates and Tigris. This eventually had dramatic consequences, with vast quantities of soil being washed downhill. Deep silt deposits have been found all over Mesopotamia and the shoreline of the Persian Gulf shifted an astonishing 130 miles in some 2,000 years.

It seems that after the flood, the people of Ur picked up the pieces and life started again. But the eventual demise of Ur and other cities, such as Kish and Lagash, is linked to another environmental factor: the injudicious use of irrigation water that led to the salinisation of farmland, with catastrophic consequences for its food supply.

In 3,500 BC, roughly equal amounts of wheat and barley were grown in Sumeria. But wheat can only tolerate a salt level of 0.5 per cent in the soil, whereas barley can still grow in twice this amount. The increasing salinisa-tion of the soil can be deduced from the declining amount of wheat cultivated and its replacement by the more salt-tolerant barley. By 2,500 BC, wheat had fallen to only 15 per cent of the crop; by 2,100 BC, Ur had all but abandoned wheat production and overall wheat had declined to just 2 per cent of the crops grown in the region:[20]

By 1,800 BC, when yields were only about a third of the level
obtained during the Early Dynastic period, the agricultural base
of Sumer had effectively collapsed. By 1,700 BC salt levels in the
soil throughout the whole of southern Mesopotamia were so high

*that no wheat at all was grown. The focus of Mesopotamian
society shifted permanently to the north, where a succession of
imperial states controlled the region, and Sumer declined into
insignificance as an underpopulated, impoverished backwater.*[21]

Eventually the only food plants that would still grow were date palms. Are
we in danger of repeating these impacts—except on a global scale? Says the
director of the Earth Policy Institute, Washington, Lester Brown:

> *Today we can study the archaeological sites of earlier civilisations
> that moved on to an economic path that was environmentally
> unsustainable and could not make the needed course corrections.
> One example is the early Mesopotamian civilisation. It had a very
> sophisticated irrigation system, was producing a large surplus
> of food in the countryside, enough to sustain the first cities.
> Well-planned cities had the first written language. The
> Mesopotamians were probably as excited by that as we are by the
> Internet. It was a remarkable civilisation but it did not last
> because it had a basic flaw in the design of its irrigation system,
> that eventually led to the rising water tables, waterlogging,
> salinity, declining food production and collapse. Today you can
> still see the remnants of the canals, but no cities, no people,
> almost no vegetation. It's a wasteland. We may think that because
> our technology is so advanced this can't happen to us. The
> Mesopotamians may have felt the same way.*[22]

Today salinisation of soil is becoming a huge problem in farming in tropical
and subtropical countries as increasing populations and crops grown for
export require the ever-greater intensification of food production. Typically
only 15 per cent of irrigation water is actually taken up by crops. The rest
either evaporates or escapes through broken pipes and unlined channels. This
inefficient management of water leads to both waterlogging and salinisation.
When too much water flows over the land it can become waterlogged and
crops will rot and die. Salinisation occurs when natural salts contained in
irrigation water seep into the ground, making it too saline to grow crops.

   The very wealth accumulated by Sumerian city-states lead to jealousies
and wars between them, as well as to attacks by nomadic tribes. Even the
strongest fortified walls could not protect these proud cities. In the end they

all succumbed to a combination of deteriorating soil conditions and hostile invasions. Apart from Uruk and Ur there were 30 other cities, such as Eridu, Kish, Lagash, Nippur, Sippara, Babtibira, Larak and Shuruppak in Sumeria. These cities were on a downward spiral by 1,600 BC when the Hittites attacked from the north, coming on horseback and using iron weapons for the first time. After their conquest, the Hittites adopted Sumerian culture. Ironically, they were primarily responsible for transmitting Sumerian legal, political, economic and religious ideas around the Mediterranean.

As the cities of Sumeria declined, Babylon, in northern Mesopotamia, took over as the dominant city-state. Hammurabi, king of Babylon from 1799–1750 BC, produced the famous code named after him that included laws on social relations, conflict resolution, irrigation, farming, navigation and more. It remained highly regarded, in Greece and Rome and also in ancient Egypt.

The Nile Valley is also full of the ruins of ancient civilisations and these are even better documented than those of Mesopotamia. Giza, Buto, Amarna, Karnak, Hotepsenusret, Elephantine, Ubar, Memphis, Thebes and Alexandria are some of these ancient settlements. From 3,000 BC onwards, cities were built both in the Nile Delta in Lower Egypt as well as in the valley of the Nile in Central and Upper Egypt. They were usually located on the edge of farmland adjoining the Nile.

With the exception of Alexandria, Egypt's primary seaport built by Alexander the Great, all ancient Egyptian cities faded into dust. Unlike Sumeria, it was not damage to farmland by inappropriate irrigation or other environmental reasons, but wars or simply the passage of time that obliterated their mud-brick buildings. Of course, the remnants of ancient Egypt's great temples, such as those at Karnak, Memphis and Abu Simbel and the great pyramids, continue to attract visitors in large numbers.

An interesting aspect of Egypt's environmental history is that the narrow strip of farmland along the Nile has been productive for some 7,000 years. From the time of the Pharaohs, through the period of the Ptolomies, the Romans, the Mamluks and the Arabs, the farmers of Egypt have cultivated the desert continuously, utilising both silt and water from the Nile. More prudent irrigation systems than in Sumeria assured that salinisation never became a problem until recent times. Today, of course, the Aswan High Dam intercepts the river's silt and farmers have to use artificial fertiliser instead. But more about this in Chapter 5.

THE ENIGMA OF ANCIENT GREECE

The rise of the cities of Greece from 750 BC onwards draws heavily on the *hardware* breakthroughs achieved in Sumeria, though it went beyond these, particularly in developing iron and weapons technology and shipbuilding. But ancient Athens in particular made a novel contribution to the *software* of civilisation. The Agora, the living heart of ancient Athens, was where the citizens met to trade, to participate in religious processions and sporting events, and to administer the city's affairs and philosophise. The Greeks developed the alphabet, oratory, democracy, mathematics, theatre, aesthetics and the arts. These contributions did not remain anonymous. Names such as Homer, Socrates, Plato, Aristotle, Aeschylus, Euripides, Aristophanes, Herodotus, Phidias, Archimedes, Euclid, Pythagoras, Hippocrates, Sappho and many others are all permanently inscribed into the collective mind of humanity. (Most are even recognized by my computer spell check.)

Urbanisation in Greece, as elsewhere, was made possible by the bio-productivity of forests and farmland outside the cities. But its hilly land is not very fertile and is easily eroded. With a growing population, Greece soon needed to diversify its economy, exporting pottery, wine and olive oil in exchange for grain. Greek merchants traded throughout the Mediterranean, gradually replacing barter with money transactions. This trade also advanced Greek culture and influenced in the Mediterranean region. In addition, a highly expansionist civilization, backed by well-organised armies and navies, continually established new colonial cities all around the Mediterranean, to ease overcrowding in mainland Greece and to extend its power base.

Athens, of course, was dominated by the Acropolis and the Parthenon, the temple of the Athena, goddess of war and wisdom. Its ruins are still the destination of millions of tourists to this very day. Most Athenians lived in modest houses. The warrior class dwelt around the temple of Hephaestos, the divine blacksmith. Below the Acropolis, there lived artisans and farmers who tilled the land nearby. On the north side, there were communal dwellings, gymnasiums and dining halls.

On land northwest of the Acropolis Solon, the law-giver established the Agora in the 6th century BC. This cradle of consensual democracy was the heart of Athens's political life. The most successful democratic revolution in history was made possible by a citizenry that felt responsible for their community and society. However, of a population of some 317,000, only around 43,000 held full citizenship in 431 BC.[23]

The fundamental presupposition of Greek political life was that the community, the polis, should have priority over the individual. Citizens who participated in its political life enjoyed freedom and, through their actions, sustained its existence and furthered its welfare. The key principles were: a) all citizens had the right to vote and hold office; b) the duty of all citizens is to participate actively in the political process; and c) majority votes should make decisions.

All citizens could attend civic assemblies that were held more than 40 times a year. Every citizen could speak and vote, directly influencing the decision-making process. Special councils drew up the agenda of the assemblies and these were composed of citizens that were drawn by lots and served on each council for a year. This system established some key principles that were followed by later democracies, and for this reason ancient Athens is seen as the birthplace of democracy. However, because of its limited membership, it was really more an aristocracy than a democracy.

This is not the place to discuss the complex history of the cities of Greece, and Athens in particular, in any detail. Here it may be of interest, however, that the success of Greek cities was achieved at considerable environmental cost. The impact of Athens on its local hinterland, Attica, is vividly described in Plato's dialogue *Critias*, written in 360 BC:

The earth has fallen away all round and sunk out of sight . . . In comparison of what then was, there remain only the bones of the wasted body . . . all the richer and softer parts of the soil have fallen away, and the mere skeleton of the land is left. But in the primitive state of the country, its mountains were covered with soil, and the plains . . . were full of rich earth, and there was abundance of wood in the mountains . . . Not so very long ago there were still to be seen roofs of timber cut from trees growing there, which were of a size sufficient to cover the largest houses; and there were many other high trees, cultivated by man and bearing abundance of food for cattle.

Moreover, the land reaped the benefit of the annual rainfall, not as now losing the water which flows off the bare earth into the sea, but, having an abundant supply in all places, and receiving it into herself and treasuring it up in the close clay soil . . . providing everywhere abundant fountains and rivers, of which there may still be observed sacred memorials in places where fountains once existed; and this proves the truth of what I am saying.[24]

Our story starts and ends with the impacts of urban development on forests. Civilisation and deforestation seem to be two sides of the same coin. This theme will continue to accompany us throughout this book.

CHAPTER 3

From Rome
to Edo

This chapter is a journey across 2,500 years from the days of ancient Rome
to Edo, predecessor to modern Tokyo. Both were cities of just over a million
people, yet in terms of their use of resources, they were very different places.
Comparing Rome and Edo, and tracing the environmental and cultural history
of cities over two millennia, allows us to catch a glimpse of the very varied
ways in which cities related to their host environment.

In many ways Rome is the prototype of the large modern city—minus the
fossil fuels. It grew to 1.2 million people in about 1,000 years—no other city
anywhere on earth reached that sort of size for another 1,200 years or so. At
first, Rome drew its sustenance mainly from its immediate hinterland. But
to become an opulent city of over a million people, with hundreds of smaller
satellite cities, Rome required an empire the size of the United States.

Rome's story starts in about 750 BC, with a small village inhabited by
Latins, Sabines and Etruscans. Rome thrived because it straddled a trade route
linking the Etruscan region in northern Italy and the Greek colonies in the
south. Being located on the banks of the Tiber was also of major benefit.
Rome's water supply was sufficient until the 4th century BC. Then as the city
grew larger, the Tiber became polluted and the Romans started building a
system of underground water channels to supply the city.

At around the same time the Romans started building a complex road
network across Italy—the Via Appia was soon followed by Via Aurelia,

Flaminina, Fulvia and Flavia. Their paved, central roadbeds were constructed for ox-drawn carts and wagons, the main land-based transport system of the ever-expanding Roman economy. Marching armies, horsemen and pedestrians kept to the side paths. The new road system facilitated the rapid movement of Rome's armies and their supplies, and this was crucial for bringing Italy and colonial territories elsewhere under Rome's control.

The First Punic War, 263–241 BC, was a great turning point in the history of Rome, as it expanded the empire beyond Italy's shores for the first time. The great prize in the victory against Carthage was the annexation of Sicily. This island with its rich farmland was declared 'an estate of the Roman people'. Its industrious population became slaves on its own land, and was forced to produce crops for Rome.

Victory in the First Punic War brought about profound social change in the Roman Republic. For 200 years, Roman farmers had struggled for freedom and a share in Rome's government, and for 100 years they had enjoyed their hard-won privileges. But the war robbed them of much of what they had won as they now had to compete with cheaper produce from the new 'latifundia', the estates of the rich that were tended by slaves. Many farmers were forced to become full-time soldiers, manning the legions and partaking in the loot of Rome's colonial adventures. In 89 BC all free inhabitants of Italy officially became citizens of Rome, but in reality it was the rich who controlled a feudal state largely for their own benefit.

By 100 BC, Rome had conquered Greece, Macedonia, parts of western Asia and Egypt. By 230 years later, it controlled most of Europe, including Britain, and its empire stretched a long way into Asia and across northern Africa. At that time, the city reached a population of about 1,200,000. It became a sort of welfare state with some 300,000 people receiving grain rations. More and more resources were expended on entertaining Romans with a great variety of extravagant spectacles.

Rome itself had become a magnificent city, built largely by slave power. The Circus Maximus, mainly used for chariot races, could seat some 200,000 and the Colosseum, with its spectacular gladiatorial displays, over 50,000. The Forum Romanum was the central hub of the city, with magnificent public buildings, palaces, temples, sacred sites and monuments of conquest symbolising Rome's political, economic and religious power.

The majority of Roman citizens now chose not to live in the countryside, but in the city itself, with its paved roads, aqueducts, schools, temples, libraries, markets, arenas and public baths. Most people were housed in insulae, apartment blocks shared by several families. There were some 45,000

Colosseum, Rome
The colosseum is the prototype of the sports stadium that can be found in most contemporary cities, though sports today are less brutal than in Roman times.

of these, with some rising up to ten storeys high. Building regulations deliberately limited the height of apartment blocks, but some did collapse and there was a constant danger of fires.

The satellite cities that were built across the empire tended to be miniature versions of Rome itself. To connect these colonial outposts with the mother city, a complex network of naval transport routes and paved roads was organised. In Britain alone, some 10,000 miles of roads were built. To make people feel they had a stake in the empire, every free man was granted Roman citizenship in AD 212. But many more people were kept as slaves to supply Rome's insatiable demands—for food, timber and precious metals.

RESOURCES AND ENVIRONMENT

To meet the needs of the ever-growing city, Rome had to keep improving its water supply system. The first elevated aqueduct was completed in 144 BC as the demand for water increased with more and more bathhouses being built across the city.[1] In another great engineering feat, the Cloaca Maxima and its tributaries were built to drain the Forum and the valleys between the city's seven hills, and to flush the sewage into the Tiber. The writings of Sextus Julius Frontinus bear testimony to the Romans' extraordinary know-how on urban water management. Nine separate aqueducts were built as water demand in the city grew:

> The supply . . . suffices not only for public and private uses and purposes, but also for the satisfaction of luxury; we have listed to how many reservoirs it is distributed and in what wards; how much water is delivered outside the City; how much is used for water-basins, how much for fountains, how much for public buildings, how much in the name of Caesar, how much for private consumption.[2]

The conquests of its armies gave Rome access to a great variety of trade goods that contributed to affluence and luxury back home: pottery and wine from

Library at Ephesus, Turkey
Ephesus was one of Rome's most important satellite cities around the rim of the Mediterranean. As the best preserved classical city in the region, it has become a major tourist attraction.

France, gold, silver, copper and olives from Spain, olive oil from Greece, linen from Egypt and Tunisia, tin and gold from Britain. In addition, the Romans received goods from lands they had not conquered, such as iron from Germany, amber from the Baltic, myrrh from Arabia, muslin, gems, pepper and ivory from India, and silk from China.

Rome did not have the benefit of coal, oil or gas. Like Uruk, it needed forests for timber and fuel. To start with, the Romans mainly exploited the forested slopes in the city's hinterland. Firewood was required for cooking and heating, for metal smelting, brick making, pottery and glass and for producing olive oil. Wealthy Romans used central heating systems and needed copious amounts of firewood for both their villas and public baths. Pliny the Elder wrote:

> We plough the ground, plant trees, trim the trees that prop our
> vines, build houses and quarry rocks and accomplish other useful
> tasks . . . We likewise use iron for wars and slaughter, not only in
> hand-to-hand encounters but as a winged missile.[3]

With its massive use of resources, Rome pioneered a highly developed economy but it also caused major environmental problems. Deforestation around the catchments of the Tiber led to soil erosion as tree roots were no longer there to absorb the rainwater. Downpours quickly turned into torrents, washing soil down from the hills and silting up the river bed of the Tiber, and eventually the port of Ostia. As this became useless for larger vessels, Emperor Trajan had to construct a new harbour at an inconvenient location at Civitavechia, which was twice as far from Rome as Ostia.

As the empire grew, Rome needed access to ever-larger areas of forest for metal smelting, for constructing houses and for building ships. John Perlin's book *A Forest Journey* gives a vivid account of how Rome systematically exploited the forests of France, Spain, North Africa and the Mediterranean islands. Elba was Rome's main supplier of iron implements, whose production swallowed vast quantities of charcoal. It was nicknamed 'Athaelia', the Greek word for smoky, because its furnaces spewed out such a lot of fumes. When Elba's forests had been obliterated, the iron ore had to be shipped over to be smelted at Populonia on the Etrurian coast. According to the Roman writer Strabo, 45 million pines had to be felled there to keep up the iron production at Populonia.[4]

Rome itself had a variety of environmental problems, starting with air pollution from hundreds of thousands of fires that were burning during the winter months. The writers Juvenal and Martial complained about the dirt, animal excreta and dead bodies in the streets of the overcrowded city. There were many open drains and canals full of smelly sewage, an ideal breeding ground for mosquitoes. But there is little evidence that the Romans made a connection between a dirty urban environment and diseases such as cholera or typhoid.[5]

Much of the city's waste was simply discarded in situ. Archaeological excavations have revealed a huge variety of broken everyday objects in the remnants of buildings, drains and small rubbish tips, though of course, much less was thrown away in Rome than in modern cities.

The Romans did know about the benefits of recycling. For instance, workshops located near slaughterhouses turned bones and ivory into pins, tokens, buttons, hinges and other items. Rather surprisingly, some of the cables used in Roman war machines were made from women's hair and animal nerves. In the final days of ancient Rome, broken glass was recycled to reduce the need for fuel. As firewood ran short, the quality of bricks used in Rome gradually deteriorated.[6]

TIMBER AND GRAIN FROM NORTH AFRICA

With its large population, Rome consumed hundreds of thousands of tonnes of grain per year. Having depleted the farmland of Italy as well as Sicily, it was Caesar who decided that North Africa would be a suitable region for supplying grain to Rome. Caesar's armies conquered most of the territory north of the Sahara. In many places, particularly on the slopes of the Atlas Mountains, the Romans found wooded landscapes and an abundance of fruit trees. Pliny the Elder describes the exuberant tribes that lived there: 'The night was filled with the music of drums, cymbals, flutes and the sounds of people dancing.'

After 'pacifying' the local tribes, the Romans started cutting down forests for building houses and ships, or for timber exports to Rome itself. Vast numbers of wild animals were captured. Just for the opening of the Colosseum in AD 70, some 5,000 lions, elephants, leopards, panthers and bears were shipped to Rome to kill Christians or to fight gladiators.[7] In North Africa, the Romans terraced large areas of farmland and used irrigation systems to increase its productivity. Many barrages have been found in what is now semi-desert land. For over 300 years North Africa, and particularly Tunisia, supplied about 500,000 tonnes of wheat and barley a year to Rome, as well as grapes, olives, dates, wool and leather goods.

Roman veterans who settled in North Africa often married local women. They administered the latifundia owned by Roman nobles. Some 600 towns were built or expanded to act as epicentres of Rome's economy. Carthage was the greatest, with a population of up to half a million. But others, such as Leptis Magna, Thysdrus, Caesarea, Sabratha, Timgad, Cirta and Uthina, were substantial cities of tens of thousands of people, with amphitheatres, aqueducts, public baths and schools. Their main function was to collect taxes and to safeguard Rome's colonial territory.[8]

But over the years, deforestation and salinisation from imprudent crop irrigation took their toll. Crops were grown year after year but the fertility of the land was not replenished. The Romans ate the bread made with grain from North Africa, and for centuries they flushed their bowel contents through the Cloaca Maxima into the Mediterranean Sea. There is no doubt that this continual loss of plant nutrients impaired the fertility of North Africa's soil. Around AD 250 St Cyprian, bishop of Carthage, wrote this note:

> *The world has grown old and does not remain in its former vigour.*
> *It bears witness to its own decline. The rainfall and the sun's*
> *warmth are both diminishing . . . The husbandman is failing in his*
> *fields. Springs that once gushed forth liberally now barely give a*
> *trickle of water.*[9]

DECLINE AND FALL

In the 3rd century AD, the Romans began to feel increasingly insecure. They started building protective walls around many of their colonial cities because of the growing threat of invasions by barbarians. In around AD 300, Emperor Hadrian decided to consolidate the territory of the empire by building a series of defensive walls, such as Hadrian's Wall across northern Britain, and the Limes between the Rhine and the Danube. At the same time, the construction of massive new walls around Rome itself got under way.

In AD 306, Constantine became emperor of Rome. He decided to convert to Christianity and, at last, Christians were safe from persecution. Constantine found subtle ways of combining pagan worship with Christianity. He made December 25th—the holy day of Apollo, the Roman god of the sun, the arts, prophecy and healing—into the official birthday of Jesus Christ. He also decided to make his new city, Constantinople, the capital of the Eastern Empire. It was easier to defend than Rome and continued under Christian rule until 1453, when it was conquered by the Turks.

The Western Empire succumbed to shifting, wandering confederacies of mainly Germanic tribes that Rome had never been able to control. In 409, the Visigoths, led by Alaric, occupied Rome for three days, burning many buildings and taking with them as many valuables as they could carry. In 455, the Vandals, led by Gaiseric, had another go at looting Rome and transported much booty back to their base in Carthage. In North Africa's cities, the Vandals lived it up in the villas and baths of Roman noblemen. They proceeded to build a pirate fleet, playing havoc with trade in the Mediterranean, and increasingly intercepting Rome's faltering grain supplies. In 476, Romulus Augustulus abdicated and the Western Empire was at an end. Between 500 and AD 1,000, Rome contracted to a town of just 30,000 people.

There were many reasons for Rome's decline and fall—invasions, punitive taxes in the colonies, civil wars, corruption, famines and plagues. The Romans had overextended their supply lines and lost the capacity to safeguard their vast empire, partly because many soldiers were foreign legionnaires who had no stake in Rome itself. Another factor in Rome's fall was the fact that its enemies learned many new military tricks that increasingly allowed them to challenge its power. Knowledge always has the tendency to spread, and in this case it helped Rome's opponents to acquire new weaponry and military tactics. In the end, Rome collapsed like a tower that had grown too tall for the foundations on which it was built.

One thesis, by American historian Ellsworth Huntington, cites climate change as a major factor in Rome's fall. He writes that reduced rainfall and unstable climate became a massive problem for the latter day Romans, forcing them to invest in costly irrigation projects, particularly in North Africa. Water was stored in reservoirs full of stagnant water, an ideal environment for malarial mosquitoes. Malaria rose to epidemic levels, killing millions, initially in North Africa and then in Rome itself.[10]

Given today's knowledge and our present concerns, there is little doubt that environmental factors such as deforestation, soil erosion and salinisation played a major part in the demise of the Roman Empire. Rome's ecological footprint must have been massive even by today's standards—I venture an informed guess of up to 100 times its own surface area (see also Chapter 6).

A major difference between ancient Rome and today's cities is that it ran largely on biological resources—the forests that it required for its sustenance were severely depleted but, once the pressure of Rome's demands was off, some of these would have regenerated. Others, of course, were permanently removed as forests were turned into farmland. The landscape of

North Africa in particular was changed into a severely degraded landscape with a permanently altered—hotter and drier—climate.

Drawing on the example of Athens, Cicero, Cato and Scipio represented the republican principle in Roman history, which was then superseded by imperial rule, first tried by Caesar. Augustus, Nero, Hadrian, Diocletian, Claudius, Constantine and Caligula are some of the emperors whose names—for better or worse—are etched in the annals of history. But there were also writers and philosophers—Virgil, Ovid, Livy, Pliny the Elder and the Younger, Tacitus, Seneca, Vitruvius and others—who are still read and appreciated today. Rome's triumphs, monuments, literature, gladiatorial displays and Christian martyrdom are all mixed together in a grand picture that is astonishing: monstrous as well as dignified.

Ironically, the final days of ancient Rome saw the rise of a new kind of 'ethical internationalism', in the form of Christianity. It was this that became the basis for the city's revival in the Middle Ages. Rome was the home of the Pope and as Christianity spread across Europe, the religious power of Rome came to grow in a resurgence of its former glory.

AFTER ROME

The collapse of Rome's Western Empire left a power vacuum in Europe, the Middle East and North Africa. The so-called Middle Ages that followed are the 1,000-year period that started around AD 570. The immediate aftermath, the so-called Dark Ages, were a time of much uncertainty. Towns all over the former territory of the Roman Empire tried to lead local, autonomous lives, with a much-reduced scale of trade in goods. Interestingly, Rome's main legacy turned out to be a trade in ideas—including the spread of Christianity, which increasingly replaced long-established pagan belief systems and local religions.

After a couple of hundred years of upheaval, Charlemagne, king of Franconia, was crowned emperor of his new Holy Roman Empire in AD 800 and sought to establish unified order across Europe. He brought a fresh sense of culture and learning to Europe and is especially remembered for his efforts in spreading education beyond a small social elite. Throughout his empire magnificent Romanesque cathedrals sprang up in the centre of cities, inspired by Roman architectural styles.

At the same time, the rise of Islam introduced its own sense of order and religious fervour in the Middle East, North Africa and parts of Spain. Cairo,

Baghdad, Damascus and Granada, with their magnificent mosques and palaces, all became symbols of the power of Islam. The important contributions of Islam to architecture, mathematics, astronomy, navigation, crop cultivation and medicine are well known. The fierce competition between Christianity and Islam caused great upheaval as well as a powerful cross-fertilisation of ideas.

During the Middle Ages, the majority of people in Europe lived in villages or on small farms, often controlled by feudal landlords. Its thousands of towns and cities, were increasingly attractive to rural people. *Stadtluft macht frei*—'city air makes you free' was a theme that gained widespread credence. In many cities, new inhabitants could gain their freedom after one year, as long as their feudal landlords did not demand their return to the land. Economic prosperity was closely linked to social innovation. At the end of the Middle Ages, there were few serfs in western Europe and the thriving new burgher class played an increasingly important role. Despite the continuing dominance of the church and the local nobility, many cities in Europe offered a semblance of democracy.

Medieval cities were 'walking cities' and short distances make for intensive social interaction. The division of labour was highly developed. Blacksmiths, tanners, harness makers, saddlers, shoe makers, tailors, masons, sculptors, carpenters, roofers, book binders and sellers, rug makers, weavers, rope makers, chandlers, bakers, butchers, fishmongers, innkeepers, merchants and doctors all had their own guilds. Bookkeepers, scribes and clerks proliferated as new companies were formed and trading activities increased. City life was punctuated by religious ceremonies centred on saints and holy days. Popular festivals and funfairs were usually enlivened by travelling musicians, jugglers and theatre groups.

Defensive walls were a prominent feature of the towns and cities of the Middle Ages, defining their compact layout with their many narrow lanes. Some walled cities survive largely intact today. In France, cities such as Carcassonne, with two concentric walls and 52 towers, and Aiges-Mortes with its square configuration are showcases of medieval planning. In Germany, Rothenburg and Dinkelsbuehl possess perfectly preserved medieval walls and buildings. In Spain, Barcelona, Burgos, Avila and Toledo still have large sections of their Roman and medieval walls. In Britain, portions of walls remain standing in places like York and Canterbury, with magnificent Gothic cathedrals taking pride of place in the city centre.

The Gothic church was a great invention of the 12th century. The underlying concept is attributed to Suger, abbot of St Denis near Paris, and Bernard of Clairvaux, a key figure in the Cistercian monastic order. In their opinion, religion was a mystical experience that needed to be reinforced by the very structure of the house of worship and especially its use of space and light. This idea was first tested in the redesign of the Abbey of St Denis. Starting with the Cathedrals of Laon and Noyon, Gothic churches soon became a must for towns and cities all over northern Europe. Britain has a particularly rich variety of Gothic cathedrals. Perhaps the most powerful expression of gothic design is Chartres Cathedral in France, whose astonishing multicoloured windows are still largely intact. Rheims Cathedral, where France's kings were crowned, is a magnificent example of the High Gothic.

Cathedrals fostered community ties within their own citizens but they also had a great impact in their hinterland. Their awesome spires could be seen from miles around and could lure in village people and pilgrims. The great cathedral windows, illuminated by the rays of the sun, vividly told the story of the bible and the salvation of Christ. Craft guilds usually donated the windows, which tended to reflect their particular skills in their visual narrative. Thus the cathedral was an expression of religious devotion as well as shared civic pride in a magnificent building.[11]

Bernard of Clairvaux was abbot of the Citeaux monastery, centre of the Cistercian monastic order. During his 38 years as abbot, he personally saw to the establishment of 66 of the 300 Cistercian monasteries founded across Europe. The Cistercians were not only interested in spreading Christianity, but also in helping to develop and improve farming and rural living. They preferred setting up their monasteries in forest or swampy areas, which they cleared and drained for agriculture. By developing the local farming and crafts economy, they played a key role in extending medieval technology. They harnessed water power for milling but also for working bellows used in making iron and steel. This was utilised to make new, efficient ploughs and shoes for the horses that were used in farming for the first time.

In medieval cities, drainage or sewerage arrangements were often rather basic, compared with Rome's elaborate water supply and sewage disposal systems. In some places privy vaults and cesspools were used, but more often people dumped their wastes into gutters to be flushed away by rainwater or collected as fertiliser. Inadequate sanitation played its part in the repeated outbreaks of the plague. During the worst episode, in 1347–8, nearly half of Europe's population died.

Rheims Cathedral
Gothic cathedrals, such as here in Reims, became the central feature of thousands of European cities from the 12th century onwards. Their tall, perforated structures were a highly innovative achievement of architectural design.

LOCAL SELF-SUFFICIENCY

Europe's medieval smaller towns were first and foremost self-sufficient local economic entities. For many, trade was the icing on the cake of an otherwise self-sustaining local economy. They mostly fed themselves from their immediate hinterland, returning organic waste back to the soil and maintaining their own forests for a sustained supply of timber, firewood and charcoal. Chimneys first made their appearance in the 13th century, revolutionising building design.[12] The first uses of coal are also reported at that time.

Despite their reputation for mediocrity, the Middle Ages was in fact a period of considerable technological change. One innovation stands out: the widespread use of watermills. Because of its steady rainfall, northern Europe was particularly suitable for this technology. In 1066, the Domesday Book mentions 5,624 watermills in Britain alone. These would continue in use right up to the industrial revolution in the 18th century. Two other important innovations in energy technology occurred: windmills and the ever more widespread use of horse power in both farming and transport.[13]

The integration of cities into their hinterland is well described by geographer Johann Heinrich von Thuenen in his book *The Isolated State*, published in 1826. He was the founder of 'location economics' and the first to develop an analytical model of the relationships between markets, farming systems and their location.[14] The medieval town represents his model perfectly. Concentric rings of market gardens, forests, orchards, farmland and grazing land usually surrounded it. Cows were often stabled within the city and herded out to the fields in the morning and back into the city for milking at dusk. The townspeople helped to maintain the fertility of the farmland that fed them by returning animal manure and night-soil to it.

In his famous diagram[15] von Thuenen is concerned with the inherent logic by which towns are encircled by clearly defined systems of farming and forestry. The innermost zone is used for horticulture and milk production, where cultivation is very intense, with regular applications of manure and night-soil from the town. The second is the wood products zone, for both firewood and timber. The third zone is for intensive crop rotation, where the land is fertilised annually. The fourth zone is a less intensive rotational cropping system with fallowing and dairying. The outer zone is extensive livestock grazing for meat and wool. When a major transport route such as a navigable river (or a motorway) is available, the circles are 'bust open' and replaced by an increasingly linear arrangement.

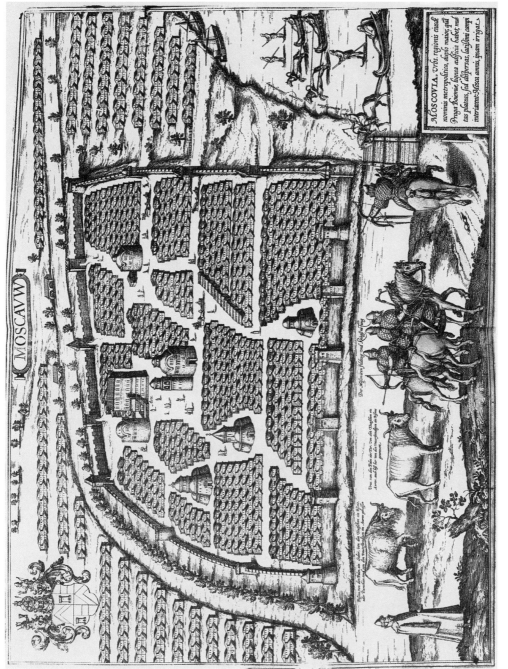

Medieval Moscow

Like many major cities, Moscow used its river for transport and water supply as well as protection against invasion. Beyond the periphery of the walled city, unprotected suburbs sprawled into woodland and farmland.

This analytical model is still of great relevance today as the availability of cheap transport systems, bringing in food and goods from long distances, is beginning to be questioned because of their wasteful use of energy, particularly when airplanes fly in food from halfway around the world.

The medieval city state depended on the countryside for its food supply and it always controlled a large area of land, the size of which varies according to the needs of the city . . . the growth of the cities meant that the rural areas began to change at an ever increasing rate. The mercantile cities imported foodstuffs and raw materials, while at the same time exporting industrial and commercial goods, and the countryside, because of the reciprocal nature of this trade and because of the growth in population, was forced to raise its levels of agricultural production by putting new land under cultivation and by using the existing land more efficiently.[16]

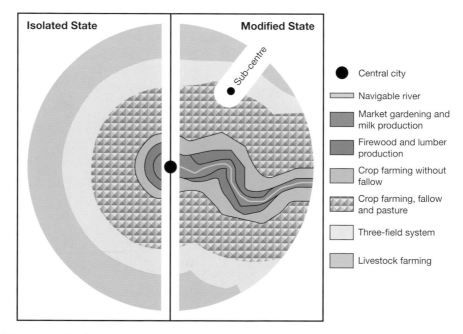

The geographer Heinrich von Thuenen made a major contribution to the understanding of the relationship of cities to their local hinterland. Once significant transport connections are established, their linkages to local farmland and forests tend to be weakened.

CITIES OF THE RENAISSANCE

The triumph of the Gothic in northern Europe was not replicated in Italy, where Roman ruins dominated the appearance of many urban areas. The rise of major new cities such as Venice, Milan, Florence, Siena and Pisa in northern Italy in the medieval period revived the fortunes of the country through their banking- and trade-based economies. The new churches and palaces that appeared in these cities owed their architectural inspiration as much to ancient Rome as to newer fashions of architectural design.

As proud new cities emerged in northern Italy, the last remnant of the old Roman empire, Constantinople, was about to fall. It was the prime example of a fortress city, defended by triple walls some 22 kilometres long. But in 1453, it fell to Sultan Mehmed II and his Ottoman armies. Its massive walls could not withstand the onslaught of his large cannons, the most powerful weapons of his large army.[17] Soon modern cannon technology made city walls obsolete everywhere. Over the coming centuries, they were taken down in

Medieval Prague
Europe's traditional cities, such as Prague, attract visitors from all over the world. Their compact design is being copied in some new urban development.

most cities and recycled into building materials. Their location was often used for building urban ring roads, as in Vienna's Ringstrasse.

After the collapse of Constantinople, many scholars of Greek and Roman texts had to find new careers. They emigrated to Italy and started to translate the classics into modern languages. Johannes Gutenberg begun printing Luther's German Bible in 1450 and thus helped to spread the ideas of the Reformation. Then he and other printers proceeded to bring out translations of Greek and Roman classics, which were widely circulated across Europe, giving rise to a new cultural movement, the European Renaissance.

In the Renaissance, architecture was the supreme art. Writers such as Vasari believed that it represented the highest level of artistic achievement. It was not considered a specialist profession, but was also the realm of painters and sculptors such as Michelangelo, or aristocratic amateurs with a lot of time and money on their hands. In the Renaissance, the new idea of public space was implemented, in which civic pride and organisation could be displayed on a city-wide scale.

The growth of Renaissance cities was accompanied by major environmental impacts. The example of Venice is particularly interesting. In the 14th century it became a major power, trading salt, glass and other manufactured goods. Its growth to a city of over 100,000 people is directly linked to the deforestation of the islands in the Mediterranean. Hundreds of thousands of oak piles were needed to build this island city on swampy ground, and vast quantities of timber were used for building galleons and merchant ships for its highly successful maritime trade. After the fall of Constantinople, when the Ottoman Empire challenged its maritime supremacy, Venice had to redouble its shipbuilding efforts using vast quantities of oak, mainly from the slopes of the Alps. The Venetian writer Guiseppe Paulini explained how the deforestation of the Italian Alps caused massive soil erosion, with local rivers carrying silt right into Venice's lagoon.[18]

As timber ran short in the Mediterranean, Amsterdam started to replace Venice as Europe's leading shipbuilding centre, mainly using timber from the Baltic to supply ships for city-states as far away as Venice. The cities of the Hanseatic League—Luebeck, Hamburg, Bremen, Danzig and others—grew larger and more powerful as they came to control trade in the Baltic and the North Sea.

After 1500, the cities of Spain, led by Madrid, grew on the back of the new colonial trade with America. Between 1550 and 1800, Mexico and South America produced more than 80 per cent of the world's silver and 70 per

Aztec mural
South America has its own unique ancient urban traditions. After the arrival of the treasure-hunting Spanish conquistadors, the Mayas, Incas and Aztecs fled their cities and retreated into mountains and forests.

cent of its gold. Bolivian historian Eduardo Galeano estimates that between 1503 and 1660, Spain extracted 185 tons of gold and 16,000 tons of silver from its South American colonies. The total European reserves quadrupled and this contributed greatly to the continent's economic development, ultimately helping to finance the industrial revolution.[19]

South America had its own large cities, such as Teotihuacan, Tikal and Tetnochtitlan. In 1492 Tenochtitlan, the capital of the Aztec empire, had some 300,000 inhabitants. To supply a city that size, the Aztecs had developed sophisticated food production and distribution systems. The city region was agriculturally self-sufficient, with farmers working the land communally and producing enough to feed its entire population. The Spanish conquistadors destroyed much of the city, but the ruins of Tetnochtitlan are the location of modern Mexico City, one of the world's largest cities today.

THE RISE OF BEIJING

The cities of the European Middle Ages are quite small in comparison to urban growth in the Far East. The Chinese in particular had a great tradition of city building. The city of Xian, straddling the Silk Route, was built during the Tang Dynasty, AD 618 and 907. At its zenith its population was about one million people. Xian's 22 kilometre-long walls with their 12 gates enclose a nine-square grid, the ideal Chinese urban plan since ancient times. Today the walls are still well preserved.

The creation of Beijing is a particularly astonishing example of Chinese urban development. In 1404, Emperor Zhu Di embarked on the extraordinarily ambitious project of transferring the capital of China from Nanjing to Beijing. A vast army of workers one million strong was taken on for the purpose. To feed them, and to feed the new city, Zhu Di proceeded with repairing and enlarging China's Grand Canal into a water system stretching 1,800 kilometres, all the way to the Pearl River Delta, China's rice bowl in the south. Most of the food needed in Beijing was imported from there. Timber for constructing the city had to be brought from as far as Jianxi, Shanxi and Sichuan provinces, and from Annam and Vietnam. In 1421, the new capital was inaugurated, with envoys from many countries—India, Japan, Vietnam, Siam, Java, Sri Lanka, Sumatra, Arabia, East Africa—invited to participate.

After the end of the ceremonies, they were taken back to their native countries in probably the world's largest fleet ever assembled until that time. This was also intended to explore foreign lands. Shockingly, as soon as these 'treasure fleets' had set sail, a lightning strike set alight the city of Beijing and much of it burned down within a few days. Zhu Di was devastated. He believed that emperors ruled with the mandate of heaven and the fire could hardly have been more ominous for him. He never recovered from the shock and it took a long time to rebuild the city.[20] Nevertheless, Sir George Leonard Staunton, secretary of the British Mission to China in the 18th century, estimated that Beijing had a population of some three million people at that time. It was by far the world's largest city.

THE STORY OF EDO

The story of Tokyo is equally as interesting and it will be useful to discuss it in some detail. It used to be called Edo and its history dates back the 10th century BC. Until the 17th century, it was far less important than Japan's imperial capital Kyoto. All that changed in 1603 at the start of the 'Edo Period', which lasted 264 years until 1867. At the start of this era, Shogun Ieyasu of the Tokugawa clan together with his allies transferred the country's government to Edo, leaving the emperor marginalised in Kyoto. In 1720, Japan's first census indicated a national population of about 30 million people, and this figure changed little throughout the period. Edo's population at the time was 1.25 million people, about the same as ancient Rome.

Edo is located in a well-watered, fertile agricultural region on Honshu Island on the shores of Tokyo Bay, an enclosed coastal sea extending to some 1,000 square kilometres that teamed with a huge variety of fish and crustaceans. These formed a reliable source of protein for the people of Edo and those of other important cities such as Yokohama and Kawasaki nearby.

During the Edo Period, Japan had little exchange with other countries and ocean-going ships were outlawed. It was an introspective, peaceful period of remarkable cultural development. New art forms like *kabuki*, a lively and highly stylised kind of dance, and *ukiyo-e*, a sensual form of painting, became very popular. Porcelain and lacquerware also thrived. Advances in printing and education led to a highly literate population. The dominant philosophy of Neo-Confucianism stressed the importance of morals, education and hierarchical order in society. A four-class social system had the samurai at the top, followed by merchants, artisans and peasants. Ironically, because the Edo Period was so peaceful, many samurai were out of a job and became martial arts teachers, scholars, writers, poets and artists instead.

Novelist Eisuke Ishikawa has researched the Edo Period and describes it as a highly sustainable society. He found that when the city of Edo was first established, great piles of rubbish disfigured it and created very unhealthy conditions. But by around 1790, the people of Edo had created an extremely clean and hygienic if rather static urban environment. In the absence of mass production and consumption, the economy grew by only 0.3 per cent a year.

The sustainable utilisation of limited resources in a continuous circular system had become the norm, with extensive reuse and recycling of waste materials. An ever-growing number of businesses reused the city's waste materials. 'End-of-life' goods were not discarded: instead, tens of thousands of specialised traders and craftsmen were engaged in their reuse and recycling. Tinkers repaired old pans, kettles and pots. Ceramic repairers glued broken pieces of ceramics. Others fixed tubs, barrels, lanterns, locks, inkpads, pots and pans, wooden footwear, umbrellas or mirrors. There were some 4,000 old clothes dealers in the city. Candle wax buyers even collected candle drippings and made them into new candles.

Tokyo Tea House
The architecture of Edo was highly stylised and adapted to the region's humid climate. In modern Tokyo such beautifully crafted buildings have given way to western-style functional, angular blocks that are often devoid of character.

Temple of Heaven, Beijing
This extraordinary building reflects the imperial splendour of Emperor Zhu Di's Beijing. Set in a park away from other buildings, it is a survivor of the great fire of 1421.

Others collected wood ash for farmers to use as fertiliser. Farmers themselves regularly visited homes and offered money or vegetables in return for night-soil, to be used as fertiliser. City landlords with many tenants made good money from the night-soil collected from their premises. There are even stories of arguments between landlords and tenants about ownership of the night-soil. Some farmers would only collect it from up-market districts for growing exclusive kinds of tea.

The first westerners who saw the city were astonished at its cleanliness. But, in fact, few had access to it. There was only one small trading post at Nagasaki. However, Edo's splendid isolation did not last. In 1853 things began to change. The United States had started to take a serious interest in the Pacific. US President Fillimore sent Navy Commodore Matthew C. Perry to Japan in one of his steam-powered 'black ships'. He came demanding trade and soon the British and other westerners followed. Japan could no longer maintain its isolation and in 1858 it signed trade treaties, soon beginning to interact with western governments and commercial agents. After a show of force in 1864, the Shogunate surrendered power to the Emperor Meiji. The age of the samurai ended with the Meiji Restoration of 1868 and a system of government centred on the emperor.[21]

The new government changed the course of Japan's history, promoting modernisation, adopting western political, social and economic systems. It set out to create an industrialised country in a fraction of the time it had taken the countries of the West. In 1872, Japan's first railway line connected Tokyo and Yokohama, and other lines soon followed. Japan greatly strengthened its military power and negotiated new treaties with the West. In 1889, a new constitution enshrined Japan's modernisation process. The newly introduced industrial and military technologies gave Japan the power to dominate the rest of Asia. Victory in wars with Russia, China and Korea made it the dominant force in the region. Japan's new economic and military power centred on Tokyo and it soon started to grow into a vast city.

As we will see in Chapter 5, in the 20th century Japan, with Tokyo at its heart, continued to increase its economic interaction with the rest of the world. In the last 50 years Tokyo, with 28 million people, has become the largest city region on the planet.

LESSONS OF URBAN HISTORY

One way or another, nearly all the cities described in this chapter still exist today. Those that have managed to retain some of their traditional buildings and public spaces appeal to us because of their beautifully detailed architecture, their quality of craftsmanship, local identity, civic pride and compactness. The physiology of traditional towns and cities was very different from that of modern conurbations. It was defined by production and transport systems based on muscle, water and wind power, which inevitably limited their outward and upward growth. People from all over the world come today to admire and walk about in old cities, particularly those with their old walls still intact (and those that have particularly horrible torture chambers). They reflect a sense of continuity that is often absent in the cities we build today. Stone and brick as used in the construction of old cities have a more lasting quality then today's concrete and glass facades. The cultural and religious history of cities makes each one of them very different and unique in its own way.

But the continuity of human settlements is first and foremost reliant on their successful adaptation to their host environment. The environmental history of ancient cities is certainly a chequered one. In admiring them we should not forget that they grew because of a tremendous exploitation of nature, particularly timber resources. Some cities destroyed both themselves and their hinterland, while others maintained a thriving, sustainable relationship with their host environment. What can modern cities learn from the history of Rome and Edo?

CHAPTER 4

Technology — Triumph and Tragedy

This chapter deals with the economic, social and environmental history of urbanisation from the giddy days of the industrial revolution onwards. The modern city arose, above all else, out of major innovations in combustion technology. But where there is fire there is smoke; where there is urban growth there are housing shortages and congestion; and where there is food consumption there is sewage. These are some of the great new problems that the cities of the industrial revolution had to deal with.

The primary differences in social organisation and the uses of technology between traditional and modern cities can be summarised as follows:

	Traditional city	Modern city
Social organisation	Community	Society
Building materials	Stone, bricks	Concrete, steel
Fuel	Firewood, charcoal	Coal, oil, gas
Production	Crafts	Industry
Transport	Carts, coaches, boats	Trains, automobiles
Food	Mainly locally produced	Globally supplied
Human waste	Open drains and cesspits	Sewage systems
Solid waste	Mainly reused and recycled	Dumped in landfills

The industrial city started to develop in Britain in the 18th century. Millions of people had been squeezed off the land because of the enclosure of farms and they were moving, or being moved, to the colonies and to Britain's own new cities. They also helped to dig the canals that were built to connect these cities.

In the past, the slow development of technologies had limited the growth of cities. Most cities had to obtain the bulk of their resources, including food and energy supplies, from their own immediate hinterland. Until the 18th century muscle, water and wind power, firewood and charcoal were the only energy sources. Only some of the largest cities, such as Rome and Beijing, were able to supply their food and timber requirements using canal barges and merchant vessels.

But modern cities function very differently from traditional ones. These differences arise, first and foremost, out of innovations in energy technology. When only charcoal was available for smelting metals, a limited range and quantity of tools and metal objects could be produced. The introduction of coking coal in the 18th century made it possible to create an unprecedented

Pig-iron smelting
The smelting of iron using coking coal became the basis of the industrial revolution and dramatically increased human power over nature.

range and quantity of new metal objects, including rails, iron girders and all kinds of machines. When coke made from coal came to replace charcoal for smelting iron ore, the production and availability of iron and steel increased dramatically. In 1712, Thomas Newcomen built the first steam engine, which was used to pump water out of a Cornish tin mine. In 1781, James Watt started producing his revolutionary rotary-motion steam engines. Soon they were driving factory machinery and powering trains and ships. In 1802, William Murdock brightened up a Birmingham city street with coal gas lights for the first time.

Urban writer Louis Mumford says this about coal gas lighting:

> *during the next generation its use widened, first in factories, then in homes; first in big cities, later in small centres; for without its aid work would frequently have been stopped by smoke and fog. The manufacture of illuminating gas within the confines of the towns became a characteristic new feature: the huge gas tanks reared their bulk over the urban landscape, great structures, on the scale of a cathedral: indeed, their tracery of iron, against an occasional clear lemon-green sky at sunrise, was one of the most pleasant aesthetic elements in the new order.*[1]

The routine use of steel caused a revolution in several key facets of urban life, particularly building construction, industrial production and transport systems.

In addition to these technological changes, major social changes also occurred. Steam engines, in particular, caused a major concentration in the ownership of the means of production and the organisation of labour. Small producers could not afford to buy the large and expensive engines. Consequently, more centralised patterns of ownership and production emerged, with large factories predominantly located in cities. And because the great cost of investing in steam engines made it crucial to run them continuously, shift work and regimented labour became the norm.

The new urban-industrial working class was very different from the peasants, feudal serfs or self-employed craftspeople that had preceded them. Legions of miners and industrial workers, many of them displaced from farms and villages, manned the new urban production centres, often located near coalfields. People were serving machines with endlessly repetitive labour. The development of machine-based production, in turn, necessitated rigid organisation of labour and tight managerial control. The vast range of new manufactured products brought unprecedented riches for a few, new prosperity for many and great misery for many more.

Steam engines soon became indispensable for pumping water into cities and sewage out of them. Steam technology was not static but was continuously improved on, sharply decreasing the consumption of fuel use relative to the 'horsepower' produced. In 1698, Savery's rudimentary steam engine had used 14 kilograms of coal to generate 1 horsepower. In 1768, James Watt's first engine used only 4 kilograms. In 1798, Oliver Evans's high-pressure engine used 3 kilograms and 100 years later the compound steam engine required only 1 kilogram to generate 1 horsepower. This fourteenfold improvement in energy efficiency and the increasing sophistication of the technology allowed an ever-wider range of applications.

The first passenger railway line, financed by Quaker money, opened in 1825 and ran between Stockton and Darlington. It was still rather experimental, as carriages kept derailing and locomotives exploding. The first 'serious' passenger railway, the Liverpool and Manchester Line, opened in 1830 and after that the world changed forever. George and Robert Stephenson built the line and the locomotives and were then given charge of many other new railway lines. The railways challenged the canal network that had connected the cities of Britain and provided a steady but slow means of bulk transport. Despite many teething problems, the speed and cost-effectiveness of rail transport made it victorious. Every town wanted a rail connection to increase its prosperity. As the demand grew, the length of rail tracks in Britain went up, from nothing in 1824 to nearly 14,000 miles in 1870.[2]

By the end of the 19th century, steam engines were given yet another new role: to drive generators, brightening up buildings and city streets with electric lights for the first time. This required machines of great power. The largest ones ever built were eight engines used to power electricity generators for New York City's new subway train system in 1898. Each 535-ton engine produced 11,000 horsepower. However, after just a few years such large steam engines became obsolete, as steam turbines started to take over for large electricity generators, and diesel engines for smaller ones.[3]

INDUSTRIAL DEVELOPMENT AND THE LOCAL ENVIRONMENT

The growth of urban factories in Britain was primarily due to the steam-powered new industrial technologies such as Arkwright's Spinning Jenny in 1769 and Cartwright's Power Loom in 1785, which were used to mass produce cotton into clothes, sheets and towels for the first time. These spinning and weaving mills, of course, had to be fed with vast quantities of raw cotton, which was produced by African slave labour on thousands of farms in the southern United States.

Britain's cotton industry developed in three places: North West England, centred on Manchester; the Midlands, centred on Nottingham; and the Clyde Valley in Scotland, between Lanark and Paisley. By the 1780s, it became concentrated in Lancashire, with many mills springing up in the Oldham–Bolton–Manchester triangle. The livelihoods of most people in the country came to be dependent on cotton. By 1802, the industry accounted for between 4 and 5 per cent of Britain's national income. By 1812, 100,000 spinners and 250,000 weavers were working in the cotton industry, which had overtaken the woolen industry. By 1830, more than half the value of British home-produced exports consisted of cotton textiles.[4]

The growth of this industry, in turn, contributed to unprecedented urban-isation. For instance, Manchester grew 33-fold in 90 years, from 12,000 people in 1760 to 400,000 people in 1850. The downside of this astonishing growth was appalling environmental and housing conditions that are familiar today from Third World cities.

In 1844, Friedrich Engels reported what he saw in Manchester:

The working people's quarters are sharply separated from the sections of the city reserved for the middle-class . . . Of the irregular cramming together of dwellings in ways which defy all rational plan it is impossible to convey an idea . . .The confusion has only recently reached its height when every scrap of space left by the old way of building has been filled up and patched over until not a foot of land is left to be further occupied . . .

The courts, which lead down to the Irk . . . contain unqualifiedly the most horrible dwellings which I have yet beheld. In one of these courts there stands a privy without a door, so dirty that the inhabitants can pass into and out of the court only by passing through foul pools of stagnant urine and excrement . . . Below it on the river there are several tanneries which fill the whole neighbourhood with the stench of animal putrefaction . . . Allen's Court was in such a state at the time of the cholera that the sanitary police ordered it evacuated, swept, and disinfected with chloride of lime . . . At the bottom flows . . . the Irk, a narrow, coal-black, foul-smelling stream, full of debris and refuse, which it deposits on the shallower right bank.[5]

Since there are few drawings or prints available to illustrate conditions in industrial cities, here is another quote. In 1862, the English author Hugh Miller wrote this about Manchester:

> Nothing seems more characteristic of the great manufacturing city, though disagreeably so, than the river Irwell, which runs through the place ... The hapless river—a pretty enough stream a few miles up, with trees overhanging its banks and fringes of green sedge set thick along its edges—loses cast as its gets among the mills and print works. There are myriads of dirty things given it to wash, and whole wagonloads of poisons from dye houses and bleach yards thrown into it to carry away; steam boilers discharge into it their seething contents, and drains and sewers their fetid impurities; till at length it rolls on—here between tall dingy walls, there under precipices of red sandstone—considerably less a river than a flood of liquid manure.[6]

In the new industrial towns and cities, municipal services were all but absent. In many places, the poor could be seen going from house to house in the middle-class districts, begging for water. Because of inadequate sewage systems, waste water was then flushed down open drains and into the streets. Yet ironically, despite their foulness, such urban environments were places of comparative affluence.[7]

In 1846, George Weerth, a young German, said this about Bradford in a newspaper article:

> Every other factory town in England is a paradise in comparison to this hole. In Manchester the air lies like lead upon you; in Birmingham it is just as if you were sitting with your nose in a stove pipe; in Leeds you have to cough with the dust and the stink as if you had swallowed a pound of Cayenne pepper in one go—but you can put up with all that. In Bradford, however, you think you have been lodged with the devil incarnate. If anyone wants to feel how a poor sinner is tormented in Purgatory, let him travel to Bradford.[8]

Bradford was widely regarded as England's most polluted town, with 200 factory chimneys continually churning out black, sulphurous smoke. From 1801 to 1851 its population grew eightfold, from 13,000 to 104,000. Bradford's raw sewage was dumped into the River Beck. Because people had to obtain their drinking water from the river, frequent outbreaks of cholera and typhoid occurred. Only 30 per cent of children born to textile workers reached the age of 15 and life expectancy, of just over 18 years, was one of the lowest in Britain.

Sheffield was another centre of industry. Its growth in the mid-19th century was largely due to Henry Bessemer. In the 1850s, he had patented a process turning molten pig-iron into steel by blowing air through it. This dramatically reduced the cost of steel making. In 1859, he established a company to produce steel for cannons and rails, using his Bessemer Converter. By 1879 Sheffield was producing about 10,000 tons of Bessemer steel weekly, nearly a quarter of Britain's total output. This was the answer to the dreams of engineers, who needed metals that were more durable than wrought iron but without the high cost of crucible steel.

Bessemer's cheap steel greatly stimulated the development of railways and the construction of iron steamships for commerce and warfare. Engineers were laying rail tracks all over the country. By 1885, Britain had about 18,000 miles of railways. In the same year, Blackpool inaugurated Britain's first electric street tramway.[9]

Dudley, Sandwell, Walsall, Solihull and Wolverhampton were all cities that grew on the back of coal and steel in a region that is now called the Black Country. It also encompassed Birmingham, though its own growth was based mainly on smaller-scale industries. In the final decades of the 19th century, its many factories produced guns, wire, nails, buttons, pens, saddles, bedsteads, spectacles, and gold and silver jewellery, which were exported all over the world.

The concentration of industry in central areas of Birmingham led to increasing demand for working-class housing close to the factories. The poor needed to be near the available work and so living in overcrowded areas was the norm. Old middle-class houses were divided up to accommodate several families. New, cheap back-to-back housing was often built on low-lying land prone to flooding. Usually several houses shared a common yard, washhouse, water pump and an uncovered privy.

The deplorable lack of adequate water supply and sanitation, reminiscent of 21st-century Third World cities, is vividly described by Louis Mumford:

The most elementary traditions of municipal service were absent.
On occasion, the poor would go from house to house in the
middle-class sections, begging for water as they might beg for
bread in a famine. With this lack of water for drinking and
washing it is no wonder that the filth accumulated. Open drains
represented, despite their foulness, comparative affluence.[10]

However, there is much evidence that poverty, bad housing and sanitation did not usually make the poor inhuman, but made them more aware of one another's needs. Poverty-stricken neighbourhoods were not slumped in despair—there was friendship as well as dislike, laughter as well as sadness. But the closeness of people to each other both in the factories and in the community, also led to another important development: the trade union movement, which set out to change fundamentally the living and working conditions of labouring people.[11]

At the other end of the social scale, the rich had their own way of social-ising. Birmingham, for instance, was the location of a monthly gathering of famous entrepreneurs and scientists known as the Lunar Society. Its meet-ings were timed 'to enable distant members to drive home by moonlight'. Its membership included the potter Josiah Wedgwood, scientist and philosopher Dr Erasmus Darwin, steam engine manufacturers Matthew Boulton and James Watt, Sir William Herschel, Sir Joseph Banks, Samuel Galton, James Keir and John Baskerville. The primary purpose of their meetings was to exchange ideas on science, technology, health, literature and art. Between them, the members of the Society did much to invent the key ideas and technologies that shaped the century.[12]

THE *LONDON* EMPIRE

The German poet Heinrich Heine said after a visit to London in 1827:

> *I have seen the greatest wonder which the world can show to the astonished spirit . . . and ever will there remain fixed indelibly on my memory the stone forest of houses, amid which flows the rushing stream of faces of living men with all their varied passions, and all their terrible impulses of love, of hunger, and of hatred—I mean London.*

Authors such as Charles Dickens eloquently depict the living conditions of poor Londoners. In *The Old Curiosity Shop* he talks about air pollution: 'Tall chimneys . . . poured out their plague of smoke, obscured the light and fouled the air.' Like in the industrial towns of the north, Londoners preferred to live near their work, with overcrowding reaching the most astonishing levels. But all that began to change as London's suburban railway network and its pioneering underground system stared to develop. Rapid travel profoundly changed London's physiology.[13]

Chimney belching black smoke
This sort of image may have represented the march of progress a few decades ago.
Today it is a symbol of the collision course between humans and nature.

In 1836, the city's first passenger railway, the London and Greenwich, was inaugurated, the first of numerous lines to be built during the 19th-century railway boom. Soon major train stations connected London to the rest of Britain: Waterloo was opened in 1848, King's Cross in 1851–2 and Paddington in 1854. Then, in 1863, the world's first steam-powered underground railway, the Metropolitan Line, was completed. After the introduction of electric trains a decade later, the Underground transformed London and was soon copied in other cities such as New York.

In 1800, London was a city of one million people. By 1850, it had reached four million, overtaking Bejing to become the world's largest city. London's astonishing growth represented a new scale of urbanisation. By 1939, it had grown to 8.6 million, with an urban region accommodating a further four million. London's growth was made possible by the technologies of the industrial revolution in Britain's industrial cities, and above all else steam power and its use in production and in local, regional and global transport. It soon became an essential component of the ever-greater expansion of the British— or the London—Empire.

Of course, London's growth was not only driven by new urban technologies, but also by the fact that it was at the heart of a global empire. By 1790, it was already a port city with some 14,000 ships bringing in goods and taking out exports to the rest of the world. London, with its global tentacles, was doubtless the world's greatest trading centre. When Isombard Kingdom Brunel launched his revolutionary *SS Great Britain* in Bristol in 1843, with its steel hull and its novel combination of sails and steam power, a global transport technology was born that transformed trade across the world.

London, of course, had also become the world's leading financial centre. Operations such as the East India Company were immensely profitable. The company financed the tea trade from India with illegal opium exports to China. Opposition to this trade precipitated the first Opium War, 1839–42, in which the Chinese were defeated and forced to extend British trading privileges. According to author Nick Robins, the East India Company reversed the ancient flow of wealth from West to East, and then put in place new systems of exchange and exploitation:

The impacts of this huge siphoning of wealth were immense, creating a misery of 'an essentially different and infinitely more intensive kind than all Hindustan had to suffer before', in the words of a columnist writing for the New York Tribune *in 1853, one Karl Marx.*[14]

St. Paul's Cathedral
London's empire was the product of a combination of industrial revolution technologies, military and financial power.

The satellite cities that had been created all over the empire were the bridge-heads of a highly profitable trade. Calcutta, Bombay, Hong Kong, Singapore, Sydney, New York, Toronto, Nairobi, Lagos and many others became even more accessible with the introduction of steamships. London's unprecedented access to resources and products from across the planet resulted in ever-greater accumulation of wealth by London entrepreneurs—traders, bankers and speculators. Steam-powered ships rendered distances increasingly irrelevant, plugging London into a global hinterland 'on which the sun never set'.

Meanwhile the abolition of the Corn Laws in Britain, which had protected British farmers against cheap food imports, meant that food, and particularly grain, was increasingly brought in from countries such as Canada and the USA rather than grown at home. When refrigerated ships became available, even meat and fruit could be imported long distances, from places such as New Zealand and Argentina. Compared with the food supply system that emerged in 19th-century Britain, ancient Rome's food imports from North Africa pale into insignificance.

Economic globalisation, much talked about in the early 21st century, actually made its debut in the mid-19th century. William Stanley Jevons wrote in his book *The Coal Question*:

The plains of North America and Russia are our cornfields;
Chicago and Odessa our granaries; Canada and the Baltic are our
timber forests; Australasia contains our sheep farms; and in
Argentina and on the western prairies of North America are our
herds of oxen; Peru sends her silver, and the gold of South Africa
and Australia flows to London; the Hindus and the Chinese grow
tea for us. And our coffee, sugar and spice plantations are all in
the Indies. Spain and France are our vineyards and in the
Mediterranean are our fruit gardens, and our cotton grounds,
which for so long have occupied the Southern United States, are
now being extended everywhere in the warm regions of the Earth.[15]

Jevons's own concern was Britain's growing dependence on supplying essential goods by using cheap coal for long-distance transport. He thought that this could have a highly detrimental effect on he country's economic stability in the long term.

In today's language, London could be described as a great pioneer in unsustainable development. Many of the processes of mega-urbanisation that started in London are still unfolding today.

SMOKE, WATER AND SEWAGE

In addition to dangerous trade dependencies, London also developed major local environmental problems—notably smog from a million coal fires. Mark Twain said that 'in London . . . you can't persuade a thing to look new; the coal-smoke turns it into an antiquity the moment you take your hand off it'.[16]

Like Rome, London had to develop a complex water supply system, though it had the benefit of steam-powered pumps. It used to supply itself from the groundwater table underneath the city, but 150 years or so of economic activity there had resulted in accumulations of heavy metals or chemicals from gas works and factories in the soil. This made the use of groundwater for drinking purposes increasingly problematic. London is lucky in having another water supply close at hand in the form of the River Thames. However, other cities are not so fortunate.

As London grew larger and larger, the condition of its main artery, the river Thames, became an increasing cause for concern, due to contamination from industrial activity and the accumulation of human excreta. From the early 19th century onwards, flush toilets had been installed in London houses. Initially these were usually connected not to sewers but to cesspits. In 1848, of 16,000 dwellings less than half were connected to sewers. But because the cesspits frequently overflowed, environmental conditions in the densely populated city were often intolerable. In 1853–4 a cholera epidemic killed nearly 11,000 Londoners. Eventually, in a pioneering feat of medical detective work, Dr John Snow traced a major outbreak in Soho to well water contaminated with human waste from local cesspits. Nevertheless, as more and more houses were connected to sewers, the pollution was flushed into the Thames instead.

In 1855, eminent scientist Michael Faraday described the condition of the river:

> I traversed this day by steam-boat the space between London and Hungerford Bridges . . . The appearance and the smell of the water forced themselves at once on my attention. The whole of the river was an opaque pale brown fluid . . . The smell was very bad, and . . . the whole river was for the time a real sewer . . . I have thought it a duty to record these facts, that they may be brought to the attention of those who exercise power or have responsibility in relation to the condition of our river . . . If there be sufficient authority to remove a putrescent pond from the neighbourhood of a few simple dwellings, surely the river which flows for so many miles through London ought not to be allowed to become a fermenting sewer. The condition in which I saw the Thames may perhaps be considered as exceptional, but it ought to be an impossible state, instead of which I fear it is rapidly becoming the general condition. If we neglect this subject, we cannot expect to do so with impunity.[17]

The year 1858 was notorious for the 'great stink'—the sewage pollution of the Thames halted debates in the Houses of Parliament for days on end. Yes, something had to be done: but how could London deal with the sewage produced by so many people? A long and passionate debate ensued and various schemes were discussed. One was a recycling system consisting of metal pipes arranged like the spokes of a wheel, through which the sewage would be transported to fields at the edge of the city to be used for growing crops.

Justus Liebig, a famous chemist, favoured such a scheme. He was called over from Germany to advise the British government. While most people were simply concerned with cleaning up the Thames, Liebig was preoccupied with the loss of plant nutrients from farms supplying food to London. He had studied Rome's environmental history and had become convinced that the export of large amounts of grain from North Africa over hundreds of years had permanently depleted its soil fertility (see Chapter 3). If the minerals contained in the excreta of millions of Londoners—nitrogen, potash, phosphate, magnesium and calcium—were to be removed and never to be returned to the farmland feeding Londoners, how could the land be kept productive? In a letter to Prime Minister Sir Robert Peel, he expressed his concerns about London repeating Rome's mistakes, but on a much larger scale:

> The cause of the exhaustion of the soil is sought in the customs
> and habits of the towns people, i.e., in the construction of water
> closets, which do not admit of a collection and preservation of the
> liquid and solid excrement. They do not return in Britain to the
> fields, but are carried by the rivers into the sea. The equilibrium in
> the fertility of the soil is destroyed by this incessant removal of
> phosphates and can only be restored by an equivalent supply . . . If
> it was possible to bring back to the fields of Scotland and England
> all those phosphates which have been carried to the sea in the last
> 50 years, the crops would increase to double the quantity of
> former years.[18]

In Paris a famous contemporary, Victor Hugo, echoed Liebig's views in his novel *Les Misérables*. He, too, advocated the use of sewage as fertilizer:

> Paris throws five millions a year into the sea. And this without
> metaphor. How, and in what manner? day and night. With what
> object? without any object. With what thought? without thinking of
> it. For what return? for nothing. By means of what organ? by
> means of its intestine. What is its intestine? its sewer . . . Science,
> after long experiment, now knows that the most fertilizing and the
> most effective of manures is that of man.[19]

Back in London, Liebig failed to persuade the Metropolitan Board of Works to build a sewage recycling system. After much debate, it was decided to dispose of the sewage in the North Sea instead. From 1858, the engineer

Joseph Bazalgette was put in charge of a huge sewage disposal project, during which 20,000 men worked for 13 years to construct a very ambitious and expensive sewage system. The 1866 Sanitary Act enforced the connection of all London's houses to Bazalgette's sewer network, whose outlets into the Thames were downriver at Crossness and Beckton. When the system was up and running, the exposure of Londoners to sewage ended for good and cholera became a thing of the past.

But as a direct consequence of London deciding to build a sewage *disposal* rather than a *recycling* system, Liebig and others set to work on the development of artificial fertilisers, to find a way to replenish the fertility of farmland feeding cities such as London by artificial means. The age of artificial fertilisers and chemical agriculture had arrived. I would argue that this historic development significantly contributed to the unsustainability of both agricultural and urban systems today.

On British farms in the late 19th century, guano, cheaply available from Chile and Peru, temporarily became the primary source of soil fertility, until artificial fertilisers, containing phosphates, nitrates and potash, had been fully developed.

London's decisions, taken in the 19th century, still have a profound effect around the world today. Most cities have built sewage disposal rather than recycling systems and the farmland feeding them is being kept productive artificially by the use of chemical fertilisers. The consequences are there for all to see: in many countries coastal waters are laden with urban sewage and industrial pollutants, as well as the fertiliser and pesticide run-off from farms feeding cities. Surely there must be more sustainable ways to manage urban systems, particularly in new cities where major investments in sewage infrastructure have yet to take place (see Chapter 11).

THE INDUSTRIAL REVOLUTION SPREADS

In Germany, the Ruhr region went through a transformation similar to that of Britain's Black Country. On the back of coal mining and steel, industries were developed by industrialists like Krupp and Thyssen and massive urban growth occurred. From 1852 to 1925, the Ruhrgebiet increased its population tenfold, to 3.8 million people. Like in Britain, most people who came to work in the mines and the steel mills were farmers and craftsmen. At first they mainly came from Germany itself, but soon also from Poland, Slovakia, Croatia and Italy, creating an ethnically very diverse society.

Refinery
Refineries and chemical works have given us the power to make a new world of industrial products. But pollution has become a major legacy.

The Ruhrgebiet was transformed from a landscape of small farms, villages, towns and forests into an industrial landscape of mines, steelworks, slag heaps, tenement buildings and railway lines. The speed of change was so rapid that proper planning was well nigh impossible. The mining and steel industries caused small towns such as Essen, Duisburg, Dortmund, Gelsenkirchen and Bochum to grow into a cluster of large cities. From time to time attempts have been made to bring them together into one single, giant Ruhr metropolis, but this has never succeeded.

The industrial revolution in the Ruhr in turn contributed greatly to economic development in Germany as a whole and, ultimately, to the growth of Berlin, which became the capital city in 1871. In the 100 years from 1755 to 1855 it more than quadrupled to 440,000 people and in 1871 its population was 825,000. Really massive growth occurred in the next 40 years, with Berlin becoming Germany's administrative centre and also as a result of rapid industrialisation, with major companies such as Borsig and Siemens locating there.

In 1837, August Borsig had founded his steel works, which soon started producing steam locomotives and rails, completing Berlin's first railway line to Potsdam in 1838.[20] In 1847, Werner Siemens had established his company in Berlin, to produce electricity generation and communications equipment, and quickly established a reputation as a leading innovator in these fields. Both companies grew massive by playing central roles in marketing transport, electrification and communications systems, which were used in Berlin itself and elsewhere in Europe. (In 1873, Siemens's English subsidiary laid the first undersea cable linking Britain and the US, spawning the age of intercontinental telecommunication.)

By 1914, Berlin had 3,700,000 people. It reached its maximum population in 1933 with 4.24 million, extending to an area of 88,000 hectares which, at that time, made it the third most extensive city in the world after New York and London. Today its population has stabilised around 3.5 million.[21]

Like all large cities, Berlin had to deal with the consequences of its rapid growth, including the problems of dealing with waste water, which was causing pollution in the city and its rivers. In the 1870s, Berlin's chief engineer, James Hobrecht, was charged with developing a new sewage system for the city. Working closely with the doctor and hygienist Rudolf Virchow, he chose a radial system of pressured steel pipes connected to the sewers, similar to the sewage recycling system that had been proposed but rejected in London.[22]

The purpose of the radial pipe system was to transport the waste water from Berlin to 12 large 'trickle fields' extending to thousands of hectares on the edge of the city, which were to receive and 'digest' the waste water. Using the plant nutrients contained in the sewage, substantial horticultural and orchard enterprises were set up on the periphery of Berlin, which operated for about 100 years. The system was only abandoned and replaced by conventional sewage treatment systems after 1985. Subsequent investigations have shown substantial accumulation of heavy metals and chlorinated hydrocarbons in the soil, caused by the contamination of Berlin's sewage from industrial and commercial activities. Ironically deindustrialisation, as has been occurring in cities such as Berlin in recent years, will make it safer again to use urban sewage in farming.[23]

OVER IN THE USA

The many technologies pioneered during the industrial revolution were eagerly adopted abroad. In the USA, industrial entrepreneurs such as Andrew Carnegie, a Scottish immigrant to America, made his fortune by setting up Bessemer Converters in Pittsburgh after a trip to Britain. He greatly contributed to the growth of Pittsburgh, which had all the right ingredients for industrial development: it was rich in coal, had abundant forests and its rivers provided good access to the Great Lakes and to new manufacturing cities such as Detroit. Pittsburgh soon turned into the 'steel capital of the world' and also became known as 'Smoky City'. The author James Parton said of Pittsburgh that it was 'hell with the lid taken off'. On some days the air was so sooty that streetlights and automobile headlights had to be lit during the day and office workers had to change their shirts at noon.

Pittsburgh had a very heterogeneous working class with workers from all over the world. Carnegie knew how to exploit their labour for his own benefit. In 1892, he defeated a strike by skilled craftsmen, which gave him almost complete freedom to shape the iron and steel industry exactly as he wished. He set about the task of redesigning his mills to maximise steel production and minimise workers' control. With the formation of US Steel in 1901, an age marked by competition gave way to monopoly control over the industry. The employers felt secure in their mastery of the workforce and their increasing domination of the political landscape of the United States.[24]

THE RISE OF NEW YORK CITY

HG Wells said of New York: 'To Europe, she was America. To America, she was the gateway of the earth. But to tell the story of New York would be to write a social history of the world.'

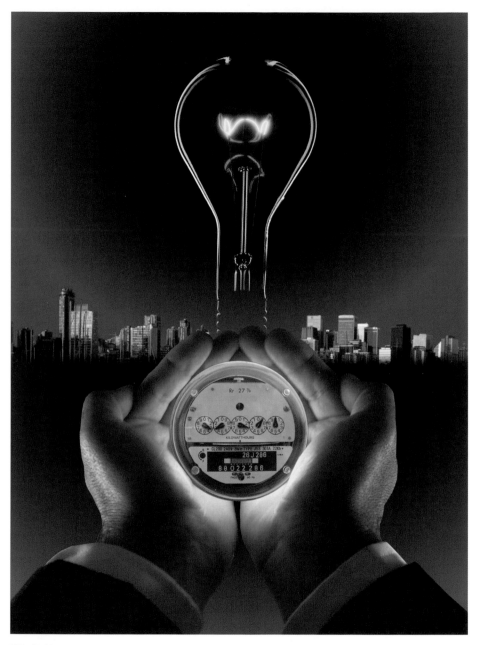

City lights
Electricity is a non-negotiable ingredient of the modern world. But can we produce enough of it sustainably?

New York City is located at the mouth of the Hudson River and originated as a Native American settlement. Ever since the Dutch started settling there in the late 16th century, it had been a city of immigrants. British settlers soon followed and thereafter the city found it hard to keep up with waves of immigration that came from all over the world. For two years, 1789–90, it was the US capital. By then, it was already the largest US city.

New York City consists of five boroughs—Brooklyn, Queens, Staten Island, Manhattan and The Bronx. Its grid plan echoes 'ideal' urban layouts dating back to ancient China. Like Beijing, New York prospered partly because of to a new canal that connected it to its hinterland. The 363-mile Erie Canal, opened in 1825, linked New York with the Great Lakes and started a fresh, prosperous era. New York shook off a reputation as a squalid urban centre and soon acquired the image of a city of superlatives: in 1870 Thomas Edison lit up the city's streets with arc lights for the first time. New York buildings soon became the tallest, in 1883 its 1,600-feet Brooklyn suspension bridge became the longest, and its subway system, started in 1904, became the most extensive in the world, extending to 368 kilometres. With 337 hectares, Central Park, created by 3,000 men over 10 years, was one of the largest parks in the world. And New Yorkers needed it badly: the city's population grew from 79,000 in 1800, to 700,000 in 1850, to 3.4 million in 1900, to 7.9 million in 1950.[25]

At the turn of the 20th century New York City no longer just grew outwards—it started growing upwards. Using steel girders made in Pittsburgh, its first tall buildings had 'made in America' stamped all over them. Ironically, while the design and construction methods were revolutionary, many early skyscrapers are actually topped with retro fantasy castles derived from medieval European architecture.

Skyscrapers crucially depended on the development of elevator technology. In 1903, Otis installed the first ever electric lifts in New York's 55-metre Beaver Building. In 1913, the new 241-metre Woolworth Building was hailed as New York's 'Cathedral of Commerce'. In 1930, the 320-metre Chrysler Building, with 77 floors, was briefly the world's tallest. But in 1931, the 443-metre Empire State building, with 102 floors, became the tallest of them all. Its lift speed reached 366 metres per minute, nearly double that of the elevators in the Woolworth Building.[26] Because of fast elevators, top floors in New York City and elsewhere, originally difficult to let, became the most desirable and expensive floors of tall buildings.

In 1817, the New York Stock & Exchange Board was created and, as its power grew, it turned New York into a centre of finance to rival London. Wall

Central Park, New York
New York's Central Park is surrounded by a girdle of skyscrapers. Nature should be at the heart of every city to make people aware that they are not just creatures of modern technology.

Street became a world power in its own right, and the ultimate example of a global information-based industry. The financial power of megacities such as New York is a major driver of worldwide industrial and urban growth and the impacts of these developments need to be better understood.

CITIES AND THE ENVIRONMENT

The modern city is the product of a range of breathtaking innovations that emerged from the industrial revolution. As new technologies spread across the world, large cities started to spring up in many places. Problems of pollution, traffic congestion and overcrowding became ubiquitous. In many areas attempts have been made to deal with these by social innovation and planning. A pleasant urban environment with public spaces, parks and gardens came to be regarded as crucial for assuring a positive social life (see also Chapter 8).

Cleaning up urban pollution has often been achieved by regulations that forced factories to improve their environmental performance or by moving them away from city centres. In addition to increasing local environmental impacts, the industrial revolution also caused dramatic changes in the relationship between humans and nature. Unprecedented access to the earth's subterranean stores of resources, and particularly fossil fuels, profoundly altered the way we inhabit this planet. These issues will be dealt with in subsequent chapters.

The next chapter focuses on the continuing process of urbanisation and how it is spreading across the world.

CHAPTER 5

Globalisation and Megacity Growth

We have entered the urban millennium. At their best, cities are engines of growth and incubators of civilization. They are crossroads of ideas, places of great intellectual ferment and innovation . . . cities can also be places of exploitation, disease, violent crime, unemployment, and extreme poverty . . . we must do more to make our cities safe and liveable places for all. (Kofi Annan, 2000)

We live in astonishing times. From 1900 to 2000, the global human population increased fourfold, from 1.5 to 6.2 billion. During that time, the global *urban* population expanded thirteenfold, from 225 million to 2.9 billion, or to about 47 per cent of the world population. In 2000, the more developed nations were about 76 per cent urbanised, while the figure for developing countries was about 40 per cent. By 2007, urban dwellers are likely to outnumber rural dwellers for the first time. By 2030, 60 per cent of the world population, or 4.9 billion people, are expected to live in urban areas, more than three times more than the world's entire population in 1900. In the coming decades, virtually all the world's population growth will occur in cities, and about 90 per cent of this will take place in developing countries.[1]

From 1995 to 2000, urban populations in the more developed countries grew by just 0.6 per cent, whereas those in developing regions grew by 2.9

per cent per year and will continue to grow by 2.3 per cent until 2030. In 2000, two-thirds of urban people lived in cities of half a million or less, and only one-third in larger cities.[2]

Only a few per cent of people live in megacities with 10 million inhabitants or more, yet the unprecedented growth of cities of this scale is still a very important trend. Their numbers rose from just one (New York) in 1950 to five in 1975, to 19 in 2000, with 16 of them in developing countries. By 2015, there will be some 23 megacities, of which 15 will be in Asia.[3] Urban landscapes such as Tokyo, São Paulo or Mexico City, which sprawl across hundreds of thousands of hectares, are unprecedented in human history and are by far the largest structures ever created by humanity. Their emergence would have been impossible before the age of coal, oil, steel, industrial mass production and global trade.

At the start of the 21st century, urban growth is most rapid in two areas: in the Asia-Pacific region it is around 4 per cent a year, but in parts of Africa, at 5 per cent a year, it is even higher.[4] All over the world, population growth within cities is a major factor in overall urban growth. Whereas in Asia it is caused primarily by new urban opportunities, in Africa it is often driven by

Shanghai
Shanghai, with over 10 per cent urban and economic growth per year, is well on its way to joining the elite group of the world's premier cities.

acute crises in rural areas. The continuing worldwide inmigration of people from rural areas results from a combination of factors: labour-saving farming technology; deforestation, soil erosion, subdivision of farms or lack of water; or competition from subsided, imported crops. People are being 'pushed' away from farms and villages, but also being 'pulled' towards cities, which promise new opportunities.

There are ten main factors that contribute to urban growth:

- migration due to job and business opportunities,
- urban education, health and other services,
- reproduction of urban populations,
- cheap energy supplies,
- technological development,
- import substitution and economic growth,
- economic globalisation,
- urban political and financial power,
- urban-centred transport systems,
- easy access to global food supplies.

Urbanisation is driven above all else by economic factors, and particularly the creation of international production centres and markets backed up by global transport systems. In the last 50 years, the global economy has grown many times and is becoming ever more integrated. In 1950 most of the world's workforce was employed in agriculture; by 1990 most worked in services.[5]

Because urban growth can have detrimental effects on rural areas, some countries have initiated policies to try to counter rural–urban migration, and to improve living conditions in villages—by rural education and health programmes, improved water supplies and sanitation, road construction, electrification and investment in rural economies. But such policies can be counterproductive because they tend to introduce urban cultural values into rural areas. The spread of satellite dishes and TV to remote rural communities, in particular, can increase local people's fascination with urban living.

CITIES AS DEPENDENT SYSTEMS

As we saw in the last chapter, the emergence of large cities is very much the result of new technical options such as combustion technology, steel making, motorised transport and long-distance communication systems. Large modern cities depend on large infrastructures for their energy, raw materials, water and food supply. Their tall buildings require continuous electricity supplies to operate lifts, pump water, light rooms and power air conditioning and domestic electrical equipment. They require elaborate internal transport infrastructures, as well as regional and global transport systems to take goods and materials into and out of cities.

Such developments are not *determined* but *made possible* by an array of new technologies. New building technologies, in particular, have helped accelerate urban growth. Bulldozers, cranes, road-building machinery and ready-mixed concrete are the 'headline technologies' that make fast urban construction possible. Buildings are usually no longer made of local materials, but from steel, glass and cement.

Where cities grow, so does the demand for cement for making buildings, roads, parking lots, bridges and dams. Worldwide cement production is about 1,800 million tonnes, with a turnover of US$144 billion forecast by 2006. China, the world's biggest manufacturer, produces 700 million tonnes of cement and accounts for 37 per cent of global demand. Turkey, India, Brazil and Thailand are other major producers and consumers. The US uses about 260 million cubic metres of ready-mixed concrete each year, with cement and sand as its main ingredients.

Concrete has become the most widely used construction material in the world and its use has major environmental implications. Compared with traditional buildings made of brick and stone, concrete structures are far more immutable and difficult to dismantle. Concrete seals soil surfaces and its production also requires vast amounts of energy: for each tonne of cement about one tonne of carbon dioxide is emitted into the atmosphere. Cement production is a major source of greenhouse gas emissions, accounting for some 8 per cent of carbon dioxide discharge globally.[6]

In the process of urbanisation, we are profoundly changing our relationship to our host planet. The growth of modern cities and urban economies means increased demands on *natural capital*, as well as increased discharge of wastes. Cities suck in resources and dump wastes in nature, and in an urbanising world it is crucial to create a better match between urban resource use and the world's ecosystems. The environmental impact of increasing urban resource use is becoming the dominant feature of the human presence on earth.

This can be witnessed in developing countries, where urban people have much higher disposable incomes than rural dwellers. For instance, in China in 2003 the disposable incomes of urban people were four times higher than those of rural dwellers—$8,000 as compared with $2,000.[7] This inevitably increases their consumption of fossil fuels, water, meat, cement, metals and manufactured products. Cities require a continuous supply of all manner of materials and products, yet the environmental costs of increased consumption are not reflected in the price of the goods that people buy.

In many modern cities, a direct connection to the land that supplies them with food or forest products has all but ceased. Long-distance food supplies are becoming the norm. The same is true for water supplies. Construction of large dams in distant river valleys has become commonplace, to supply water (and electricity) to far-away cities. But as cities abstract water for themselves, they often deprive local rural communities of water supplies, further contributing to rural–urban migration (see also Chapter 11).

TOKYO—THE WORLD'S LARGEST CITY REGION

The UN's seminal book *An Urbanizing World* states:

> the countries with the most rapidly growing economies since 1950 were generally those with the most rapid increase in their level of urbanisation while the world's largest cities are heavily concentrated in the world's largest economies.[8]

Throughout the 1980s and 1990s Asia's economies and cities, in particular, grew at a record rate and were catching up with the per capita levels of consumption in the previously developed countries. Perhaps the most striking postwar example of rapid urban-industrial growth is Tokyo, which also illustrates the problems of dealing with growth-related pollution and waste.

Since the 17th century, Tokyo has been Japan's economic and political centre (see Chapter 3). After the intensely creative but somewhat introverted culture of the Edo Period, the Meiji Period in the 19th century turned Japan into an industrial and military power with global ambitions. But these came to grief as the Second World War left its economy and many of its cities in ruins. Then the Korean War presented Japan with new opportunities for rapid industrial growth. Before long, companies, benefiting from a large, loyal and hard-working labour force, put an ever-wider range of new industrial products on the world market—from motorbikes to cars, cameras, hi-fis, fax machines and computers. For 25 years, from 1950 to 1975, Japan had annual economic growth of up to 10 per cent, though from 1976 till 1992 this gradually dropped to 4 per cent, and has been somewhat less since then.[9]

Tokyo has been the hub of Japan's economic miracle. During the postwar period, the Tokyo Metropolitan Region became its largest manufacturing centre. Economic and urban growth were closely interlinked. Tokyo's population doubled in 53 years, from 6 million in 1949 to 12 million in 2002, as people moved in from villages and farms to take advantage of new job opportunities. The Tokyo Metropolitan Region, also known as the Tokyo–Yokohama–Kawasaki Area, became the world's largest conurbation with a population of 28 million people, and now houses nearly a quarter of Japan's population.

All this growth occurred with little city-wide planning. Housing costs soared and housing shortages and overcrowding became endemic. Chronic traffic jams were only gradually overcome by the construction of a new metro and a system of fast suburban trains. In 1966, the Tokyo prefecture drew up a series of plans to solve the city's many problems. New provisions were made to improve and expand public housing. Suburban development was encouraged to reduce inner-city overcrowding. For instance, Tsukuba, 30 miles northwest of Tokyo, was developed as a new housing area and also as a centre for scientific research. It now has 50 research institutes and two technical universities.

As a global trading city, Tokyo has relied heavily on imported energy, food and timber supplies. Japan, the world's second largest economy, imports 78 per cent of its energy, 60 per cent of its food and 82 per cent of its timber from other countries.

The Tokyo Metropolitan Region is not only Japan's economic powerhouse but also one of the world's largest consumer markets, with an average disposable household income of around US$30,000 per year. While this makes it a very attractive market, such a high concentration of consumers also causes major waste disposal problems. For many years, much of the metropolitan region's waste was dumped in Tokyo Bay, with some of it being used to create new land for more urban growth.

As industrial production and consumption increased, so did pollution. Air pollution became a major problem. The Sumida and Onagi rivers, which flow through Tokyo, became heavily polluted with industrial effluents as well as sewage and with mineral fertiliser run-off from farmland, since farmers had phased out night-soil for growing their crops. Around Tokyo Bay, where fishermen once had their picturesque villages, oil tanks, refineries, factories and power plants now proliferated on reclaimed land. In a couple of decades of industrial and urban growth, the bay's fragile marine ecosystem was severely damaged. Fishing collapsed as Tokyo Bay became heavily polluted.[10]

During the Edo Period and before, Tokyo Bay had yielded huge amounts of fish and shellfish. However, after 1955 the population density in the Tokyo Metropolitan Region grew rapidly, and large-scale development and reclamation destroyed much of the original shoreline. A gradual increase in public pressure led the Tokyo prefecture to implement various measures to deal with water pollution, encouraging local companies to clean up their effluents, and building new sewage works to counter the eutrophication of Tokyo Bay. Since the 1973 oil crisis, more and more has been done to clean up the bay and its water quality has improved substantially.

Tokyo's large industrial production capacity as well as its huge consumption also caused major solid waste disposal problems. This was further compounded by the fact that most people like to own the latest electronic gadgets and have no room to keep their old equipment, even if it still works. Due to its limited land area and lack of space for landfills, Japan has started to take recycling seriously. Glass, metals, green waste, paper and cardboard are increasingly collected separately and recycled. Much of Tokyo's combustible waste is burned in 18 incinerators and the ash is deposited in landfills. But there has been growing public concern about this practice, and the avoidance of incineration and a transformation to a full-blown recycling society are now widely debated.

From the 1980s onwards, heavy industries in Tokyo have gradually been replaced by high-tech light and knowledge-based enterprises. More and more manufacturing companies have relocated from the coastal zone to areas of the interior that have good access to high-speed transportation. Tokyo's economy is increasingly focused on finance, wholesaling, information and service industries. Of course, it is also the seat of Japan's government and of foreign embassies.

Some Japanese are beginning to remember the days of the Edo Period when the country had an economy based on renewable resources. It was self-sufficient in all the resources people needed for a comfortable life. Many Japanese today are eager to learn more about the social and economic system of that time and to apply the 'wisdom of the Edo Period' in contemporary living.[11]

GLOBAL CITIES, TRADE, FINANCE AND COMMUNICATIONS

The growth of Tokyo in the last 50 years was initially driven largely by industrial development, but it has been transformed into a prime financial services centre. As a leading player in the global financial system, it has joined London and New York in the exclusive club of the world's 'premier cities'. The financial power of these three cities is unprecedented, with information technology giving their financial institutions a global reach as never before. The daily money-go-round from Tokyo to London to New York is the most striking example of this.[12]

In the New York Region, the service sector makes up 85 per cent of its GDP, while in Greater London the figure is 82 per cent, and in Greater Tokyo 74 per cent. The computerisation of stock exchanges in the 1980s brought about a process of rapid change, globalising the financial markets. Previously protected national markets were forced to compete for internationally mobile investors, as protective regulations and transaction taxes were abolished or reformed. These developments have made investors increasingly footloose, as they learned to avoid expensive national regulations and to shift their activities to low-cost locations.

In the global hierarchy of cities, Hong Kong, Singapore, Seoul, Taipei, Shanghai and Mumbai represent an increasingly important second rank. Hong Kong, for instance, grew after 1945 as a centre for cheap manufacture. But more recently services have become the largest sector of its economy, accounting for nearly 85 per cent of its 1996 gross domestic product.[13]

In Singapore, manufacturing is still the largest employer, with 2,000 companies employing some 145,000 workers, mainly in engineering, chemicals and electronics. Nine out of the world's 20 leading semiconductor manufacturers operate 13 wafer fabrication plants. But Singapore is also a major centre for shipping and air transport and is becoming a major financial trading centre. Its financial sector has rapidly expanded in areas such as risk management, financial engineering, securities trading and investment banking.

A few large cities are becoming the command centres of an information-centred global economy. According to Manuel Castells, 'the new economy is organised around global networks of capital, management, and information, whose access to technological know-how is at the roots of productivity and competitiveness'.[14] From a similar perspective, Saskia Sassen has developed a 'global city hypothesis'. She argues that a handful of global cities have become:

- concentrated command points in the organization of the world economy by the use of advanced telecommunication systems,
- important centres for finance and specialized producer service firms,
- coordinators of state power,

Singapore
Singapore, a major centre of manufacturing and trade, has become one of the world's major cities in a matter of decades.

- sites of innovative forms of industrialization and production, and
- markets for the products and innovations produced.[15]

Manuel Castells sees the emergence of a global network society:

[Power] is no longer concentrated in institutions (the state), organizations (capitalist firms), or symbolic controllers (corporate media, churches). It is diffused in global networks of wealth . . . information and images, which circulate and transmute in a system of variable geometry and dematerialised geography. Yet it does not disappear.[16]

The impact of the information revolution seems set to become as large as that of the industrial revolution, profoundly changing the way we live, work, learn and recreate. Due to Internet technology, networks are replacing communities, with virtual meeting places, forums and markets that have no rootedness in place. In a world of social networks, the virtual equivalents of the Greek agora, the Roman forum, the village green and the town square are beginning to emerge as websites and Internet chat rooms. A global do-it-yourself interactive information society is transcending communities based on location and shared experience. But powerful companies are using the same technology very effectively outside any democratic control.

URBAN-INDUSTRIAL GROWTH IN CHINA

Until recently a few developing countries, such as China, deliberately prevented rural–urban migration. After 1949, the Chinese government's introduced a closed-city policy and for 30 years population mobility was strictly controlled by issuing local passports to stop people from moving away. A person's place of residence was determined by their role in the local agricultural or industrial labour force. In 1978, China was still an essentially rural society. However, Deng Xiaoping's economic reforms during the 1980s and 1990s dramatically changed this situation. It encouraged the growth of rural industries and triggered a process of 'rural urbanisation', during which many towns multiplied their populations. For instance Shenzhen, on the border with Hong Kong, grew from a few thousand to a few million people in a couple of decades.

From the 1980s onwards, China experienced a dramatic increase in rural–urban migration, one of the largest flows of labour migration in human history. By 1995 there were probably over 80 million rural–urban migrants in China's major cities. People longer needed on the land migrated into cities to take up jobs in factories, construction, restaurants, transportation, urban agriculture or as household servants. The settlers soon demanded the same privileges as older urban residents. The latter often resent migrants and hold them responsible for traffic congestion, housing shortages, competition for jobs and increasing crime. Many also want a slowdown in urbanisation, because rapid growth requires major investments in basic infrastructure such as sewage, energy distribution, water supply and waste disposal.[17]

What is happening in China today loosely follows patterns of growth arising out of the industrial revolution in Europe, America and then Japan. A specific feature in the growth of the Chinese economy, however, is that global investors benefiting from cheap labour are substantially contributing to the country's boom.

Today, China is probably urbanising faster than any other country in history. This is directly linked to the growth of its manufacturing sector, driven by the emergence of a consumer society as well as a huge export-driven economy. For two decades, China's economic growth has been around 8 per cent per year and urbanisation is on a similar scale. By 2010, China expects to build no less than 400 new cities. Some 300 million people—a quarter of the country's population—will be moving to cities, converting from peasant farming and craft-based living to urban-industrial lifestyles. The increased purchasing power of hundreds of millions of people is driving greatly increased demand for consumer goods and also for meat (see Chapter 6).[18]

But what are the likely environmental impacts of urban development in China? Will it undergo the same 'dirty' development familiar from Europe and North America, or will it be able to avoid soil, water and air contamination? Can urbanisation in China be reconciled with its acknowledged goal of sustainable development, expressed, for instance, in the country's 'Trans-Century Green Project Plan'?[19]

Large-scale urbanisation is profoundly resource demanding. As we have already seen, peasants switching from rural to urban lifestyles greatly increase their per capita resource use. In China's cities, factories are proliferating, making products such as plastic toys, household equipment, computer parts, and using toxic and hazardous materials in their production processes. Storage tanks for oil, diesel and gasoline, natural gas, ammonia, chlorine and sulphur compounds, acetone and chemical cleaning agents sometimes leak. Air and water pollution is becoming a growing problem.

Boom cities like Shanghai or Tianjin look like large, modern cities anywhere, with new factories and warehouses, new roads full of new cars and a skyline dotted with cranes supplying building materials for new tower blocks. The rapid industrialisation in the Shanghai area is symbolised by its huge new container terminal, with ships leaving day and night for destinations across the planet. In China, urban growth and economic globalisation are intimately connected. This is also evident in Shanghai's new stock market, with its vast electronic display board indicating the fluctuations of stocks and shares. Not surprisingly, Shanghai is a leading candidate to join the ranks of the world's premier financial service centres.

East Asia as a whole—including countries such as Korea, Thailand, Vietnam, Laos and Cambodia—has seen a rapid growth in private income with an accompanying growth in public infrastructure and services. Poverty has certainly been reduced. According to World Bank statistics, 10 per cent of the region's population now live in poverty compared to 30 per cent in 1970. Along with high income growth, population growth rates have fallen markedly. East Asian population growth rates were 2.3 per cent a year from 1965 to 1990 and are expected to fall to 0.7 per cent a year for the period from 2000 to 2030.

Fundamental to the income growth has been rapid industrial development. Between 1965 and 1990, the industrial sector in East Asia as a whole grew by an average of 9 per cent a year to nine times its 1965 size. But how environmentally sustainable are these developments, driven as they are by the massive growth in the use of non-renewable resources, and particularly fossil fuels?

CITIES IN THIRD WORLD COUNTRIES

Living conditions for a billion or more urban people today in many parts of the world are comparable to those in the cities of the industrial revolution, often lacking even the most basic amenities. In cities such as Nairobi, Manila, Calcutta or Jakarta, squatter camps can accommodate up to half of the urban population. People in search of new opportunities in the city often end up living in appalling housing conditions, in cardboard or tin shacks, with no sewage or waste collection, infested by flies, lice, rats and other vermin. Poorer cities often cannot afford to import or maintain appropriate infrastructure technology. Many Third World urban neighbourhoods lack any effective infrastructures for water supply, sewage disposal and waste management, with people having to live in festering, health-threatening environments.

Unhealthy conditions have become the degrading reality of life for hundreds of millions of people. Infectious diseases such as cholera, typhoid and tuberculosis are now commonly occurring in developing cities, with epidemics threatening particularly the poorest neighbourhoods. Tackling urban environmental problems is one of the great challenges in the age of the city.[20] But approaches differ greatly according to the circumstances. In poor cities the 'brown agenda' is the primary issue and environmental problems are seen primarily as local, immediate and health threatening. In middle-income cities they are often regarded as regional, delayed and threatening to people's health as well as to ecological sustainability. Only in affluent cities are the impacts seen as global and inter-generational in scale.[21]

In India, 50 years of post-colonial development have spurred extensive industrialisation and much 'spontaneous' urbanisation. India is still a mainly rural country and yet it has the world's second largest urban population, more than the total urban population of all countries put together barring China, USA and Russia. Over the last 50 years, while India's population has grown 2.5 times, its urban areas have grown fivefold. In 1947, only 60 million people, or 15 per cent of the total population, lived in urban areas. By 2000, some 305 million Indians lived in nearly 3,700 towns and cities, or nearly 30 per cent of the country's population, and 71 million people, or about one-third of urban India, live in metropolitan cities of a million or more. These cities have increased from one in 1901, to 23 in 1991 and 40 in 2001. Metropolitan cities grew by 28 million people.[22]

Now 3.7 per cent of India's population live in four megacities—Mumbai, Delhi, Calcutta and Chennai. They offer a wide range of commercial and job opportunities. In telecommunications Mumbai stands out, representing 40 per cent of India's overseas phone calls. Mumbai and Bangalore have carved out a niche for themselves as major international media and telecommunication centres. But in spite of the economic strength of India's large cities, population pressures and deterioration in the physical environment and quality of life are serious problems. Slums have grown in all major cities. Nearly one-third of urban Indians live below the poverty line, about 15 per cent do not have safe drinking water and about 50 per cent have no sanitary facilities. In most cities, traffic congestion has reached critical dimensions, with inadequate road space and lack of public transport. Across urban India, the gap between the demand and supply of essential services and infrastructure is widening.

Latin America, too, has changed dramatically in the last 50 years, from being a predominantly rural to a highly urbanised continent. Between 1995 and 2000, Latin America's urban populations grew at over 3 per cent a year. At first, national capitals grew the fastest, but then secondary urban centres also expanded: 74 per cent of the population of Latin America and the Caribbean are urban and 80 per cent of Latin America's population live in just 600 towns and cities.

In recent years Latin America's old-established function of selling raw materials and buying manufactured goods has been substantially modified. Indigenous industrialisation centred on cities such as São Paulo, Mexico City and Buenos Aires has been replaced by a globalised system dominated by industrial assembly. Large reductions of custom duties during the 1990s are an important feature of the new system, which centres on the import of capital goods and the export of agro-industrial products.

In much of Africa, rapid urbanisation is often not driven by new urban opportunities but by declining rural conditions. This is particularly vividly illustrated by the example of Nouakchott, capital of the Republic of Mauritania, which has been one of the world's fastest-growing cities. In 1957, when it was founded, it had just 2,000 inhabitants. Only 43 years later, in 2000, it had grown to 600,000 people. This exponential urban growth was driven by massive rural–urban migration, mainly of cattle- and camel-herding nomadic tribespeople who had lost their grazing land because of persistent droughts and desertification. In 1962, Mauritania as a whole was only 4 per cent urbanised. By 2002, the figure was 61 per cent—1.4 million of a total population of 2.3 million. The growth was so rapid that adequate city planning could not occur and squatter camps occupied more than 40 per cent of Mauritania's urban land. Half the population exists below the poverty line.

Lagos in Nigeria is another example of urban growth driven by a combination of decline in rural areas and lack of economic development. It is the premier city of one of the world's major oil exporters. But instead of being fabulously wealthy, its dominant features are unemployment and poverty. Nevertheless, Lagos has become one of Africa's largest cities. At first it grew quite slowly, from 25,000 people in 1866 to 74,000 in 1911. After the Second World War, rural–urban migration in Nigeria, combined with huge waves of migrants from other African countries, produced a population growth rate of some 14 per cent a year until the early 1970s and 4.5 per cent per annum in the late 1980s. Lagos grew from 665,000 people in 1963 to 7.9 million people in 1990 and to around 15 million people in 2003.[23]

Unlike the rest of Nigeria, 90 per cent of the population of Lagos have access to electricity. But despite the region's substantial endowment of water, the city suffers from acute water supply problems as well as inadequate sewerage. Much of its human waste is disposed of through open ditches and discharged onto tidal flats. Traffic congestion is also a daily problem—it can take people three hours to travel 20 kilometres.

Lagos has a great lack of adequate housing and it is common for up to six people to live in one room. During the 1970s, a man earning an average salary could build his own house. But in recent years, high inflation and declining wages have resulted in workers living barely above subsistence level, with no money left for investment. Only the rich can now afford to build their own houses. Up to 50 per cent unemployment, linked to overdependence on a limited number of government and oil-related jobs, has led to very high crime rates and an escalation of armed banditry.

Apart from its oil production, Nigeria has become largely irrelevant to the world economy. Like in many other parts of the Third World, development has stagnated and an increasingly volatile underclass has emerged that plays its part in global drug trafficking, smuggling, money laundering and prostitution. Ironically, this criminal economy has started to make heavy use of information technology to build and maintain its own worldwide connections.

THE GEOGRAPHY OF INEQUALITY

The extremes of rich and poor in cities all over the world have had a variety of local consequences. The American urbanist Mike Davis has coined the term 'ecology of fear' to describe the condition of people living in islands of wealth surrounded by poverty. In cities such as Los Angeles, Lagos, Jerusalem, Nairobi and Delhi, protected home zones with guarded entrances and high walls topped with electric security fences are becoming commonplace. In some cases, such as in São Paulo's Alphaville, entire neighbourhoods complete with schools, swimming pools and shops have been walled off, with access only through heavily guarded entry points. The 'siege mentality' in these modern feudal fiefdoms is a manifestation of ever-growing insecurity, with wealthy inhabitants forming block watches and vigilante groups. Private security firms have taken over from police forces where the state can no longer provide adequate security.[24]

Perhaps the most extreme example is post-apartheid Johannesburg, in which the city centre has become a virtual no-go area for non-residents. Well-to-do people have moved out into gated communities in suburbs such as Sandton equipped with all manner of modern security systems and 24-hour armed response teams. In these privileged areas, poor blacks have taken to carjacking, often using Russian AK-47 assault rifles smuggled in from Mozambique as the tools of their trade.

Journalist Sarah Sally writes these comments from Johannesburg:

Home is in a compound surrounded by an electric fence. There's a guard on the gate, and every unit is fitted with panic buttons. There's a button next to the sink in the kitchen and another one next to my bed. There's even a portable version that you can wear as a necklace if your paranoia isn't satisfied. Set off the panic alarm and an armed response team arrives within minutes. It's like a suburban cavalry patrolling the streets of Johannesburg. It's

*an industry in itself. There are guards to look after your car while
you shop and even guards inside the change rooms at the gym . . .
Many locals avoid going into the city centre because it's regarded
as unsafe. Instead, they exist in suburbia. They crowd into secure
shopping centres on the weekends. They eat at al fresco tables,
which are actually inside rather than out in the street. People
drive from one bubble of security to the other.*[25]

South Africa's 1996 constitution states that everyone has the right to have
'access to adequate housing'. By 2002, over a million houses had been built
and services were extended to millions of people. But a further two to three
million units were still needed. In addition, the housing programme has been
criticised, houses are often badly built and very small and are frequently in
locations that lack social or economic infrastructure.

In many townships, unemployment is as high as 50 per cent and millions
of people can't afford basic necessities. The Congress of South African Trade
Unions recently noted:

Johannesburg slum
Apartheid may be over but the cities of South Africa are still blighted by townships with
minimal services and where unemployment, AIDS and crime are rife.

*While Africans make up 76 per cent of the population, their share
of income amounts to only 29 per cent of the total. Whites, who
make up less than 13 per cent of the population, take away 58.5
per cent of total income.*

In 2003, 117 murders per 100,000 people were recorded in Johannesburg. In
1999, the police recorded almost 24,000 murders, making South Africa's
murder rate more than 10 times that of the US. Violent crime affects not only
white South Africans but people from all backgrounds. A Johannesburg crime
victim survey showed that the vast majority of victims of violent crime were
black. While constituting 67 per cent of the population in the metropolitan
area, black South Africans made up 85.7 per cent of victims of rape, murder
and assault without a weapon, and 74.5 per cent of serious assault.[26]

The HIV/AIDS pandemic is another huge problem, with 4.2 million South
Africans infected. It is estimated that by 2010 South Africa's GDP will be 17
per cent lower than it would have been without AIDS.[27]

LIVEABILITY IN DEVELOPING CITIES

'By the time the next century passes its first quarter, more than a billion
and a half people in the world's cities will face life and health-threatening
environments unless we can create a revolution in urban problem solving.'
So reported the 1996 UN Nations City Summit, Habitat II. At this conference
and the 2002 UN Earth Summit in Johannesburg, the conditions of people in
Third World cities were top of the agenda. High unemployment and appalling
living conditions of hundreds of millions of people were seen as a disgrace,
but also as a potential source of social unrest and international terrorism.

Many different initiatives have been launched to deal with these problems,
among them the Cities Alliance, which was founded in 1997 by the World
Bank and UN Habitat. It states:

*The Alliance seeks to advance the collective know-how of local
authorities and their international partners on ways to reduce
urban poverty and to improve the quality and impact of urban
development cooperation.*[28]

The focus is on city development strategies and on slum upgrading to make
marginalised residents into partners in a city's development. The goal is to

create 'cities without slums'. For that purpose slum upgrading programmes, infrastructure improvement, housing improvements and small-scale job creation are being funded in cities around the Third World.

The Cities Without Slums Action Plan was endorsed by 150 heads of state and government in 2000 and is reflected in the United Nations Millennium Declaration, the goal of which is to have achieved a significant improvement in the lives of at least 100 million slum dwellers by 2020. It is a consortium of ten bilateral donors, three multilateral development agencies and four international city associations that are jointly promoting city development strategies and advancing collective know-how on urban poverty reduction. To achieve these goals, the Alliance facilitates cooperation at the community level among city governments, slum dwellers and the private sector, while also coordinating cooperation among international donors. The Alliance's funds are catalytic: they are seed funds used to help partners build strong foundations for slum upgrading and city development strategies. They also leverage the public- and private-sector capital investment required for implementation.

Slum upgrading consists of physical, social, economic, organisational and environmental improvements undertaken cooperatively and locally among citizens, community groups, businesses and local authorities. Actions include:

- installing basic infrastructure, e.g., water and waste water systems, flood prevention, electricity, security lighting and public telephones,
- removing or mitigating environmental hazards,
- providing incentives for community management and maintenance,
- creating community facilities, health posts and community open space,
- regularising security of tenure,
- home improvement,
- relocating/compensating residents dislocated by improvements,
- improving access to health care and education as well as social support programmes to address issues of security, violence and substance abuse,
- enhancing income-earning opportunities through training and micro-credit,
- building social capital and institutional frameworks to sustain improvements.[29]

Initiatives such as the Cities Alliance can do much to ameliorate deplorable social and environmental conditions in Third World cities, but they cannot counter the mega-trends that have caused these conditions to occur in the

Mumbai slum
Some 840 million people worldwide live in urban slums and squatter camps. Whilst people aim to improve their lot and build permanent houses for themselves, appropriate sites to build them are rarely affordable.

first place. It remains to be seen whether the international community can find and share new creative ways in which to counter socially and environmentally detrimental urban development. In a few places, such as Curitiba, enlightened planning policies have greatly contributed to the emergence of a liveable urban ambience.

A WORD FROM JAIME LERNER, FORMER MAYOR OF CURITIBA

Curitiba in southern Brazil is often lauded as a city in a developing country that has managed to combine a variety of considerable achievements. In the 1960s, the Brazilian government held a competition for a master plan for expanding the city. The idea was to link land use and transport needs together into one integrated concept. Jaime Lerner led the winning team and subsequently was elected mayor three times. His team pushed ahead with a strategic planning concept that has five main structural transport routes leading away from the city centre. Growing rapidly to 1.7 million people in 30 years, Curitiba is particularly well known for its highly integrated bus system that services the entire city (see also Chapter 7).

Former mayor Jaime Lerner says in an interview for the TV series *People's Planet*:

> *I have been asked 'what makes a city human?' The vision I have is for a city is to create structures of living and working together, assuring integration of functions, incomes and age groups. The more you mix, the more human the city becomes. It is the balance between addressing the daily needs and the potential of the city. If you only address the needs you won't change the city. If you work only with the potential, you will be far from the people. That is what I call a strategic view of the city.*
>
> *In Curitiba we don't have a paradise—we have slums, we have many problems as in other cities in Brazil and other parts of the world. But the main difference is the respect given to people. We try to foster citizenship or co-responsibility—where the city and its residents share a common, sustainable target. The people understand that they can change the situation for the better if they can act locally in their city.*
>
> *I always say, if you want to help the environment try to do just two things. First: use your car less. And second: separate your garbage. The problem is making people understand the impacts of their actions. I believe that in less than two years every city can make very important and positive changes. If everyone in every city in the world could do the same, the global problems would be very much diminished.*

A VIABLE URBAN FUTURE?

The 20th century saw extraordinary changes on the face of the earth. The implications of these developments for people and planet will become fully apparent as the 21st century unfolds, as people continue to flock to the cities of the world and as their populations expand through reproduction within cities.

Moscow housing estate
In the 1960s and 1970s many Le Corbusier-style 'machines for living' were built in and around
the cities of Eastern Europe. While they provided much needed housing, it remains to be seen
whether these faceless blocks will stand the test of time.

As the Cities Alliance states:

*Well managed urban centres are important for economic prosperity
for all nations—and also for meeting social and environmental
goals. Urban areas in developing countries currently concentrate
some of the world's most serious environmental problems but
provide the potential to combine healthy and safe living
environments with resource-conserving, waste-minimising patterns
of production and consumption.*[29]

The viability of an urbanising world will depend above all else on what is
done to achieve such aims. The situation in Third World cities, where some
840 million people are slum dwellers, is particularly urgent. These cities are
pressured by everyday crisis situations to which the response is sometimes not
particularly creative. Despite all the pressures, planning is crucial. As never
before, it is vital to create high-density but pedestrian-friendly cities, with

pedestrian and play streets, public spaces and parks. It is crucial to create well-thought-out cities that combine density with limited suburbanisation.

Cities also should offer:

- good chances of finding jobs that pay a living wage,
- sufficient access to good educational opportunities,
- good access to basic transport services,
- affordable supplies of safe water and adequate sanitation,
- adequate and affordable health care provision,
- secure tenure in affordable housing,
- clean air and a safe, diverse and healthy environment,
- ready access to public parks, neighbourhood gardens and public spaces,
- good opportunities for leisure and recreation,
- an active stake in local democratic governance,
- opportunities for enjoying nature.[31]

In pursuing sustainable development, we need to deal with the reality of an urbanising, industrialising and globalising planet. Developing a sustainable relationship between people and planet while transforming local environmental conditions in cities all over the world is one of humanity's greatest challenges for the years and decades to come.

CHAPTER 6

Cities as Eco-Technical Systems

The history of ancient cities shows the dangers of depleting the natural capital of their local and regional hinterland. Large modern cities draw on natural resources on a global scale. To make a contribution to creating a sustainable world, they need to take stock of the capacity of global ecosystems to supply them with resources and ecological services on a continuous basis. Cities are centres of knowledge, culture and creativity, and these urgently need to be applied to urban resource management to establish a sustainable relationship between cities and the planet.

Biological metaphors are widely used for describing cities. As long as 2,300 years ago Aristotle commented that urban society could be regarded as a *single organism*. The American planner Fredrick Olmstead referred to the city as a *social organism* whose future welfare is in large part determined by the actions of the people who inhabit it today. Louis Mumford repeatedly referred to the *organic growth* of medieval cities that developed at a measured pace over centuries. Other authors have written about the urban organism more recently. In my own writing, I have referred to modern cities as *superorganisms*.[1] This term is widely used to describe colonies of ants, termites or honey bees that behave like a single organism. Each contributes to the well-being of the whole—to feeding, growth, respiration and reproduction—by responding to internal and external stimuli. For instance, individual bees dance for the benefit of their entire colony to convey the direction of pollen sources, and ants communicate the location of prey to each other by drawing pheromone trails.[2]

The term superorganism can also describe a complex living body with a great variety of interacting organs. In the case of cities, roads, railways and waterways can be compared to a body's arteries and veins; food markets can be compared to stomachs; garbage dumps and sewage pipes to digestion systems; universities and libraries can be likened to brains; communication networks to nervous systems; and parks and gardens to the lungs of a living body. The police, at best, act like a body's immune system. Cities also have internal feedback systems to help them maintain their continuity and stability.

However, cities are far more complex than either termite colonies or single complex living creatures. Some authors, such as the urban planner Kevin Lynch, prefer the term *urban ecosystem* to describe cities. Ecosystems contain complex, heterogeneous assemblies of plants and animals that share a single environment. The dynamic interaction of living species helps to sustain the biophysical foundations of cities, by providing services such as air filtration, microclimate regulation, noise reduction, surface water drainage, nutrient retention, genetic diversity, pollination, seed dispersal, insect pest regulation, recreational spaces and living soil for food gardens. In a study of Stockholm, it was found that its green spaces assimilate no less than 40 per cent of all traffic emissions.[3]

Cities are 'fossilised' structures superimposed on living landscapes, but their existence is not just based on local ecosystems, but also on land surfaces elsewhere and on a great variety of technical systems. The dramatic, pulsating quality of modern cities has been stunningly portrayed in the film *Koyaanisqatsi*, Godfrey Reggio's 1983 visual poem about New York and Los Angeles. Because modern cities are multi-layered biological and technical systems, they might be most usefully described as *eco-technical systems*.

The very morphology of modern cities is characterised by a huge array of technologies that emerged from the industrial revolution. They power urban transport, commerce, buildings, water supply and waste disposal. In recent decades, many new technologies have been added: telephone exchanges, server farms and radio and TV stations. Cities are at the centre of a vast web of communication systems that has speeded them up and given them a global reach. The larger and richer a city, the more complex and varied its array of technical systems and the range of activities associated with them.

Concentration of intense economic processes and high levels of consumption in cities both increase their resource demands. Apart from a monopoly on fossil fuels, metals and concrete, an urbanising humanity now uses nearly *half* the world's total photosynthetic capacity as well. Cities as eco-technical systems are the home of the 'amplified man', an unprecedented amalgam of biology and technology, transcending his biological ancestors on an epic journey into the unknown.

Large modern cities make the shared human existence feasible on a unprecedented scale. The intense economic and cultural activities that define them give them a proud identity all of their own. But urban eco-technical systems differ profoundly from nature's ecosystems in that they are essentially linear systems. They transcend local ecological boundaries by importing ecological services from elsewhere, using nature as a source of materials as well as a sink for their wastes. But as I shall discuss below, cities can only exist on a continuous basis if they learn to mimic the essentially circular metabolism of living ecosystems.

Carajas mine
The Grand Carajas mine in the Brazilian Amazon is the world's primary supplier of iron ore: megatechnolgy for supplying the demands of megacities.

CITIES, COMMERCE AND RESOURCE USE

The coming together of large numbers of people in one urban location is triggered by a variety of key factors:

- location near a concentration of resources,
- convenient river or coastal setting,
- transport connections with good access to markets,
- opportunities for manufacturing for local consumption and trade.

Urbanist Jane Jacobs pioneered the view that the intense interaction of people in villages, towns and cities is the basis for economic development. Agglomeration of economic activities causes urban growth to take place. Significant reductions in production costs occur as related enterprises locate close to one another and this, in turn, leads to an intense accumulation of local know-how. The location becomes attractive to businesses that move in to take advantage of the new opportunities. Import substitution then leads to the growth of further local enterprise and expertise. The intense human interactions that result, in turn, stimulate local cultural and social activities. By 'proximate co-habitation' we learn about one another's strengths and weaknesses and we come to share and divide tasks according to our own unique skills. Economic growth derives from such a multiplication of options, from collaboration and specialisation, from comparative advantage and from the development of appropriate standards.[4]

Manuel Castells has updated and modified Jane Jacobs' insights in creating the concept of the 'space of flows'. He writes:

> Our societies are constructed around flows: flows of capital, flows of information, flows of technology, flows of organizational interactions, flows of images, sounds and symbols. Flows are not just one element of social organization: they are the expression of the processes dominating our economic, political, and symbolic life ... Thus, I propose the idea that there is a new spatial form characteristic of social practices that dominate and shape the network society: the space of flows. The space of flows is the material organization of time-sharing social practices that work through flows. By flows I understand purposeful, repetitive, programmable sequences of exchange and interaction between physically disjointed positions held by social actors.[5]

As centres of economic and social activity, modern 'network' cities have a highly developed division of labour, though social stratification distributes the benefits of this unequally, undermining social solidarity within internal relationships. They have unique characteristics of their own with 'the fine specialisation and extraordinary diversity of skills . . . firms will tend to congregate where there is a large market, but the market is large precisely where firms' production is concentrated'.[6]

The downside of urban concentrations is that congestion inevitably occurs, with resulting cost increases undermining the benefits of location. And if manufacturing is the primary activity, environmental contamination can also hamper and undermine local economic development. As we have seen in Tokyo, in affluent cities there is a tendency for manufacturing to be replaced by knowledge-based activities, while manufacturers tend to relocate to convenient out-of-town transport nodes.

Cities are centres of production as well as consumerism, closely linked to economic prosperity. In recent years, the development of vast shopping malls with hundreds of department stores and shops has become a global trend, and this usually occurs on greenfield sites well connected to major transport routes. The clustering of stores gives them access to large numbers of potential customers with minimal advertising costs. In the age of the motor car, out-of-town shopping malls have become a tremendous competition for traditional inner-city shopping centres.

LOCAL CONSUMPTION, GLOBAL IMPACTS

Shopping is a key feature of urban eco-technical systems. Its impacts extend far beyond city boundaries. This is clearly demonstrated by food shopping. Food is a biological resource, but its production has become a predominantly technological process—from the uses of farm technology to distribution, processing and preparation. Yet we are hardly aware of its origins, the environmental impacts of its production or the energy expended in processing and transporting it to our homes. There are major externalities that are not reflected in the price we pay for food, particularly the carbon dioxide discharged in powering modern food systems.

An ever-increasing proportion of the fruit and vegetables we eat is transported to our cities in the bellies of jumbo jets. By the time a mango or a papaya flown in from India or East Africa arrives on a London dinner table, it will have consumed several hundred times as much energy as the calories it actually contains. Modern long-distance trawling similarly requires around 100 times as much energy as the calories actually contained in the fish. Our food production and distribution system as a whole expends 10–15 calories of energy for every calorie of food energy produced.

A crucial question for premier cities such as London, Tokyo or New York is how they can reconcile their status as global centres of consumption and trade with the imperative of sustainable development. As described in Chapter 4, London pioneered the long-distance import of food, spices, tea, coffee and timber. It 'grew' a global hinterland. Since then other cities have copied these patterns and the whole world has become an urban hinterland. Urbanisation has been changing the very way in which the 'web of life' functions, from a geographically distributed interaction of a myriad of species into a system dominated by the resource use patterns of a few hundred large cities. Their demands are causing the world's ecosystems to become increasingly stressed.

The responsibility of cities in reducing this stress is now widely acknowledged. Agenda 21 and its prescriptions for local action to tackle global environmental problems were agreed by the world's nations at the 1992 Rio UN Earth Summit. This was followed by the Habitat Agenda, signed by 180 nations at the 1996 UN Habitat II conference in Istanbul. It states:

> Human settlements shall be planned, developed and improved in
> a manner that takes full account of sustainable development
> principles and all their components, as set out in Agenda 21 . . .
> We need to respect the carrying capacity of ecosystems and
> preservation of opportunities for future generations. Production,
> consumption and transport should be managed in ways that
> protect and conserve the stock of resources while drawing upon
> them. Science and technology have a crucial role in shaping
> sustainable human settlements and sustaining the ecosystems they
> depend upon.[7]

THE ECOLOGICAL FOOTPRINTS OF CITIES

As city people we need to know what levels of production and consumption are sustainable; that is, are within the earth's environmental limits. In order to assess our impacts, the Canadian ecologist William Rees and his colleague Mathis Wackernagel developed the concept of the *ecological footprints* of nations and cities.[8] They define these as the areas required to supply them

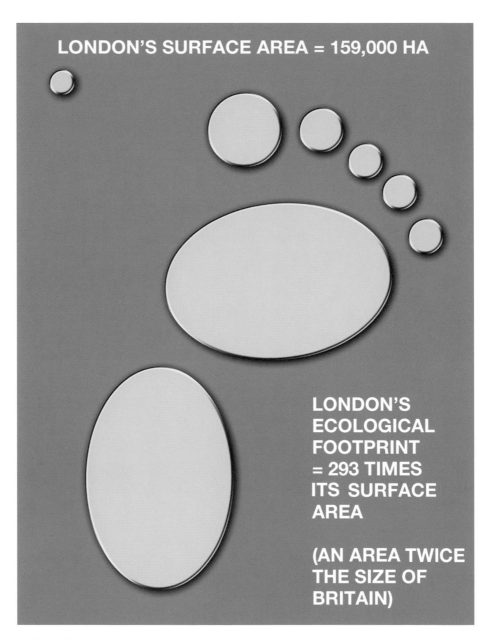

LONDON'S SURFACE AREA = 159,000 HA

LONDON'S ECOLOGICAL FOOTPRINT = 293 TIMES ITS SURFACE AREA

(AN AREA TWICE THE SIZE OF BRITAIN)

Ecological footprint
The ecological footprint of rich cities can be up to 300 to 500 times their surface area, or six to ten hectares per person. The much more frugal cities of developing countries usually have a much smaller per capita footprint.

with food and forest products and to absorb their output of wastes, and particularly their output of carbon dioxide.

They estimate that a North American city with 650,000 people requires some 30,000 square kilometres of land to meet domestic needs, without even including the environmental demands of industry. In comparison, an Indian city of this size would require just 2,800 square kilometres, or less than 10 per cent of an American city.[9]

Using this methodology in a study in 1995, I made an attempt to quantify London's footprint. I found that this extended to around 125 times its surface area of 159,000 hectares, to nearly 20 million hectares. I calculated that London, with seven million people or 12 per cent of the population of the UK, required the equivalent of its entire productive land.[10] Of course, in reality this area stretches to far-flung places such as the wheat prairies of Kansas, the tea gardens of Assam, the forests of Scandinavia and Amazonia, and Spanish and Californian orange groves. According to my figures, each individual Londoner had a footprint of some three hectares of land.

London is one of the world's most thoroughly researched cities and a more recent study called 'City Limits' conducted in 2000 went into much more detail than my own. Unlike my study, it also calculated the energy used in agricultural production, transportation and processing, the land surface required for producing pet food and the sea surfaces required for fisheries. If these additional factors are included, London footprint is actually more than double my original figures, adding up to twice the UK's surface area, or 6.63 hectares per Londoner.[11]

With 6.3 billion people now living on this planet, this is well over three times the land area available per capita. If every human being used resources the way we do in London, we would need three planets rather than the single one we have. Canadian, Australian and American cities have even larger footprints, extending to between eight and ten hectares of productive land per person. If everybody lives like Los Angelenos, we would need five planets. Clearly people across the developed world have a major job on their hands to reduce their ecological footprints.

*The ecological footprint of the world's average consumer in 1999
was 2.3 hectares per person, or 20 per cent of the earth's
biological capacity of 1.9 hectares per person. In other words,
humanity now substantially exceeds the planet's capacity to
sustain its consumption of renewable resources. We are able to*

maintain this global overdraft on a temporary basis by eating into
the earth's capital stocks of forest, fish and fertile soils. We also
dump our excess carbon dioxide emissions into the atmosphere.
Neither of these two activities are sustainable in the long term—
the only sustainable option is to live within the biological
productive capacity of the earth.[12]

A wide range of studies have been conducted in recent years focusing on the ecological footprints of cities. The Swedish academic Carl Folke and his colleagues make this important point:

The capacity of ecosystems to sustain city development is
becoming increasingly scarce as a consequence of rapid human
population growth, intensified globalisation of human activities,
and human overexploitation and simplification of the natural
resource base. The web of connections linking one ecosystem and
one country with the next is escalating across all scales in both
space and time. Everyone is now in everyone else's backyard.[13]

Folke and his colleagues have done particularly interesting work on fishing. They have established that the majority of fish that is eaten worldwide is consumed in cities remote from the sea. In 1996, the largest 744 northern European cities alone consumed 25 per cent of the world's annual sea fish catch. And for their resource consumption and waste assimilation, the cities of Baltic Europe appropriate an area of forest, agricultural, marine and wetland ecosystems that is 565–1130 times larger than the area of the cities themselves (see note 13).

OVER IN THE RAINFOREST

The spatial impact of affluent modern cities is well illustrated by what is happening to the world's rainforests. In recent years, there has been ever-growing concern about the vast, deliberate fires set in the rainforest areas of Amazonia, Malaysia and Indonesia. There is a direct connection between these events and our daily urban lives, as the ecological footprints of our cities expand across the world. The issue is not only direct resource consumption but also the role of cities as global financial service centres.

A colleague of mine, Mark Campanale, summarised a recent experience:

*I attended a meeting typical of those which take place every day
in the city of London. A group of Indonesian businessmen
organised a lunch to raise £300 million to finance the clearing of a
rainforest and the construction of a pulp paper plant. What struck
me was how financial rationalism often overcomes common sense;
that profit itself is a good thing whatever the activity, whenever
the occasion. What happened to the Indonesian rainforest was
dependent upon financial decisions made over lunch that day. The
financial benefits would come to institutions in London, Paris or
New York. Very little, if any, would go to the local people.
Therefore when thinking about the environmental impact of
London we have to think about the decisions of fund managers
which impact on the other side of the world. The rainforest may
be geographically located in the Far East, but financially it might
as well be located in London's Square Mile.*[14]

BOOM AND BUST IN THE AMAZON

In the late 1980s, when filming at the port of Belem for a documentary on
deforestation in the Amazon basin, I saw a huge stack of mahogany planks
with 'London' stamped on them being loaded into a freighter. I started to make
the connection between urban consumption patterns and their impact on the
biosphere. The logging of virgin forests, or their conversion into ranches and
farms, did not seem an appropriate way of supplying distant urban markets.

During the same trip, I also visited the city of Paragominas in the state of
Para. It was strikingly similar to the frontier towns of Wild West movies. For
30 years it was the fastest-growing boom town in the Brazilian Amazon with
an annual growth rate of some 17 per cent. At its peak it had to a population of over 100,000 people. Its economy was based on timber, charcoal and
cattle ranching. With more than 200 sawmills, it came to be called the sawmill
capital of the world.

Sawmills dominated the city, but the pall of smoke hanging over it was
from kilns in which timber offcuts were converted into charcoal for European
barbecues and for smelting iron ore from the vast Grand Carajas iron mine,
which supplies the steelworks of Europe and Japan. The workers in the kilns

Paragominas, Amazonia, Brazil
Rainforest timber was the feedstock of this city's economy. The story of Paragominas is one of
boom and bust. Bust came when the timber ran out, leaving a devastated forest landscape and
a desolate city without an economy.

are mainly women and children with scarred, bewildered faces straight out of Dante's inferno.

The people of Paragominas are settlers from elsewhere in Brazil who have the gritty determination to stay put. Millions of people have moved in along roads cut into the forest by the Brazilian government to claim their small plots of land. Despite gunmen, malaria, infertile soil and hostile world opinion, the number of settlers in the Brazilian Amazon exceeds ten million. Several large cities, such as Belem and Manaus, have over a million inhabitants.

Between 1952 and 1982, the number of licensed sawmills in the Brazilian Amazon increased 17 times. Paragominas, like other sawmill centres, sits like a spider at the middle of a road network cut deep into the virgin forest. At its economic base were chainsaws and bulldozers, as well as vast fires—set to clear the forest and blanketing huge areas with acrid yellow smoke. But the future of cities with economies that depend on devastating fragile rain-forest ecosystems is bound to be bleak.

This is clearly evident in Paragominas. Only 20 years ago the city was surrounded by thick forest. In the early 1990s, it produced $1 billion of cut timber a year, out of a total of $2.5 billion for Brazilian Amazon as a whole. There were up to 7,000 jobs in the 200 sawmills. But they ate up the very resource on which their existence depended. By 2002, only 60 were still operating and the city had become a junkyard of rusting sawmills. After decades of boom, Paragominas had gone bust. Unemployment and anger have been translated into crime and violence. The city's mayor, Sidney Rosa, says that his city may be less smoky than it used to be, but it has become a shameful symbol of violence and environmental devastation. In just 20 years, millions of hectares of primary forest around the city have turned into degraded scrubland and pastures on which only a few cattle and the occasional burnt-out tree remain.

Paragominas was a leading supplier of timber to cities like London, Paris, Frankfurt, Tokyo and Shanghai. Their insatiable appetite for timber and fine veneers is now being met by sawmill towns elsewhere in the Amazon, in central Africa, Indonesia or Malaysia, until they, too, have denuded their local forests. And so virgin forests all around the tropics are literally disappearing into our cities.

GETTING INTO THE MEAT-EATING HABIT

Until a few years ago, Chinese people might have had small pieces of pork, duck or carp as part of their mainly vegetarian meal. But with rising affluence, much larger helpings of meat are becoming the norm in China's booming cities. Economic growth is bringing major innovations in the way people live and eat. By 2000, 120 million out of China's current population of 1.2 billion were considered as affluent and China may soon have the largest number of wealthy consumers in the world. With a whopping 8 per cent economic and urban growth across China, and 12 per cent in Beijing and Shanghai, diets are changing fast and beef is definitely on the menu.

Those who can afford it buy processed foods in supermarkets. Japanese-style marbled beef is becoming very popular. To produce it, the right sort of feed is all important. Traditionally, cattle in China are fed on hay and the stalks of rice or wheat. But increasing quantities of marbled beef are being produced in American-style beef lots, requiring a feed mix that includes soybeans, maize and barley—cereal normally used for direct human consumption. Feedlot beef production is spreading fast and most feed is imported because China itself cannot provide sufficient quantities.

Increased meat eating dramatically expands a country's per capita ecological footprint. The world's population can be divided into three groups according to their meat consumption. One billion people in the rich countries eat large amounts of meat. A further billion people in the poorest countries eat hardly any meat at all. The remaining four billion people in developing countries are consuming more meat, milk and cheese as they get richer. Much of Asia and the Middle East are in this third category. But meat production requires huge amounts of feed: one kilogram of feedlot beef requires seven kilograms of feed, and a kilogram of pig meat requires four kilograms of feed. Supplying the world's consumers with more meat requires grain and soybean imports from the US, Australia and Brazil. In the US, the world's biggest producer, more land is now under soybeans than under wheat.[15]

People are rarely aware that their meat consumption endangers virgin rainforests. In the state of Mato Grosso in Brazil, soybean fields now stretch to the horizon and farmers export 'soya cake' as cattle feed all over the world. To create farmland, savannah and forest are burned and then ploughed up.[16] Some of the world's largest farms have been created in Mato Grosso, meaning 'Big Forest'. Until 25 years ago most of it was covered with *cerrado*, a mixture of savannah and forest. By 2000, more than 60 per cent of the state's virgin land had been turned into fields. With booming demand, farmers are now ploughing up not just savannah but also forest land further north in the Amazon. Some 60 per cent of the region's soybean crops go to Asia and

Burning rainforest
The Amazon is one of the last remaining areas where forest can be converted into cattle ranches and farmland. The destruction continues as cities across the world demand ever greater quantities of meat.

exports to China are increasing especially fast. The government is encouraging soybean production to increase Brazil's export earnings. The Amazon basin is one of the few places left on earth where new farmland can be created, but only at great environmental cost.[17]

In the second half of the 20th century, global meat production increased fivefold. Beef eating consumes huge quantities of grain. Americans, the world's top beef consumers, get through some 900 kilograms of grain per person, currently three times as much as the average Chinese. But as affluence there increases, Chinese consumers could catch up with America. This has huge implications for the rest of the world given China's vast population. Lester Brown estimates that if everyone on earth had a meat-centred diet similar to that of the average American, all grain currently produced on earth could feed less than half the world's current population, and only a quarter in 50 years' time. He says:

> If we are living high on the food chain, as many affluent people are in the world, then we can move down the food chain, consuming less livestock products and become healthier in the process, whilst reducing our environmental impact at the same time. If we reduced our consumption of feedlot beef by one kilogram we would free up seven kilos for direct human consumption. Producing seven kilograms of grain takes 7,000 kilograms of water. So the effect on the earth's land and water resources of consuming feedlot beef is very substantial.[18]

CREATING AND MAINTAINING CARBON SINKS

The bulk of the fossil fuels we burn are used to power cities and their transport systems. Carbon dioxide emissions have increased from about 2.5 billion tonnes in 1960 to 6.2 billion tonnes in 2000, in line with global industrialisation, urbanisation and expansion of transport systems. While it is of the essence to stabilise and reduce the quantities we burn in the coming decades, it is also crucial to assure that the capacity of the biosphere to absorb carbon dioxide is increased rather than diminished. A major component of the ecological footprints of cities consists of areas of land that would need to be set aside as 'carbon sinks'. There are three main terrestrial approaches to absorbing carbon: 1) protecting ecosystems that store carbon; 2) manipulating ecosystems to increase carbon sequestration; and 3) creating new carbon sinks by planting new forests and enhancing carbon storage in farmland.

Currently land and ocean sinks remove 30 to 50 per cent of the carbon dioxide released into the atmosphere from combustion. Increasing concentrations of carbon dioxide can accelerate tree growth by a process of 'carbon fertilisation'. However, they can also affect ecosystems such as the Amazon rainforest by reducing rainfall and converting forest into savannah, thus diminishing its carbon dioxide sequestration capacity. As carbon dioxide concentrations in the atmosphere increase, more and more ecosystems are expected to become increasingly unstable.[19]

Enhancing natural processes that remove carbon dioxide from the atmosphere is a cost-effective means of reducing atmospheric levels of carbon, and in some places reforestation and deforestation abatement efforts are already underway. Some parts of the world, such as Australia, have a very large potential for tree planting both for carbon sequestration as well as for countering soil erosion, salinisation and desertification. It remains to be seen whether large-scale tree planting initiatives can help sequester significant amounts of carbon dioxide currently being discharged by cities.

THE METABOLISM OF CITIES

The vast environmental impacts of global urbanisation, encapsulated in the ecological footprint concept, need to be met with a wide range of creative responses. Can we transform cities into much less environmentally demanding and damaging places? Can we establish a sustainable relationship between cities and the planet, while improving the quality of urban life at the same time? Can modern cities reduce their discharge of wastes by enlightened self-regulation and self-limitation?

Understanding cities as dynamic and ever-evolving eco-technical systems helps us formulate strategies for a sustainable urban future. It is clear that cities would be well advised to model themselves on the functioning of ecosystems to assure their long-term viability. Nature's own ecosystems, such as forests or coral reefs, have an essentially *circular* metabolism in which every output discharged by an organism also becomes an input that renews and sustains the continuity of the whole. The whole web of life hangs together in a 'chain of mutual benefit', connected by the flow of nutrients that pass from one organism to another.

The term *metabolism* can be defined as the sum of all the biological, chemical and physical processes that occur within an organism or ecosystem to enable it to exist indefinitely. The metabolism of nature's ecosystems is circular, while the metabolism of rich, modern cities is essentially linear, with resources being 'pumped' through the system with little concern about their origin or about the destination of wastes. Food is imported into cities, consumed and discharged as sewage into rivers and coastal waters. Raw materials are extracted from nature, combined and processed into consumer goods that ultimately end up as rubbish that nature cannot beneficially reabsorb. Wastes end up in landfills, where organic materials are mixed indiscriminately with metals, plastics, glass and poisonous residues.

This linear model of urban production, consumption and disposal undermines the overall ecological viability of urban systems. To improve the urban metabolism, and to reduce the ecological footprint of cities, the application of ecological systems thinking needs to become prominent on the urban agenda. In future, cities need to adopt circular metabolic systems to assure their own long-term viability and that of the rural environments on whose viability they depend. Outputs will also need to be inputs into the urban production system, with routine recycling of paper, metals, plastic and glass, and the conversion of organic materials, including sewage, into compost, returning plant nutrients back to farmland feeding cities to keep the soil in good health. There is more about this in the coming chapters.

FROM THEORY TO PRACTICE

What does a circular metabolism mean in practice? The town of Kalundborg, in Denmark, provides an interesting example of what can be done when waste is used as a resource rather than discarded as a nuisance. In Kalundborg, 20 companies and the municipality cooperate, exploiting each other's waste and by-products on a mutual basis. Over several decades they have developed a symbiotic, circular system in which each step of the chain makes a profit. The exchange benefits the municipality as well as the local companies in several ways:

- One company's waste is a cost-effective resource for another company.
- Efficient consumption of resources benefits the local economy.
- Reduced discharges of wastes reduce environmental pollution.

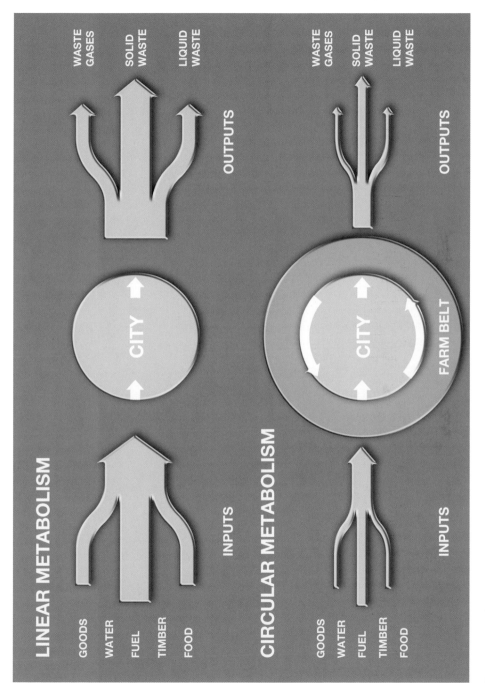

Linear vs circular

Modern cities in many rich countries have a linear metabolism – taking resources and discarding wastes without much concern about environmental impacts. Sustainable cities, by contrast, need to mimic the circular metabolism of natural systems.

Kalundborg's symbiotic web starts with Asnæs Power Station. It produces both electricity and heat for 4,500 households in Kalundborg. The station also provides process steam for three companies—the Statoil Refinery, Novo Nordisk and Novozymes. The partners have reduced their oil consumption by 20,000 tonnes per year by using process steam and have reduced their overall water consumption by 25 per cent by letting water circulate between the individual partners. Some of the power station's cooling water is also used by a fish farm that produces 200 tonnes of trout and salmon annually, with the warm water providing ideal growing conditions.

The 80,000 tonnes of ash produced by the power station is used in the construction and cement industries. The 200,000 tonnes of gypsum it produces in its sulphur scrubbers is sold to Gyproc, enough for its annual plasterboard production. Excess lime is sold to NovoGro and incorporated in fertiliser for 20,000 hectares of farmland. Novozymes, Asnæs Power Station and Kalundborg Municipality have a joint waste water treatment facility, with only minimal discharges into the Baltic Sea. Newspaper, cardboard, rubble, iron, glass, green waste and kitchen wastes from the waste stream of Kalundborg and its various companies are all recycled and turned into new products in a 'cradle-to-cradle' production system.

The 'Kalundborg symbiosis' came about through voluntary action by companies primarily for commercial reasons. Other cities have adopted similar resource use strategies employing a combination of markets and regulation as the main organising principles. The key issue is to create viable end-markets for remanufactured waste products, and for this purpose regulatory barriers, diseconomies of scale and lack of adequate information need to be overcome.[20]

COMMUNICATION AND SUSTAINABILITY

Today the plethora of new communication technologies should be harnessed for improving the way cities function, giving people the appropriate information to make well-informed decisions. Urban intranets, which are used in many cities, can improve communication flows between the various sectors of urban society and facilitate the active participation of individuals and communities in decision making affecting their future. Efficient feedback systems can improve internal interactions and can also provide information on our impacts on the outside world. Simulation and modelling can help us reinvent the city by acting on information flows about the workings of the natural world and our collective relationship to it. They can help us to manage our cities in more participatory ways, while improving their metabolism and reducing their ecological footprints.

The critical question, as humanity moves to 'full-scale' urbanisation, is whether high living standards in our cities can be maintained while curbing their local and global environmental impacts. To answer this question we need balance sheets to compare the resource use and environmental impacts of different cities across the world. Information is becoming available indicating that similar-sized cities supply their needs with a greatly varying throughput of resources and local pollution levels. The main point is that cities could massively reduce their resource throughput, maintaining high standards of living while creating much-needed local jobs in the process.[21]

CREATING CIRCULAR SYSTEMS AND REDUCING OUR FOOTPRINTS

According to British scientist and originator of the Gaia Theory James Lovelock, 'A key actor in our relationship with the rest of the world and with each other is the capacity to make the correct response in time.'

Cities may have effectively declared independence from nature, yet ultimately they are essentially dependent systems, depending on the integrity of the global cycles of life, circulation of air and water currents for their continued existence. Despite the hubris of a rather self-satisfied and self-centred urban civilisation, cities must deliberately 'construct' feedback loops with natural systems beyond their boundaries.

As indicated in the introduction, today's world is not *civilisation* in the old-fashioned sense but *mobilisation*, dependent on long-distance transport routes, by land, by sea and by air, which is, ultimately, highly vulnerable to disruption. This statement has assumed a new urgency in the 21st century, which can look forward to the future with little confidence as the ecological basis of our existence is increasingly eroded.

Understanding the connections between urban structures, systems and processes, at large and small scale, is essential for the development of a new paradigm for our cities. With Asia, Latin America and Africa now joining Europe, North America and Australia in the global urban experiment, it is of paramount importance to apply the principles of sustainability to urban

LONDON SUSTAINABILITY SCENARIOS

	'Unsustainable'	'Towards sustainability'	'Sustainable'
Resource and land use	'Factor 1': 2000 Per capita footprint: 6.6 ha = Total ecological footprint ~ 300 × London's surface area	'Factor 2': 2015 Per capita footprint: 3.3 ha = Total ecological footprint ~ 150 × London's surface area	'Factor 4': 2030 Per capita footprint: 1.6 ha = Total ecological footprint ~ 75 × London's surface area
Food	Long-distance supply of highly packaged food as norm. Intensive processing as norm. High meat consumption. High food waste as norm. Very energy intensive. Only 2% organic, most of this imported. Limited allotment growing and peri-urban fruit and vegetable cultivation.	Reduced long-distance supply. Less processing and packaging. Reduced meat consumption. Some food waste recycling. More energy efficient. 30% organic, mostly locally grown. 40% UK grains. 50% increase in allotment growing. 40% peri-urban fruit and vegetable supplies.	Regional supply emphasised. Minimal processing. Low meat consumption. Much food waste recycling. Highly energy efficient. 50% organic, incl. use of sewage. 60% UK grains. A further 30% increase in allotment growing. 60% peri-urban fruit and vegetable supplies.
Water	Water from Thames and Lea. High-flush toilets etc. No run-off storage. Single household water system. Little sewage recycling.	'Imported' and London water table. Variable-flush toilets as norm. Some run-off storage. Efficient household water system. Some sewage recycling.	'Imported' and London water table. Low-flush toilets as norm. Substantial run-off storage. Dual household water systems. Routine sewage recycling.
Energy	Reliance on fossil fuels. 18% nuclear. Low building insulation standards. Much use of inefficient appliances and systems.	Reduced fossil fuel/more CHP/ some renewable. Improved building insulation and energy efficiency standards.	CHP/solar/wind/biomass and fuel cells as main energy technologies. High building insulation, very high energy efficiency standards

	Minimal end use efficiency. Minimal renewable energy.	More efficient appliances and increased end-use efficiency.	Common use of high-efficiency appliances and implementation of high end-use efficiency.
Transport	Emphasis on private transport. Minimal car sharing. Little cycling and walking. Fossil fuel-powered transport. Low transport interconnection.	Better transport mix. More shared vehicles. Much cycling and walking. Petrol, electric and fuel cell transport. Good interconnections.	Optimal transport mix. Widespread sharing of vehicles. 'Urban village', cycling and walking. Electric and fuel cell transport. Optimal interconnections.
Materials	Wasteful use of materials. Only imported materials. Little product durability. Everything is packaged. Few regional supplies. No regional timber. Unsustainable sources as norm. No consumption limitation.	More local and reused materials. Minimal use of virgin materials. Increasing product durability. Reduction in packaging use. Emphasis on regional supplies. Some regional timber. Sustainable sources common. Some consumption reduction.	Minimal waste of materials. Maximise sustainable sources. High product durability. Minimal packaging. Emphasis on local supplies. Regional timber in common use. Shared use of products. Large consumption reduction.
Waste	Linear system. 8% recycling. Little waste separation. Minimal recycling. Most waste disposed of in landfills. Some incineration. No remanufacturing.	Towards a circular system. 25% recycling. Some waste separation: reduce, reuse, recycle. Restricted landfill disposal. Minimal incineration. New remanufacturing industries.	Circular system. 75% recycling. Waste separation as norm: refuse, reduce, reuse, recycle. Remanufacture of metals, glass, paper and consumer waste into new products has become routine.

Source: © Herbert Girardet, 2002 and 2004

development on a worldwide scale. This also implies that cities in developed countries need to reduce their ecological footprints as those of cities in developed countries expand theirs to some degree.

Cities will always be centres of consumerism. But we can profoundly change the way they utilise resources. Conceptualising cities as sustainable eco-technical systems requires us to convert their largely linear resource throughput into circular resource flows. Energy efficiency, resource productivity, urban and industrial ecology—these are the key terms in this context. These are issues for companies as well as policy makers. A major push is needed to make cities much more resource efficient, and to reduce their vast sprawling ecological footprints (see also Chapter 10).

Let us trust that we will translate a better understanding of how large cities work into appropriate initiatives on urban sustainability. The table on London sustainability scenarios suggests what an increase in resource productivity by a factor of four and a simultaneous reduction of its ecological footprint by the same amount means for a large city such as London. The next chapters are concerned with how such measures can be implemented in practical terms.

CHAPTER 7

Transport
and the City

In 2003, the Thai government announced a new measure for countering congestion in Bangkok: it was banning vagrant elephants from the city's streets. The ban affected some 250 elephants that have been roaming Bangkok with their handlers, begging for food or promoting the sale of trinkets. Wandering the city, they were prone to holding up traffic, being hit by vehicles or even falling into open drains.

Each megacity has its own remedies for congestion problems. As Bangkok banned elephants, London introduced its congestion zone. From early 2003, people driving into London's central district have to pay a congestion charge of £5. This measure turned out to be a great success, reducing car traffic by some 30 per cent and increasing average speeds to 12 miles per hour, just a little more than in the days of horse-drawn coaches and buses.

The number of traffic jams has fallen dramatically, which means quicker trips both for those who pay and those who don't because they choose to take buses or taxis instead. Buses run on more routes and perform much better. Around 20,000 more people opt to travel on buses in the morning rush hour between 8 and 9 am. However, some central London businesses complained about a loss in sales. London mayor Ken Livingstone commented:

> *Congestion is down more than 30 per cent in the zone and journey times on central London roads are 10 per cent faster. Buses and*

taxis, which don't pay charges, have increased by 15 and 20 per cent respectively.[1]

In the giant cities of the Asia Pacific region, traffic congestion is the price people are paying for rapid urban and economic growth. Bangkok is probably the world's most congested city. A metropolis of about ten million daytime population, it spreads out over 600 square kilometres. The city's 2.6 million vehicles drive on streets covering just 8 per cent of the city's surface, compared, for instance, with 16 per cent in Tokyo. Since drivers spend about 22 days a year in their vehicles, many businesspeople have customised them as mobile offices. The traffic police are trained to deliver babies and doctors go out from hospitals on motorcycle taxis. Around 15 per cent of outpatients in Bangkok's hospitals suffer from acute breathing difficulties and chronic respiratory problems.

Lack of mass transportation is a major problem. A lane of light rail can move up to eight times more people per hour than a lane of highway.[2] To deal with this, Bangkok opened its first 20 kilometre underground train route in 2004. It can carry 12,000 passengers per hour in each direction across the city centre. It has 18 stations, including three connections with the Sky Train, the elevated rapid transit system that first came into operation in 1999. Bangkok has also made a start at getting cars off a street in the city's commercial district. In early 2004 Silom Road, which had previously been flooded by traffic, was pedestrianised, to great public acclaim.[3]

Delhi is another city that is notorious for both air pollution and congestion, particularly in the boom years at the start of the new millennium. There are now 4 million cars for the city's 14 million people. To ease congestion Delhi is building a metro system and new trolleybus routes are also being implemented. But critics say that only a comprehensive regional transport plan will speed up the daily migration of millions in and out of the city.[4]

Rapid economic growth of cities invariably results in traffic chaos. This seems to be unavoidable as the transition is made from walking and animal-based transport to cars and buses. Faster vehicles get people used to covering longer distances—until the traffic becomes snarled up again. Rapid urban growth invariably means a lack of adequate transport capacity to deal with people's travel expectations, in ways that are only too familiar from 19th-century cities such as London. Easing urban congestion means massive investment in new transport systems, but as soon as more public transport capacity frees up road space, more cars come along to fill the streets once more. Further investment in public transport then causes the cycle to start all over again.

In urban living, travel time is a constant whereas travel distance is variable, depending on the mode of transport available. A reasonable amount of time to get to and from work could be 45 minutes. Cities before the industrial revolution were walking cities. A person walking 45 minutes would cover three or four kilometres. In a modern city, 45 minutes by underground or bus means a travel distance of, say, 40 kilometres. And by car it means a distance of 80 kilometres or more. In Japan, where travel on intercity bullet trains can average 300 kilometres per hour, the 45-minute commuting radius can measure as much as 220 kilometres.

And so the walking city turns into the motor city and the centrifugal force of sprawl becomes its defining characteristic. Says Paul Downton of Urban Ecology, Australia:

> When trams and railways revolutionised transport, enabling people to move further, faster and more comfortably, they changed the shape of cities from cuddly and roundish to leggy and spread out. Riding the train or tram you could still get across the city in about half-an-hour, but you travelled much further. Wherever the iron horses stopped people got off and walked, so the compact walkable city shape was repeated along the legs of the railway lines. Then along came cars. And because cars go anywhere and we build roads to ensure it, our flabby cities have begun to lose any discernible shape at all![5]

The change from micro-mobility to macro-mobility not only tends to change dense urban form into low-density sprawl, but it also changes economic activity. The capacity of people to travel greater distances is closely linked to changes in retailing arrangements. Local businesses located in city centres lose out to out-of-town shopping malls that are dominated by multinational retail chains.

Says Austrian transport planner Hermann Knoflacher:

> Because humans plan, build and operate transport systems it is assumed that they are also in control of them, but unfortunately this has proved to be a fundamental misjudgement.[6]

Transport is one of the most intractable problems in sustainable development. In the next section I shall briefly look at the history of the motor car and how it affects urban growth patterns. I shall then discuss various ways of reducing its negative impacts—through planning policy, increased urban density, road pricing, improved public transport and new vehicle technology. The combination of all of these could significantly reduce the environmental impact of urban transport, though as far as implementation is concerned most cities still have a long way to go.

WELCOME TO THE MOTOR CITY

Visitors from outer space would be forgiven for believing that cars are the 'real' inhabitants of our cities, given that they populate roads and motorways that are much wider than the pavements and sidewalks to which people are confined. Worldwide this trend is still growing as more than 40 million new cars every year demand ever more road space. As affluence arrives in the motor city, low-density sprawl becomes the name of the game.

How did all this come about? The story of the Model T Ford is worth telling here since it changed the world and turned urban transport upside down. At the start of the 20th century few people in America could afford motor cars, which cost around $5,000. Then in 1908, using interchangeable parts and a moving assembly line, Henry Ford started to mass produce his Model T cars. In 1913, he modified his belt assembly line system and was able to produce his cars eight times faster still. He sold them for just $850, less than the price for a wagon and team of horses. By 1925, Ford had perfected his production system and his workers were able to complete a new car every ten seconds. As a result, the price of a Model T could be dropped to $360. A new American dream was born. Everyone with a good salary could now afford a car. City and state authorities were obliged to 'mass produce' roads to accommodate the proliferating car population. Companies such as Standard Oil had a booming new market, pumping oil as never before.

At the same time, a few large companies with a strong interest in private transport found ways of buying up America's urban public transport. In 1925, General Motors, Ford's main competitor, orchestrated the first large-scale streetcar closure. It bankrolled the bus company National City Lines, systematically to buy up and close down streetcar companies across the country. Teaming up with Standard Oil, Phillips Petroleum, Mack Trucks and Firestone Tyres, GM tore out the streetcar tracks in no fewer than 85 American cities in just a few years. The motor city had been born.[7]

Twenty years later, after the horrors of the Second World War, people in many countries dreamed of material advancement, of a house and garden in

Traffic jam
The car is a curse and a blessing. Individual freedom for some is air pollution for others. Every car requires some 200m^2 of asphalt.

the suburbs and of a car to get there. Thus the new American dream also became the European dream. Low-density, automobile-dependent urban development became a symbol of progress, even though in densely populated Europe, with its old and compact cities and its tight planning regulations, it was harder to implement. But the proliferation of motorways, connecting cities right across Europe, became a symbol of postwar progress. However, due to planning restrictions, support for public transport and high fuel taxes, car use in Europe is still much lower than in the USA.

Transport experts David Banister and John Pucher have presented some interesting comparisons between travel patterns in the USA and Europe. In the USA, less than 10 per cent of trips are by walking, cycling or public transport, compared with around 50 per cent in Europe. In the USA, car travel per person is 23,000 kilometres per year, with Europe's average being around 10,000 kilometres. In the USA, total energy use in travel per person per year was 83,500 megajoules, over three times more than in the EU countries, with 27,000 megajoules.[8]

Now rapidly developing countries such as China are determined to catch up with the developed countries. In 2002, China had a fleet of 15.5 million cars, one car for every 84 people, compared to one car for every 1.3 people in the USA. Car sales increased by more than 80 per cent in the first half of 2003, compared with the same period in 2002. China is the world's fastest-growing car producer, with production of 4.5 million in 2003 and of 5.15 million in 2004, surpassing Germany as the world's third largest car maker. In 2020, annual demand for passenger cars in China is forecast to hit 20 million, with its car total fleet reaching 156 million vehicles. That will be a tenfold increase in 18 years.[9]

If China reached the USA's per capita level of car ownership it would have some 970 million cars, 50 per cent more than the entire worldwide car fleet in 2003. In 2002, China already imported 20 per cent of its oil, yet by 2010 it is expected to import half its oil, and this figure could go up to 75 per cent by 2020. At 225 million tonnes of oil per annum, that will be about as much oil as OPEC currently produces in two months.[10] China's authorities know that a move to alternative fuels is important but, so far, there is little indication of an active move in that direction. However, neither is there much indication of a change in the rest of the world.

The implications for China of becoming a country of car users are astonishing. In 2003, China's oil consumption rose by 11.4 per cent. In 2004, its annual consumption of crude oil reached 270 million tonnes of which 100 million tonnes were imported, making it the world's second largest oil importer after the USA.[11] With projected growth rates for car use in the coming years, global competition for oil will reach unprecedented levels.

In Germany, car producer par excellence, research into the environmental and social impacts of the motor car has been particularly intense. Researchers have established that each car, taking up an average surface area of six square metres, is responsible for 200 square metres of tarmac and concrete and produces some 44.3 tonnes of carbon dioxide throughout its life.[12] It is, as yet, unclear how much of China's farmland will be covered by tarmac if motorisation there continues apace, and how much carbon dioxide will be discharged in the process.

The British transport researcher and planner John Whitelegg, who has researched these issues for half a lifetime, has coined the term 'Road Peace' as a rallying call for a fundamental rethink on our global addiction to the motor car.

THE PROBLEMS OF SPRAWL

Research in the USA has shown how unrestrained use of cars translates into urban form. As car ownership there reached unprecedented levels, low-density suburban sprawl became the norm. Between 1982 and 1997, the area of urban and built-up land in the US grew by almost 40 per cent—two and a half times faster than its population. For instance, the population of metropolitan New York grew only 5 per cent from 1975 to 2000, yet its surface area grew by 61 per cent.

Los Angeles is the classic case of urban sprawl based on cheap fuel. Its growth along its vastly complex freeway system is a product of both cheap building land and cheap gasoline. About 90 per cent of its population live in detached houses surrounded by large plots of land and drive to work by car. A city region of about ten million people, it covers an area three times larger than London, which has a population of seven million. London itself, where semi-detached houses and smaller gardens are the norm in the suburbs, is several times larger than Hong Kong, which has six million inhabitants and where most people live in high-rise blocks. Not surprisingly, Hong Kong uses space as well as public transport much more efficiently than either Los Angeles or London. But living in tower blocks, of course, is not everybody's ideal of city living.

Yet Los Angeles looks positively dense compared with Phoenix, Arizona, the world's most sprawling city. The 3.2 million people of its metropolitan region take up 353 square miles, nearly as much as the ten million people of Los Angeles County. Everybody lives in detached houses surrounded by large irrigated gardens and drives to work by car.[13] As yet, nobody has seriously tried to curtail this sprawl. Pennsylvania Governor Tom Ridge claims:

> *Among the biggest factors contributing to suburban sprawl are the substantial federal impediments to the redevelopment of urban land. Often, businesses invade the countryside, because they can't afford to clean up and reuse polluted industrial sites in the cities.*[14]

In the USA, a wide range of government policies directly subsidise urban sprawl, and this applies particularly to road construction and other urban infrastructure schemes. Keeping up roads costs several tens of thousands of dollars per year per mile. If developers and their customers had to bear the full costs of development without any such government underwriting, they would have far less incentive to build in outlying areas and far more incentive to redevelop within cities themselves.

Cities, of course, don't sprawl only in the USA. In Australia the pattern of urban growth is very similar and this is directly linked to the fact that quarter-acre housing plots are the norm in the suburbs. Here too, the freedom and privilege of having a large garden are closely linked to high car ownership, with most people using cars for many of their journeys. The work of urban consultants Peter Newman and Jeff Kenworthy of the University of Perth has conclusively shown that there is a direct correlation between low urban density and high use of motor cars. In low-density cities 'designed by the car', personal transport is clearly favoured over public transport. Automobile dependence and convenience go hand in hand. But the huge cost of providing the road infrastructure can generate substantial public debts, which can affect the provision of other facilities.[15]

Another social downside of high car dependence and low urban density is that travelling is rather difficult for some people. Young and old people are particularly disadvantaged by having to rely on those with driving licences and routine access to a car to get around. The sense of freedom for some can become loneliness, frustration and disadvantage for others. The situation of children is not helped by the fact that they are generally discouraged from cycling on busy streets for fear of accidents, whether to go to school, to go to the shops or to visit their friends.

The urban sprawl that has characterised American, Australian and New Zealand growth patterns for the past 50 years has been held responsible for a host of problems, such as profligate energy use, urban air pollution, tarmacking of vast areas of land, proliferation of out-of-town shopping malls, and loss of commerce in city centres. The heavy reliance on the private motor car for routine travel is becoming a major environmental issue. It is clearly desirable to counter these trends.

LIVING WITH SPRAWL

Low-density sprawl makes it difficult for public transport systems to work economically. This is clearly shown in a sprawling city such as Adelaide. With 475 cars per 1,000 inhabitants, only 5 per cent of passenger trips are made by public transport. To render the city's public transport system more viable and competitive, the number of passengers needs to increase. A comfortable, clean, high-frequency service is essential for buses to be used more widely. High-quality mass transit is the only option. Further investment is therefore of the essence and a good start has been made. Low-pollution gas-powered buses operate across the city and are popular with commuters. They offer a high level of customer comfort and are wheelchair accessible and air-conditioned.

The city envisages further improving public transport and encouraging more people to choose this over their private cars. Special transit corridors are being created to speed up bus travel. These could be painted green to emphasise the environmental desirability of bus services. They could also provide higher bus priority at traffic lights, which would improve the speed and punctuality of services.

Cycling is a vexed issue in sprawling cities such as metropolitan Adelaide. There are some 2,100 kilometres of dedicated routes across the city. Some of these are exclusive bike lanes while others are shared walking/cycling paths or bicycle lanes on arterial or local roads. Yet cycling is not a common mode of transport, despite a very suitable terrain. Only 25 per cent of people own bikes. People say that they would cycle a lot more and over longer distances if continuous, well-maintained and safe bicycle lanes were provided, particularly along arterial roads.[16]

In its 2003 Draft Transport Plan, the South Australian government set out targets for doubling cycling trips by 2018 by providing suitable new

Adelaide bus
This bus has as many passengers on board as the cars around it, most of which have only one occupant. The bus uses only a small amount of road space in comparison.

infrastructure and promoting cycling as a viable alternative to cars. Key destinations such as shops, schools, transport nodes and shopping centres are included in the proposed new system of cycle routes. Benefits would be experienced by commuters, sports cyclists as well as children, whose parents would feel safer about letting them cycle in the city.[17]

One significant way in which cities can counteract low-density sprawl is to create more 'nodes of activity' across metropolitan regions. Such compact, pedestrian-scaled neighbourhoods focused on tram or train stations are known as transit-oriented developments. These are typically denser and more socially diverse than the suburban norm. In Adelaide, an opportunity for this type of development is available at waterfront locations such as Port Adelaide, ten miles from the city centre. The area is being revitalised by providing a mix of residential, commercial, cultural and tourism opportunities. High-density waterfront living there will benefit from a great variety of local facilities, while also linking the area to Adelaide city centre via a new public transport connection.

The city of Adelaide itself has launched a new Inner City Living initiative to enable people to use cars far less than if they were living in the suburbs. The intention is to double the current number of residents to 34,000 by making inner city living attractive.[18] Incentives include 40 per cent rate rebates for new owner-occupiers to support housing on sites previously used for commercial purposes. More entertainment activity is being encouraged at night and at weekends, and new shops, restaurants and markets are being attracted to the central city. Adelaide is also aiming to give over a much greater area to pedestrian precincts[19] (see also Chapter 8).

COUNTERING SPRAWL

'Motor vehicle use in metropolitan areas is vastly underpriced',[20] says American economist Edwin Mills. Figures quantifying subsidies to car use vary depending on whether, for instance, the costs of accidents and the impacts of global warming are tallied. He found that just looking at public expenditure for highway infrastructure and services, car users paid for only 62 to 72 per cent of total expenditure.

A Harvard University study found that American motorists pay only 25 to 40 per cent of the total cost of their transportation. The remaining costs are borne by employers, through such amenities as free parking; by other travellers, due to increased congestion, reduced safety and air pollution; and by taxpayers, who pay for the expansion and maintenance of streets.[21]

For Mills, it is subsidies to the car and not sprawl per se that account for the bulk of America's problems of sprawl. He thinks that the best way to deal with sprawl is to raise fuel prices by some 150 per cent to cover the full costs of car use. This would encourage people to use their cars more efficiently and factor distance from work into their housing decisions. As a result, both congestion and pollution would be reduced.

Mills acknowledges that a fuel tax would be unpopular and that only a brave government would introduce such sweeping changes. Education would be a key factor in encouraging individuals to consider the impact of their actions on society and the environment. It is hard for people to admit that they are contributing to sprawl, congestion and air pollution. In any case, the preference for single-family detached homes with a large backyard is deeply embedded in the American psyche. And yet thinking in a systemic way, beyond individual concerns, countering sprawl is crucial for building a sustainable future.[22]

Urban sprawl needs to be dealt with by several simultaneous measures:

- removal of public subsidies on suburban infrastructure,
- creation of urban growth boundaries,
- densification of urban centres,
- subsidies on public transport to help it cover low-density districts,
- support for transport systems with low environmental impact.

In the USA, the remedy for sprawl is called 'smart growth'—housing development that is dense enough to reduce the need for private car use. Researchers found that 17 dwellings per hectare support a fairly frequent bus service, 22 support a light railway network and 37 support an express bus service that people can reach from their homes on foot (see also Chapter 8).

Portland, Oregon is a city of 1.5 million people. It has become a well-known example of a city that has been trying to counter sprawl. Since 1979 a state law demarcated an urban growth boundary, deliberately confining Portland in a restricted area and preventing encroachment of forest and farmland. Energy-efficient public transport is encouraged and is enthusiastically used. A highway along the Willamette river was removed and replaced by a linear park. Portland is also famous for the convivial public spaces that have been laid out in the city centre. But all is not well: while land use has become more intensive and sprawl has been curtailed, some people have chosen to move into towns outside the growth boundary and continue to commute into Portland by car.

Nevertheless, Orenco Station in Hillsboro, just west of Portland, shows how compact development can counter the attraction of car commuting. It is a new town centre community of 1,800 homes on 209 acres, with nearby offices, shops and restaurants built alongside a new light rail line station. It is arranged as a grid of walkable, tree-lined streets and parks, featuring town-houses, cottages and condominiums in a wide range of sizes and prices. As an ambitious and very popular new community, it has turned into a closely studied laboratory of new ideas for countering urban sprawl. Says project manager Michael Mehaffy:

> Today, as Americans search for more liveable, walkable alternatives to sprawl, the old streetcar suburbs like Orenco are being rediscovered. Orenco Station demonstrates that perhaps we need look no further than our own back yard for one of the most appealing, time-tested models of liveability. Old Orenco has been reborn, with high tech Internet wiring and other new bells and whistles, but with the same timeless neighbourhood structure.[23]

GOOD PUBLIC TRANSPORT

After decades of dominance by the private motor car, public transport is making a vigorous comeback in various parts of the world. In cities such as Hong Kong, Vienna, Zurich, Curitiba, Amsterdam and Montpellier, new tram and bus systems are making a major contribution to convenient and efficient travel. They are often given priority over private vehicles at traffic lights. Good public transport contributes to a cohesive society, enabling people to have easy access to services, jobs, education and social connections. Public transport has a major role to play in social equity, providing transport for all those who don't have access to a car. It can also contribute to a healthier way of life by assuring regular exercise in people's daily routine. Good links between mass transit, walking and cycling mean fast journeys, lower transport costs and healthier people.

With freer-flowing traffic, cities become cleaner, less frustrating and more liveable. In the 21st century, traffic congestion will be tackled increasingly by the introduction by congestion charges and urban toll roads, as London, Singapore and others have already done.

Curitiba in southern Brazil, a city of 1.7 million people, is an example of good public transport planning. Growing rapidly from the 1960s onwards, the authorities decided to develop the city along dedicated growth corridors. They set about organising a very efficient and highly integrated bus system to service the entire city, making it pleasant and fast to move around without the huge expense of constructing an underground system. Curitiba created a hierarchy of bus services, from those only serving local neighbourhoods to fast, articulated buses that run across the city on dedicated routes. By replacing conventional bus stops with so-called loading tubes, bus travel was greatly speeded up: as people enter the tubes they pay the resident conductor and when the bus arrives, everyone can get on and off instantly.

The city is planned around structural roads—or axes—with a dedicated road carrying high-speed buses; normal feeder roads are located alongside these; and several blocks away, mostly parallel, are one-way roads taking traffic into and away from the city. Measures were also taken to decongest the historic city centre by spreading businesses and housing more evenly along the new structural axes. This was achieved zoning for development closer to the transport routes. The further away from the buses they were, the smaller the buildings could be. This was to discourage people from using their cars, by making it easy to use public transport.

The man who initiated the city's bus system is the city's former major Jaime Lerner. He says:

> Every city has to deal with the problem of cars and public transport. No city in the world can be feasible just by working with individual cars. In Curitiba ten bus companies own the system, but it is managed by a public–private partnership. It is run by private companies and the city pays them by the kilometre. The balance is made up by the ticket sales. The price needs to be right. If it is too high, the people won't be able afford it, if it's too low the quality of transport will go down.[24]

TRANSPORT PLANNING IN EUROPEAN CITIES

European cities have remained more compact than most US or Australian cities. There are a number of reasons for this:

- Many cities date back to before the era of the motor car.
- Urban growth was closely linked to the development of public transport.

Curitiba bus lane
From the 1960s onwards Curitiba was 'grown' along five strategic road corridors with
dedicated bus lanes to assure rapid, efficient traffic circulation and interconnection.

- The price of fuel and the cost of car use are much higher.
- Planning restrictions have limited urban growth.

The city of Vienna shows how an integrated transport policy can increase the demand for public transport. In 1997, it published a new urban development plan and traffic concept whose main purpose is to change the 'modal split'. At that time individual motorised traffic had 37 per cent, public transport 37 per cent, walking 23 per cent and bicycles 3 per cent of total traffic. By the year 2010, Vienna aims to change the modal split to 25 per cent individual motorised traffic, 45 per cent public transport, 24 per cent walking and 6 per cent bicycle use. The Vienna Transport Plan is designed to give non-motorised transport priority. The two pillars of this policy are the improvement of services in the non-motorised transport sector and a rethinking of the management of public spaces, especially car parking facilities and use of roads. It also has major environmental benefits: it aims to bring about to a 50 per cent carbon dioxide reduction in the transport sector.

The plan is designed to balance the city's development and its transport system. Public transport has the greatest potential to contribute to an environmentally compatible transport system. New housing and commercial

Curitiba bus stop
The city's tubular bus stops, complete with resident ticket seller, allow for rapid disembarkation and boarding of buses, assuring efficient traffic flow.

development areas will be allocated along high-capacity public transport routes. The policy takes into account the balanced distribution of urban functions. It prioritises public transport, cycling and walking, cuts down traffic volumes, shifts traffic loads, improves road conditions, creates pricing structures that reflect the true costs, and utilises new forms of financing. The limitation of cars and the upgrading of the city's public transport infrastructure are the main elements of the strategy, using both structural city planning and regulatory measures.

To assure the attractiveness of the public transport system, the network of tram and bus routes is improved by the following measures:

- punctual and regular service on all lines,
- separate lanes and preferential traffic signals,
- shorter intervals at low-demand hours,
- good night-time service,
- increased efficiency and frequency of the basic network,
- route extensions in connection with urban development projects,

Vienna bus and tram
Integrated transport systems with preferential treatment of trams and buses at traffic lights have been established in many European cities, such as here in Vienna.

- improvements in rolling stock,
- flexible operating modes such as collective taxis in peripheral zones,
- improved public perception of the transport service service.

The limitation of individual car use and the promotion of walking and bicycle use are achieved by the following measures:

- provision of multistorey car parks to increase road space,
- reduction of parking space on the streets,
- regular monitoring of the public parking spaces,
- additional park and ride facilities on the periphery of Vienna.

In addition to improving public transport, the bicycle track network is being continuously improved. Although at first there were local protests against parking space management, it is now widely accepted with an 89 per cent positive reaction. The results encouraged the city to pursue its transport policies with additional vigour.

Zurich is Switzerland's biggest city and its major economic centre. It has 380,000 inhabitants, with one million inhabitants in the wider conurbation. Zurich has one of the world's most enlightened transport policies. These developed from referenda in 1962 and 1973 in which the citizens rejected the construction of an expensive subway network. Offering attractive public transport is part of an integrated approach to mobility that aims to reduce the use of cars and improve the quality of urban life. In 1975, a parliamentary resolution confirmed this approach and asserted that priority should be given to public transport.

The authorities have taken a number of key measures—such as better coordination of transport services and special tickets offers—to ensure that public transport would become cheaper and easier for people to use. The 262 lines and 44 public transport operators were gathered together under the Zürcher Verkehrsverbund, Zurich's transport union, which is responsible for coordination, budgeting, financing and setting fares.

Zurich's public transport services were made attractive through a very high-quality, wide range of services, which operate at high frequency even at night and out of rush hours. The city has a very extensive public transport network, including lines serving residential areas such as the city's innovative 'zone buses', tram tracks separated from general road traffic, special fares advertised by publicity campaigns, reduced fares for young people and combined passes for special events. An important feature of the system

Cycling network
Creating cycling networks separate from streets is important to make cyclists feel secure
without the danger of being run over by cars.

is that priority is often given to trams and buses at traffic lights. As parallel measures, parking and waiting restrictions were introduced for general traffic.

The Zurich Transport Union also conducted surveys on customers' needs and social trends, addressing the needs of specific customer groups. Its communication campaign for a closer relationship with its customers uses unusual techniques such as multimedia and cinema shows, live local radio station broadcasts from trams, telemarketing, school visits and permanent contacts with the population such as annual dance parties.

The success of the initiative has been remarkable. From 1984 to 1992, the number of people using public transport increased by almost 40 per cent. The average annual number of public transport journeys per inhabitant rose to 470, the highest figure in Europe. This increase in demand means that the Transport Union is able to cover some 65 per cent of its costs, despite constantly rising expenditure. Between 1980 and 1990, the proportion of regular public transport users went up from 51 to 60 per cent, while the car commuting population dropped from 24 to 18 per cent. Similar shifts were observed among those commuting in from the outlying suburbs. Zurich's ambitious target according to which all citizens should live no more than 300 metres away from a tramway stop now stands at no less than 96 per cent achieved.

Since 1980, Zurich's motorisation rate has not increased: it has remained at an average of 370 cars per 1,000 inhabitants, or 2.7 people per car, despite the fact that Zurich's economic prosperity is among the highest in Europe.[25]

The city's target for the coming years is a further 1 per cent annual increase in the level of use of municipal transport. The Zurich Cantonal Guiding Land Use Plan aims to increase urban density further, to ensure that further urban development is defined by the metropolitan railway system, and that areas of cantonal importance are located at public transport junctions.

Under Programme Energy 2000, private and company initiatives in saving energy are strongly encouraged. The federal government has invited business and automobile associations, energy companies, environment and consumer associations, administrative and scientific circles to develop new cooperative patterns of energy use. The programme implements the following measures:

- training in fuel-efficient driving,
- promotion of fuel-efficient cars,
- encouragement of fuel-efficient freight transport,
- private parking management to reduce daily car commuting,
- often combined with concessionary public transport tickets.[26]

The city of Copenhagen is one of the best examples of recent urban transformation. In addition to major initiatives on public transport and cycling, similar to those implemented in Vienna and Zurich, perhaps the most striking change there has been in the inner city. Over a period of 40 years, a total of 100,000 square metres of the inner city that had been devoted to motorised transport was converted to traffic-free space for pedestrians. It has transformed the experience of Copenhagen for local people as well as visitors.

Says urban planner Jan Gehl:

> *The streets seem to signal: Come, you are welcome. Walk awhile, stop awhile, and stay as long as you like. City space has been given a new form and a new content . . . 80 per cent of the movement through the city is foot traffic . . . 1,500 seats on benches and 5,000 sidewalk café chairs provide ample opportunity to sit, and they are in almost constant use. Children play, young people skate on roller blades and skateboards, while street musicians, artists and agitators of many kinds attract crowds to the squares . . . The city's new care-free spaces are used for a special form of social recreation, urban recreation, in which the opportunity to see, meet and interact with other people is a significant attraction.*[27]

Jan Gehl found that people do not prefer benches in parks in front of the most idyllic spots, but those where most people walk by.

Such comprehensive initiatives on urban density, energy efficiency, public transport and pedestrian development are still rare but are gradually catching on elsewhere. Policies similar to those pursued in Vienna, Zurich and Copenhagen are being implemented in other European cities, such as Heidelberg, Karlsruhe, Freiburg, Essen and Montpellier.

REMODELLING CITIES

Says Viennese transport planner Hermann Knoflacher 'We need to know how the system functions in order to assess at exactly which point to intervene.'[28] He argues that only bad planning requires fast transport systems. They are not needed if the functions of urban life are well integrated. For instance, large mono-functional buildings generate demand for mobility. If there is no option to work or go to school or entertain yourself locally, people are forced to be on the move. Diverse local activities are of the essence to counter the need for travel.

A major change in urban planning, then, is the new emphasis on *remod*-elling and *re*generating existing cities and subtly *re*integrating the diverse functions of urban life, *re*connecting living and working in newly pedestri-anised inner city areas wherever possible. More and more planners are aiming to create compact, diverse and liveable communities by imaginative urban design. In many cities there has been a remarkable return to inner city living. Making initiatives such as these the resounding success they deserve to be is a key issue for public policy and requires the active participation of the general public.

These are key issues for urban planners all over the world, particularly for developing countries that are still desperate to catch up with private car ownership and the travel patterns of the more developed countries. Only if the need for private car ownership is lessened will alternative, public transport and urban village models prevail.

An American campaign for walkable cities summarises the issues in a useful manner:

> *Walkability is the cornerstone and key to an urban area's efficient*
> *ground transportation. Every trip begins and ends with walking.*
> *Walking remains the cheapest form of transport for all people, and*
> *the construction of a walkable community provides the most*
> *affordable transportation system any community can plan, design,*
> *construct and maintain. Walkable communities put urban*
> *environments back on a scale for sustainability of resources . . .*
> *and lead to more social interaction, physical fitness and*
> *diminished crime and other social problems. Walkable*
> *communities are more liveable communities and lead to whole,*
> *happy and healthy lives for the people who live in them.*[29]

ALTERNATIVE VEHICLES

Can cities whose transport systems are based on cheap fossil fuels switch to renewable energy-powered transport systems in the future? To improve the environmental sustainability of transport, many avenues need to be pursued simultaneously. They include the need to accept that low-density sprawling cities are now a fact of life in some parts of the world and that many people will continue to favour the use of private vehicles. In this context, the development of alternative propulsion technology for vehicles, such as electric and hybrid-electric motors, should be actively pursued. Demand for these low-pollution vehicles is growing fast and manufacturers are improving their design and performance continually.

Electric vehicles are made by a growing number of manufacturers.[30] They are particularly appropriate for sprawling cities where most car journeys are clearly defined and limited to the city region. Electric cars should be strongly promoted as particularly suited to short commuting trips. Electric charging points should become a prominent feature of public car parks, offering low-cost recharging for users of electric cars or scooters. Photovoltaic (PV) panels should be installed routinely at car parks.

But fuel cell-powered cars and buses fuelled by hydrogen are likely to be the most significant new transport technology of the 21st century. They will be widely available by 2010, offering highly energy-efficient and pollution-free travel. New technical breakthroughs in both fuel cell systems and hydrogen production are indicating that these technologies could well replace the internal combustion engine by 2020. Hydrogen production from wind power and solar energy as well as from crop- and refuse-derived ethanol could make this a sustainable transport option for both private and public transport. As demand grows, local manufacturing in larger cities may become an attractive proposition that could also offer significant new local job opportunities.

The challenge for the decades to come is to combine the best features of compact urban development, effective use of public transport and new vehicle technologies to create a mix of key components that will lead to truly liveable cities.

CHAPTER 8

Creating
Liveable
Cities

*Integral to the spirit of the good city is its public and social life, its
zest and gaiety and the capacity for intermingling . . . It should be
a place of exuberance and exaltation of the human spirit, a place
for celebration and public 'happenings', for rich and easy
encounter, for relaxation and enjoyment. It must not be simply
functional and utilitarian.* (Wickham in Milward, 1987)

In recent decades cities, and particularly inner cities, in many parts of the
world have acquired a reputation as inhospitable, unpleasant, unhealthy and
even dangerous places. This often results from several concurrent trends: loss
of industries and jobs; depopulation; sprawl; increased use of cars; decline
in public transport; pollution; crime; and dereliction. In more extreme cases
gun crime, race riots and even urban terror can be both symptoms and causes
of urban decline, mutually reinforcing one another.

Nevertheless, history shows that horror stories can have a useful transforming function: they can concentrate the minds of decision makers, the
public and entrepreneurs on problem solving and on the need to create
human-scale cities. Creating liveable cities is as much about transforming
existing, often rundown cities or city districts to give them a new lease of
life as about building completely new cities, as is currently the case in rapidly
growing countries such as China.

Key questions to which we need an urgent answer are: how can we put the pulsing heart of conviviality back into our cities? How can we make sure that we create cities of diversity for the new millennium—places of cultural vigour and physical beauty that are also sustainable in environmental and economic terms?

Modern city planning emerged at the beginning of the 20th century and is, above all else, concerned with creating liveable cities, though commercial forces linked to the ownership of development land have often undermined good intentions. This chapter traces the origins of modern urban planning and looks at some of the pioneering developments in the 20th and 21st centuries.

Fredrick Olmstead, the father of American town planning, summarises the aims of planning:

City planning may conveniently be considered under three main divisions: The first concerns the means of circulation—the

Hackesche Hoefe, Berlin
Since the fall of the Berlin Wall the Hackesche Hoefe in Berlin have become one of the most popular spaces in the city. Their attractive, compact design with a series of internal courtyards provides for a great variety of social and cultural interactions.

distribution and treatment of the spaces devoted to streets,
railways, waterways, and all means of transportation and
communication. The second concerns the distribution and
treatment of the spaces devoted to all other public purposes. The
third concerns the remaining or private lands and the character of
development thereon, in so far as it is practicable for the
community to control such development.[1]

FROM HELL TO HEAVEN

In the 19th century, the horrendous living conditions faced by working people in the boom cities of Europe and America caused much soul searching, and ultimately gave rise to the modern town planning movement. Some governments and businessmen were fearful of slums becoming breeding grounds for revolution and initiated experiments in urban improvement.

Visions of the ideal city that would create ideal citizens became increasingly common, particularly in Britain. In his book *A New View of Society*, factory owner and social reformer Robert Owen said as early as 1816:

Society may be formed so as to exist without crime, without
poverty, with health greatly improved, with little, if any misery,
and with intelligence and happiness increased a hundredfold; and
no obstacle whatsoever intervenes at this moment except
ignorance to prevent such a state of society from becoming
universal.[2]

Owen practised what he preached. His greatest success was a model community that he created at his cotton mill in New Lanark in Central Scotland. He wanted to show that the damaging effects of the industrial revolution could be tempered by a caring and humane regime. At New Lanark, Owen abolished working for children under 10 years and organised one of the first infant schools, a crèche for working mothers, free medical care and comprehensive education, including evening classes. Leisure and recreation were also important and there were concerts, dancing and music making. Pleasant landscaped gardens were created for the whole community. Not surprisingly the village attracted international attention, encouraging Owen to create a second new village, the community of New Harmony in the United States.[3]

After Owen, other urban reformers drew up blueprints for new settlements. In 1849, James Silk Buckingham published his book *National Evils and Practical Remedies* and the plans for his utopian town 'Victoria'. This would unite 'the greatest degree of order, symmetry, space and healthfulness, in the largest supply of air and light, and in the most perfect system of drainage, with the comfort and convenience of all classes'. Victoria would have 10,000 acres, of which only 1,000 acres were to be built on, with the rest of the land retained as an agricultural estate.[4]

In 1853, the mill owner Sir Titus Salt initiated the new settlement of Saltaire three miles from Bradford, which took 20 years to build. He, like other benign industrialists, extended the paternalist tradition of the British land-owning classes, who had shown some concern about the living conditions of their farm workers, into a contemporary industrial setting. The visionary community that Salt created, with 800 houses and 3,000 inhabitants, had its own shops, park, church, school, hospital and library. At its centre was Salt's textile mill, the largest and most modern in Europe, which was designed to minimise pollution and noise.

In 1861, William Morris initiated the Arts and Crafts movement with architect Philip Webb and artists Dante Gabriel Rosetti and Edward Burne-Jones. Its aim was to spread good design inspired by nature, social fulfilment, preservation of built heritage and the pleasure of good craftsmanship. The movement was above all else concerned with recapturing the lost ideal of the medieval town set in a rural idyll.

In 1876, Benjamin Ward Richardson published *Hygeia, a City of Health*, a blueprint of a model city. He stressed the importance of fresh air, light and water. In his plan, he located industry away from the town centre in an early examples of zoning. While he did not manage to build Hygeia, his ideas certainly left their mark on the budding town planning movement.

In 1880, George Pullman, founder of the American Pullman Palace Car Company, created the new town of Pullman near Chicago on 4,000 acres. He was inspired by the socially conscious industrialists in Britain, though in the context of the wide open spaces of the USA he was able to think in larger terms. Even though the houses in Pullman have been privately owned since 1907, many are being maintained in such a way so as to assure the unity of its urban design to this day.

In 1887, the Quaker soap manufacturer William H Lever established the new community of Port Sunlight near Birkenhead in northern England. He was strongly driven by the idea that workers living in pleasant conditions will be trustworthy, efficient and reliable. Built on 56 acres, Port Sunlight included extensive allotment gardens, parks, sports grounds and cultural venues, and still exists today.

In 1901, chocolate manufacturer George Cadbury, also a Quaker, implemented plans to provide decent homes and a pleasant living environment for his workers at an affordable price. He started the Bournville community on 1,000 acres, a widely influential model village that grew into a small town that today accommodates 25,000 people. Cadbury stipulated that one-tenth of the land at Bournville should be set aside for parks and recreational space.[5]

In 1906, Margarethe Krupp, widow of German industrialist Friedrich Alfred Krupp, initiated another example of benign social engineering in a new settlement in Essen called Margarethenhoehe. It was built on 125 acres of farmland on the outskirts of the city. To assure a diverse social mix, about half of the residents were to be people not employed by Krupp. The settlement continues to thrive today.

The rapid population growth and long-distance migrations in the 19th century led to new urban development in places as far afield as the USA, Canada and Australia. In South Australia, Adelaide became the prototype of the garden city. In 1837, Colonel William Light laid out a square mile of urban development set in 931 hectares of parklands, 700 hectares of which remain to this day. At first much of the land was used for farming, though only a few olive groves remain, with the rest of the land planted as lawn shaded by trees. Adelaide became the core of the sprawling city that accomodates the majority of the population of South Australia.

BUILDING GARDEN CITIES AND NEW TOWNS

These examples of 'alternative' settlement planning inspired the British reformer Ebenezer Howard to write his book *Garden Cities of Tomorrow*. His aim was to find ways to improve the lives of millions of people who were living in overcrowded, ugly and unhealthy urban environments devoid of nature. He wanted to combine the advantages of town and country living, while avoiding the disadvantages of both. He argued for creating new garden cities on greenfield sites, while opening up old cities by the partial demolition of overcrowded terraces to create new green spaces. Howard wrote: 'Town and city must be married and out of this joyous union will spring new hope, a new life, a new civilisation.'[6]

Similar to Buckingham's plans, Howard proposed garden cities located on some 6,000 acres, of which only 1,000 were to be built on. On 1,000 acres there were to be 32,000 inhabitants and an additional 2,000 people in the surrounding 2,000-hectare agricultural estate. His circular town plan had 120-foot wide radiating tree-lined boulevards that were meant to divide the town into six distinct sectors. While his garden cities were designed as largely self-contained settlements, they were also meant to be linked to each other, and to larger cities such as London, by the use of railway lines, giving residents the benefits of modern mobility.

Howard stipulated that all land was to be leasehold rather than freehold and to be owned by the whole community. Increases in land value would accrue to the community and would be ploughed back into municipal improvements. To ensure a high quality of life, Howard meticulously separated pedestrian streets and vehicle traffic, and residential and industrial areas. When a garden city had reached its optimal population of 32,000, its growth would be halted and another town of similar size would be built within its own zone of land. But the inhabitants of the one could very quickly reach the other by a rapid transit system, and thus the people of the two towns would really be part of one community.

Howard and his colleagues were able to realise two garden city projects in Hertfordshire, at Letchworth in 1903 and then at Welwyn Garden City in 1920. Both continue to be the hugely influential icons of the garden city movement and receive visitors from around the world. Today, a foundation jointly owned by the citizens of Letchworth controls 5,300 acres of land, including two farms and 118 shops. Every penny earned from these stays in the community and from 1997 to 2003 its assets trebled to £160 million.[7]

In the USA, Frederick Law Olmsted was arguably the intellectual leader of the city planning movement. In 1917, he became the first president of the American City Planning Institute. He helped to design the innovative Forest Hills Gardens project in Queens as well as the industrial town of Torrance in California. He also prepared plans for existing cities such as Detroit, Boulder, New Haven and Pittsburgh. His concern was as much with functionality as with aesthetics:

> *The demands of beauty are in large measure identical with those*
> *of efficiency and economy, and differ mainly in requiring a closer*
> *approach to perfection in the adaptation of means to ends than is*
> *required to meet the merely economic standard. So far as the*
> *demands of beauty can be distinguished from those of economy,*
> *the kind of beauty most to be sought in the planning of cities is*
> *that which results from seizing . . . the limitless opportunities*

which present themselves in the course of the most rigorously practical solution of any problem . . .[8]

The history of 20th-century town planning was a solid background from which to endeavour to create new towns after the destruction wreaked by the Second Word War. In Britain the construction of new towns, loosely modelled on Howard's garden cities, was an opportunity to replace the more than 500,000 homes that had been destroyed. Between 1955 and 1975, three million people moved from Britain's old cities to new towns, mostly in rural locations. To contain them in a defined space, they were surrounded by their own green belt. By 1990, no fewer than 28 new towns and cities had been built, such as Basildon, Bracknell, Cumbernauld, Cwmbran, Harlow, Milton Keynes, Skelmersdale, Stevenage and Telford. But sadly most did not live up to expectations, mainly due to the indifferent quality of design and building materials. By 2000, many were worse for wear, with cracking pavements, rundown buildings and crumbling concrete in urgent need of repair.

Some new towns also have serious problems of unemployment. Unlike Howard's Letchworth, few have been able to regenerate out of their own resources because in the 1980s their development corporations were dissolved by government decree and their assets were privatised. An opportunity to create and maintain financially self-sustaining garden cities had been tragically lost.

LE CORBUSIER'S LIVING MACHINE

In the mid-20th century French architect Le Corbusier also proposed 'garden cities'. Like Ebenezer Howard, he felt that contemporary cities were chaotic and gloomy prisons for many of their people, but there the similarity between them ends. Le Corbusier had a strong conviction that the 20th century was an age in which engineering and technological breakthroughs offered tremendous opportunities for progress. Like his Bauhaus colleagues Mies van der Rohe and Walter Gropius, he felt that architecture should stop aping historical styles. Why not create standardised architecture in which building components would be assembled efficiently in mass production processes?

Le Corbusier insisted on purist design without ornamentation, emphasising the importance of function over style. He was convinced that rationally planned, collective developments offered desirable and healthy housing options. He proposed massive, angular 'living machines' to be set in leafy parks, with hundreds of apartments and with thousands of people living under one flat roof—places of light and air, with cafés, restaurants, shops and nurseries.[9]

After the war Le Corbusier was given the chance to implement his ideas in the pioneering Unité d'Habitation in Marseilles, a block with 330 housing units in 23 different forms. The massive building is 135 metres long, 24 metres deep and 56 metres high and took and five years to build, from 1947 to 1952. The development was intended to be functionally superior to traditional urban forms, meeting both individual and collective needs, with each apartment spaciously arranged in two storeys:

> *The giant, twelve-story apartment block for 1,600 people is the . . . counterpart of the mass housing schemes of the 1920s, similarly built to alleviate a severe post-war housing shortage. Although the program of the building is elaborate, structurally it is simple: a rectilinear ferro-concrete grid, into which are slotted precast individual apartment units, like 'bottles into a wine rack' as the architect put it. Through ingenious planning, twenty-three different apartment configurations were provided to accommodate single persons and families as large as ten, nearly all with double-height living rooms and the deep balconies that form the major external feature.*[10]

LIVING IN THE SKY

Le Corbusier's radical ideas were widely emulated. Across Europe, the devastation of the Second World War made major urban redevelopment an urgent necessity. A new coalition of architects, planners and politicians came together, aiming to remodel the urban development scene. Vernacular buildings, often built of local materials and adapted to local conditions, fell prey to the jaws of bulldozers and the calculators of both architects and accountants. Steel frames, reinforced concrete and plate glass revolutionised the postwar building industry, not only in Europe but also in America and Asia.

But often the new high-rise developments left much to be desired. They were frequently shoddily built, too hot or cold, lacked public amenities and tended to become dumping grounds for the less fortunate in society, who were assigned housing units in huge housing blocks without much concern for their real needs. Many apartments were cramped and badly laid out, and made life particularly difficult for families with young children. In many blocks unemployment was rife and drug use, crime and vandalism contributed to deteriorating conditions on 'problem' estates. The angularity of the architecture often made the blocks feel bleak and comfortless, and alienation, loneliness and stress became common experiences. From Berlin to Dresden, from Birmingham to Marseilles, from Detroit to Moscow, and São Paulo and other developing-world cities, housing blocks were prone to vandalism and premature aging. As a result, many did not survive more than a few decades.

In some places, however, tower blocks are starting to be rehabilitated—through privatisation and renovation, or through local schemes, with residents asserting a sense of ownership. In either case, appropriate measures can rejuvenate rundown tower blocks and turn them into liveable places. But the actual regeneration of blocks is only part of the picture. In areas of high unemployment and extreme social inequality, they are unlikely ever to become liveable places.

URBAN OASIS, SALFORD

In Salford, Manchester, the Urban Oasis project shows how a rundown block can be transformed into a thriving new community. In the early 1990s Apple Tree Court, with 100 apartments, had been half empty and was surrounded by rubble and a wasteland on which nothing grew. Then a new initiative involved the remaining residents in the transformation of the building and its environment. A resident caretaker was installed at the lift entrance to keep watch on the building. A security fence was put around Apple Tree Court and the cultivation of its gardens was taken over by the residents. They divided them up and zoned their responsibilities. Some people are interested in the orchard, some in growing vegetables, others in the flower beds, the wildlife meadow and the pond. The garden is the proud creation of the residents and in a short while it became a place of beauty and peace. People now feel secure and have a sense of shared ownership as well as privacy.

Says Tony Milburn who helped initiate this transformation:

There are high-rises all over Britain and Europe. Either you pull them down, which is the most costly solution, or you find a way to enhance and improve them. If you can do that with the local people who live there, you can save enormous sums of money. There is not enough money around to tackle these problems, so this is a social issue and an environmental one, as much as it is an economic imperative. If you're going to solve a problem, you can't afford to do that without empowering people to do it themselves. What's happened here has only happened because the people who live here had a positive vision of how they could change their lives, and they've got on with it and they did it, and they learnt from it and they're proud of it.[11]

BRITAIN'S URBAN SPLASH

In Britain, a highly imaginative property developer, Urban Splash, was among the first to recognise that the many redundant historic buildings in rundown

Antonio Gaudi's Casa Mila, Barcelona
This apartment building is one of Gaudi's most striking creations, combining functionality and exuberance. Gaudi's architecture has become one of Barcelona's trademarks and primary tourist attractions, envied by other European cities.

cities such as Manchester and Liverpool had a real future and could be adapted for new, exciting uses. Its impressive portfolio includes the conversion of many old industrial buildings such as the Match Factory in Manchester, a magnificent art deco building, into a high quality business centre, and the Tea Factory in Liverpool into stunning apartments with magnificent views over the River Mersey, as well as studio workplaces for creative industries, restaurants and bars. Urban Splash is also refurbishing rundown tower blocks, and back-to-back terraces and council houses that had suffered from dereliction and depopulation.

Since 1993, Urban Splash has brought back into use over two million square feet of previously redundant city centre space and helped create over 3,000 permanent jobs, 1,000 new homes and enabled over 250 new company start-ups. By 2003, Urban Splash itself employed over 200 people and was developing projects with a total value of over £200 million.

The creation of refurbished inner city dwellings has proved increasingly popular with young professionals, particularly in Liverpool. There has been a dramatic increase in the number of people flocking back to live in the city centre. Over the past five years Liverpool has witnessed a growing trend towards what has been termed 'city centre living', with a significant increase in the amount of residential (re)development. Many young professionals now prefer to live near their place of work and enjoy being close to the plethora of bars, restaurants and nightclubs that the city has to offer.

A NEW START?

Today's planning agenda is substantially different from the concepts developed in the aftermath of the war. After decades of deindustrialisation we have to deal with a great deal of urban wasteland. In addition, urban sprawl and the proliferation of cars has blighted many cities. At the start of the 21st century the desire to regenerate rundown, shapeless cities and brownfield sites into liveable urban environments has become a major preoccupation for politicians, planners and communities. The compact cities of the past with their walkable and varied streetscapes have become a major influence on people's thinking. Worldwide, ideas are being exchanged as never before and the importance of mutual learning from best practice is growing all the time.

Because of the explosion in international travel in recent years, many people have experienced a great variety of urban environments. Coming back with holiday snaps from places as diverse as Udaipur, New Orleans, Curitiba,

Barcelona, Copenhagen or Prague, many people are asking how such examples of 'compact liveability' can be implemented in their own cities.

It is interesting that pioneering modernist architects such as Richard Rogers, while vigorously opposed to retrospective building design, strongly encourage a renaissance of compact cities. Rogers grew up in Florence where he had first-hand experience of magnificent renaissance buildings and piazzas. He states:

> Cities are centres of communication, learning and complex commercial enterprises; they house huge concentrations of families; they focus and condense physical, intellectual and creative energy. They are places of hugely diversified activities and functions: exhibitions and demonstrations, bars and cathedrals, shops and opera houses . . . Urban meeting places are still being eroded and violated by the ever-increasing intrusion and unseemly domination of the motor car . . . The essence of a city—its human vitality— is being sucked out, leaving behind ghost towns offering only physical dereliction and social exclusion.[12]

All over the world the quest is to create the liveable, compact city of the 21st century, a place that is a pleasure to live in, work in and visit. While cities are centres of economic activity, they should also be places of cultural creativity, citizenship and conviviality. They should have well-designed public spaces and buildings, large pedestrian areas, access to water, parks and gardens. High quality 'micro-environments' should enhance the experience of urban living.

The liveable city is a fine balance between community and anonymity. Most people want to live in places in which neighbours can be neighbours, but without coercion and without others interfering in their personal lives. They want leafy streets where they can sit safely on their verandas and chat to each other. They want to belong to communities, but not to be gazed at and gossiped about. They want schools, offices, markets, shops, pubs and restaurants within walking distance and, beyond pedestrian areas, affordable buses, light rails or trams that offer rapid access to other parts of the city. A 'liveable city' agenda is to:

- make places of beauty, diversity and easy contact,
- develop vibrant local communities with diverse living choices,

Pedestrian zone, Copenhagen
Cities are rediscovering the social and ecological benefits of pedestrian zones and urban
villages. Copenhagen has mastered the art of pedestrianisation.

- integrate a diverse range of economic activities,
- revitalise underutilised land for community benefit,
- protect and enhance natural environments and biodiversity,
- enhance the benefits of climate, natural setting and architecture,
- facilitate cycling, pedestrianisation and public transport,
- assure efficiency of traffic flows and minimise traffic impacts,
- enhance public participation in decision making.

SMART GROWTH AND NEW URBANISM

In the USA and Australia, the ubiquitous problem of urban sprawl (see Chapter 7) is being countered by alternative concepts such as Smart Growth and New Urbanism, which stand for a reordering of the built environment, the revival of 'place making' and the creation or restoration of compact, mixed-use cities. The New Urbanists are architects, planners and developers who are well connected internationally and who are quietly determined to implement the ideal of the liveable city. Some of their main tenets were laid down in Europe by the traditionalist Luxemburg architect Léon Krier, best known for his collaboration with the Prince of Wales on the new settlement of Poundbury in Dorset, UK.

In the USA, the Charter of the Congress for the New Urbanism states:

> We advocate the restructuring of public policy and development
> practices to support the following principles: neighborhoods
> should be diverse in use and population; communities should be
> designed for the pedestrian and transit as well as the car; cities
> and towns should be shaped by physically defined and universally
> accessible public spaces and community institutions; urban places
> should be framed by architecture and landscape design that
> celebrate local history, climate, ecology and building practice. We
> stand for the restoration of existing urban centers and towns
> within coherent metropolitan regions, the reconfiguration of
> sprawling suburbs into communities of real neighborhoods and
> diverse districts, the conservation of natural environments and the
> preservation of our built legacy.[13]

A key advocate of the liveable city is the architect and planner Christopher Alexander, the originator of the concept of 'pattern language'. He says:

*Knowing how beautiful shapes come into being is the essence of
what we do . . . Outdoor space is positive when it is shaped, just as
a room is shaped. It has a contained character; it is bounded by
walls, trees, fences, natural vegetation, enclosure of some kind.
When space is positive, passing through it one moves from space
to space, as if one were moving through a series of rooms. Each
space, individually, is a strong centre, each one has a boundary,
one feels its heart, its substance; and one passes from one of these
strong centres, to the next, as one moves around and though the
space. This is entirely different from the space of present-day
America—where a loose aggregation of parking lots, asphalt, wide
roads, yards without significant meaning and therefore without
significant boundaries, causes an amorphous substance to exist.*[14]

THE SCOPE FOR NEW URBAN VILLAGES

The European equivalent of New Urbanism is the urban village, a concept
concerned with breaking up and refocusing undefined urban areas. In recent
years Copenhagen, Freiburg, Vienna, Zurich, Heidelberg and Barcelona have
all benefited from outstanding urban redesign, with the new urban village
theme a central feature. The urban village is created around pedestrian
streets, sidewalks, public squares and parks. Every trip should begin and end
with walking, the healthiest, most environment-friendly and democratic form
of mobility. It is the most human way to meet people, to experience a city
and to take part in its life. The dense pedestrian centre is then connected to
the rest of the city with cycle lanes and well-integrated public transport.

These ideas are echoed in many cities. Says the major of San Sebastian in
northern Spain:

*Our cities are committed to becoming more liveable spaces, more
human cities where the pedestrian comes centre stage and where
co-existence, meetings, leisure and shopping all take place in
streets and squares devised and designed primarily for these ends.
Cities cannot give in to the endless demands of vehicles. . . . We
must rethink the city and give priority to the needs of pedestrians
and act on the basis of democratic consensus and correct town
planning. We need to take steps in favour of sustainable mobility
and the improved quality of urban life.*[15]

In Denmark, a more private version of urban villages is called 'co-housing'. Groups of houses are clustered together, aiming to create convivial neighbourhoods, complete with their own community cafés, playgrounds, laundries and car sharing facilities.

In Britain the Peabody Trust, London's largest housing trust, which owns 17,000 flats, has made a particularly interesting contribution to liveable, compact urban development—the urban eco-village. The Beddington Zero Energy Development (BedZED) was created on a brownfield site, a former sewage works, in the borough of Sutton in South London. It consists of 82 homes and 16,000 metres of commercial space and was completed in 2002. It has become a buzzing mixed community of homes for rent, sharing and ownership, also incorporating commercial offices and studios. It has many innovative features, including its own combined heat -and power system burning wood chips, a 'living machine' sewage system, a pool of electric cars and photovoltaic panels mounted on the conservatories of every flat.

All homes have their own small gardens. Very high levels of energy and resource efficiency have resulted in greatly reduced running costs. For instance, instead of investing in central heating systems, each flat is insulated by 30 centimetres of rock-wool like a giant tea cosy. The buildings, designed by architect Bill Dunster, have won many architectural awards. They were jointly developed by the Peabody Trust and the BioRegional Development Group, which has also pioneered a variety of other innovative schemes aiming to reestablish a sustainable local economy.[16]

The Peabody Trust is also implementing another major new urban village project, called Ladbroke Green, on the Grand Union Canal in West London, with 300 rental and leasehold homes. An important innovation is that 200 kilowatts of photovoltaic panels will make the scheme largely self-sufficient in electricity in the summer months. It is being built on the last major brownfield land left in the Borough of Kensington and Chelsea. The primary aim is to create a diverse community in a popular west London location and a working example of many of the recommendations of the UK government's Urban Task Force, which emphasises the importance of residential development on brownfield sites and a mix of properties for sale and social housing.

At the heart of the development is a canal basin around which stylish apartments will be built, with the ground floors housing offices, studios, restaurants, cafés and bars. A landscaped park looks out to the canal across an ecology garden with wetland plants and animals. The architecture, by award-winning partnership CZWG, is striking and modern. A tower at the entrance to the development will range from 15 storeys down to seven floors,

BedZED
Beddington Zero Energy Development (BedZED) in Sutton, South London, has become famous
as a new urban village in which people can enjoy sustainable lifestyles.

forming both a local landmark and providing south-facing roof space for solar photovoltaic panels. The photovoltaic system is being supported by European Union funding.[17]

PARKS AND PUBLIC PLACES

Public spaces and parks form a crucial feature of liveable cities. Unlike in many 19th-century cities, frequently not enough space is kept aside for them. Too often, attractive, safe and well-maintained spaces are located in privately owned, enclosed shopping centres. Yet public parks are important for people, from whose lives the experience of green space and biodiversity has gone missing.

Enrique Peñalosa, major of Bogotá, makes an interesting statement about this topic:

Parks and public spaces are important to a democratic society because they are the only places where people truly meet as

*equals. Parks are also essential to the physical and emotional
health of a city. However, this is not obvious from most budgets,
where parks are treated as somewhat of a luxury. Roads, the
public space for cars, receive infinitely more resources and less
budget cuts than parks, the public space for children . . .*

*As mayor of Bogotá, a city of 7 million inhabitants, I led the
creation of more than 1,300 parks. We invested in water and
sewerage supply, schools and libraries, transportation systems and
pavement. But beyond education, we didn't have a higher priority
than public pedestrian spaces: pedestrian streets, sidewalks,
greenways, bicycle-paths, metropolitan parks, neighbourhood
parks and plazas. Spaces for people but above all, spaces that
demonstrate respect for the more vulnerable of society's members:
the poor, the old and children . . . Parks are an important means to
children's happiness and therefore, to a more convivial,
constructive and civilized society.*[18]

ECO-VILLAGES—FROM DREAM TO REALITY

The virtual evacuation of whole villages in countries such as France, Italy,
Spain and Portugal has contributed to another interesting trend: restoration
of these places by newcomers and conversion into eco-villages. Hundreds of
such developments have occurred, driven by the idea that if we want to
survive as a species we have to learn to live sustainable lives close to nature.
The rapidly growing eco-village movement is intended to address these
issues. Since the 1970s, the dream of creating alternative settlements or eco-
villages has been spooking around in the minds of ever larger numbers of
people. After a very tentative start, emerging out of the 1960s commune movement, the eco-village dream has increasingly become a reality all over the
world, in both rural and urban locations.

To live in small towns or villages surrounded by nature is an enduring
desire for many people, well expressed in the words of the *Tao Te Ching*:

*Let your community be small, with only a few people;
Keep tools in abundance, but do not depend upon them;
Appreciate your life and be content with your home;
Sail boats and ride horses, but don't go too far;*

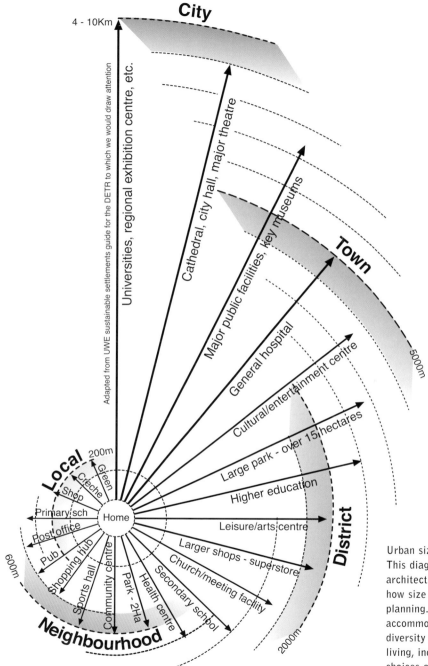

City

4 - 10Km

Universities, regional exhibition centre, etc.

Cathedral, city hall, major theatre

Major public facilities, key museums

Town

5000m

General hospital

Cultural/entertainment centre

Large park - over 15 hectares

Higher education

District

Local

200m

Green

Crèche

Shop

Primary sch

Home

Leisure/arts centre

Post office

Larger shops - superstore

Pub

Shopping hub

Church/meeting facility

Sports hall

600m

Community centre

Park - 2Ha

Health centre

Secondary school

Neighbourhood

2000m

Urban size and functions
This diagram by London architect Andrew Wright shows how size matters in urban planning. A larger city can accommodate a greater diversity of functions for urban living, increasing the range of choices available to its people.

Keep weapons and armour, but do not employ them;
Let everyone read and write,
Eat well and make beautiful things.

Live peacefully and delight in your own society;
Dwell within cock-crow of your neighbours,
But maintain your independence from them.[19]

Eco-villages aim to be living models of sustainability and examples of how action can be taken immediately. They also seek to address the degradation of our social, ecological and spiritual environments, enriching the lives of many people who profoundly lack meaningful content. According to the international Ecovillages Network, there are now some 15,000 such villages worldwide, including 11,000 existing villages with sustainable lifestyles in various parts of the world.

In terms of statistics, eco-villages have, so far, made no major contribution to housing people, with total numbers housed in the millions rather than in the billions. (The same also applies to garden cities, which have made a relatively small contribution to the development of human settlements.) However, eco-villages have made a contribution to culture and technology way beyond their numbers. They have greatly contributed to the development of renewable energy systems, waste water treatment, new forms of architecture, music and dance. As visitor centres, they have provided venues for conferences and meetings. They have made visitors aware that another world is possible and that rampant urbanisation need not be the only future option for humanity.

Each country offers different opportunities for eco-village development. In some, such as Britain and Germany, it has been exceedingly difficult to create alternative settlements in rural locations because of very strict planning regulations. In Britain, it is quite easy for people to purchase a few acres of farmland for maybe £3,000 an acre, but it is virtually impossible to get permission to build houses on that land outside existing towns and villages. Apart from Findhorn eco-village in southern Scotland, which was built on an existing caravan park, and the Centre for Alternative Technology in Wales, practically no other eco-villages have been created in rural Britain. The planning system is a major reason for this. If planning permission is granted on land currently used for farming, the value increases from around £3,000 to anything between £300,000 and £1,000,000 an acre, depending on location.

ALDINGA ARTS ECO-VILLAGE

Aldinga Arts eco-village, the brainchild of Adelaide architect John Maitland, vividly illustrates the processes by which eco-villages can be implemented. It will be completed by 2005. This residential, arts, community and commercial development is being built on 33 hectares of former farmland near Adelaide. Of this, 17 hectares will accommodate 150 dwellings surrounded by village commons, community gardens, and horticultural and recreational areas. Purchasers own their plots outright, together with a share in the common land, farm and cultural facilities. They are obliged to respect bylaws requiring environmental and social responsibility.

In the not-for-profit development, income from the sale of land is ploughed back into the project to fund the infrastructure and to increase and upgrade facilities. The community will be 'managed' by a democratically appointed group of residents.

Sustainable design principles are employed throughout the development. Houses must be energy efficient and served by a large rainwater tank. The village farm is accommodated on 16 hectares, also containing recycling sewer treatment, lagoons, tree buffers doubling as wood lots, community plots for individual planting and organic food crops, all developed on permaculture principles. Verges will be planted with food trees and ground cover vegetation. The community facility at the heart of the village is a space for markets, festivals, performances and celebrations, and a restaurant as well as an interpretive centre. Public access to the village is via walkways. The village has the following design features:

- Renewable energy—solar hot water, photovoltaic and wind power.
- Water supply from household rainwater tanks; mains needed only occasionally.
- Storm water retention in ponds, fed by swales from roads and buildings.
- Sewerage to be treated and reclaimed water used for irrigation on site.
- A sophisticated communications network to support home industries.
- Internal roads constructed for safe travel by pedestrians and cyclists.
- Edible and indigenous planting in common areas and private gardens.
- Health, financial, building and gardening services provided on site.
- A central facility for visual and performing arts and culture.
- Centralised postal services, refuse and recycling collection.[20]

MAKING IT HAPPEN

Much of this book is concerned with ways in which sustainable and liveable cities can become a reality, in both rich and poor countries. As we head deeper into the 21st century, all the creativity and ingenuity at our disposal need to be harnessed to create lifestyles and urban and economic systems that are compatible with our innermost needs for shelter, security and sufficiency—while also living within the carrying capacity of planet earth.

We need to be aware of the forces that actually shape urban development: economic power, commercial interests, transport technologies and planning legislation are, all too often, not in the hands of city people. But liveability is not just about the layout of cities, it is also about co-determination—people wanting to be actively involved in shaping their local environment. This means that liveability is also about local power and community control.

The same applies to environmental sustainability, and the next three chapters make the connection between liveability and efficient resource use in our cities.

CHAPTER 9

Solar Cities— From Theory to Practice

In a world in which climate change is becoming an ever-growing concern and in which oil and gas reserves are being rapidly depleted, we urgently need to find new ways of powering our gas-guzzling cities. Combustion technologies have made us what we are today—an urban-industrial species. In fact, the very form, functions and growth dynamics of our cities are largely due to their pervasive use of fossil fuels. This chapter explores whether our cities could run on renewable energy instead.

In the last 50 years, fossil fuel combustion has increased nearly five times, from 1,715 billion tonnes of oil equivalents in 1950 to well over 8 billion tonnes by 2002. In 1997, the global fossil fuel industry was worth over $1.4 trillion a year.[1] World oil and gas production totalled just under 5.11 billion tonnes and coal production (in oil equivalents) totalled 2.12 billion tonnes.[2] Currently we derive 85 per cent of our commercial energy from fossil fuels and 7 per cent from nuclear power.[3]

As urban citizens we are pampered as never before. In terms of our per capita energy use, the average American currently uses 110 'energy slaves', equivalent to the work of a strong human producing 100 watts in a 12-hour workday seven days a week. By comparison, a central European has 60 and a Chinese has 8 energy slaves at his or her disposal, largely based on their use of fossil fuels.[4]

Questioning a way of life based on fossil fuels seems almost unthinkable. And yet the very freedoms they give us have resulted in unprecedented environmental impacts, not just for us today but particularly for the generations to come. In the process of extracting fossil fuels we are actually reversing a key process in which the earth has been engaged for eons: absorbing carbon dioxide from the atmosphere through photosynthesis and tucking it out of harm's way within the Earth's crust. By burning fossil fuels we transfer the Earth's stores of carbon back into the atmosphere. It is estimated that we are burning fossil fuels around a million times faster than they actually accumulate in the Earth's crust.[5]

But as former Saudi oil minister Sheik Yamani has said: 'The Stone Age did not end because the world ran out of stones, and the oil age will not end because the world runs out of oil.' Fossil fuels cannot be the primary urban energy suppliers for much longer without causing irreversible climate change. Environmental campaign group Greenpeace estimates that if we burn more than a quarter of known economically recoverable fossil fuel reserves, we will not be able to stay within potentially 'safe' climatic limits.

There is widespread international agreement that unless carbon dioxide emissions are reduced by at least 60 per cent worldwide by 2050, irreversible climate change could result. The Intergovernmental Panel on Climate Change (IPCC) forecasts that this will affect most of the 50 per cent of the global population living, mainly in cities, close to the sea. It predicts sea level rises of up to 90 centimetres in the 21st century.[6] There are indications that glaciers, permafrost and ice sheets are melting faster than anticipated by the IPCC and that sea level rises this century could be even greater. Already low-lying cities such as London are under threat from increased flooding. The Thames Barrier at Woolwich is the world's largest moveable flood barrier and was completed in 1982 to be closed once every two years, but in 2003 it had to be closed 16 times. A multibillion-pound investment to build another, even higher barrier across the Thames now seems inevitable. Only rich countries such as Britain and the Netherlands can afford to protect their cities against sea levels rises by technical means over the coming decades and centuries.

The most pronounced difference between ecosystems and modern urban eco-technical systems is that the former are solar powered, whereas the latter are primarily powered by fossil fuels. In a sustainable world it is critical for them to switch increasingly to renewable energy. But can large modern cities actually exist without conventional energy technology?

Instead of relying on fossil fuels to power our cities, should we scale up nuclear energy use instead? After many years of massive financial support, nuclear power still only provides some 7 per cent of the world's energy supplies. In the USA, not a single new nuclear plant has been built since the Three Mile Island partial core meltdown accident in 1979. Across the world many plants are reaching the end of their useful life and are not being replaced. Few European countries have plans for new nuclear plants and several have started to phase out their existing ones. In its 2003 White Paper on Energy, the UK government concluded that nuclear power's 'current economics make it an unattractive option and there are also important issues of nuclear waste to be resolved'.[7] The White Paper contains no proposals for building new nuclear plants and focuses instead on energy efficiency and renewables, particularly wind power. Only a few countries, such as Japan, India, China and Iran, are still building nuclear power stations, while also vigorously investing in hydroelectric dams, as well as wind and solar technology.

Klaus Töpfer, director general of the United Nations Environment Programme, is convinced that we need to make a rapid transition towards renewables:

The alarm bells should be ringing in every national capital and in every local community. We should start preparing ourselves for the rising sea levels, changing rain patterns and other impacts of global warming. We must move ahead boldly with clean energy technologies.[8]

A major problem experienced by the clean energy industry in recent years is that unlike coal- or gas-fired electricity, which has received large government subsidies for the construction of transmission lines, it has received little support from governments. More generally, renewable energy is competing with fossil fuel technologies that have reached their economies of scale and have benefited from extensive government subsidies over many years. To stimulate renewable energy development it is crucial to create a level playing field and to include the large environmental costs of fossil fuel energy in the price we pay for it.

While local acid emissions by power stations and local air pollution in cities have been dealt with quite effectively in many countries, carbon dioxide concentrations in the atmosphere are continuing to increase relentlessly, and sooner or later we will have to pay a large price for this as the resulting climate change affects our lives. To counter these alarming trends we need to:

LA courthouse
This courthouse in LA, engineered by Battle McCarthy, will be a new departure in
'eco-modernist' design. Combining high energy efficiency with photovoltaic panels on its
south-facing facade will make it largely self-sufficient in electricity.

- give top priority to a quantum change in urban energy efficiency,
- adopt appropriate policies for renewable energy on a worldwide scale,
- link energy sustainability with local business and employment opportunities.

A canny combination of energy efficiency, combined heat and power, wind power, solar energy, fuel cell technology and new energy storage systems promises a clean and secure urban energy future. While these technologies have been introduced far too slowly until recently, the pace has quickened dramatically since the turn of the century. In many countries wind energy, in particular, has made serious inroads into the electricity market.

Solar electricity is also catching up fast: sales of solar PV systems have grown by 33 per cent annually, with PV electricity getting about 5 per cent cheaper every year. A report by KPMG for Greenpeace in 1999 calculated that 'one large-scale solar PV factory which produces five million solar panels a year (equivalent to 250,000 homes, each with a two kilowatt system) could reduce the cost of solar power by a factor of four, making it price competitive for domestic consumers with electricity produced from conventional sources'.[9]

ENERGY EFFICIENCY

In a world threatened by climate change and fuel shortages, a significant improvement in the energy efficiency of cities is a crucial first step towards a sustainable energy future. The know-how exists to bring urban energy use down by 50 per cent or more without significantly affecting living standards, while creating many new local jobs at the same time.

Major initiatives are under way to improve the energy efficiency of cities. Those such as the Cities for Climate Protection Program of the International Council for Local Environmental Initiatives (ICLEI) have set the scene. This is a performance-orientated campaign, started in 1993, that brings together local authorities all over the world. It offers them a framework to develop a strategic agenda for reducing global warming and waste gas emissions, which also has the benefit of improving community liveability. In 2004, 500 local governments were participating in the campaign, representing some 8 per cent of global greenhouse gas emissions.

Once it has become a CCPP participant, the local government proceeds to undertake and complete the five performance milestones. They are:

- Conduct an energy and emissions inventory and forecast.
- Establish an emissions target.
- Develop and obtain approval for the Local Action Plan.
- Implement policies and measures.
- Monitor and verify results.[10]

The European Climate Alliance is another major initiative. It is an association of over 200 cities, and aims to reduce the carbon dioxide emissions of its member cities by no less than 50 per cent by 2010. This is a tall order, but the benefits of dramatic energy efficiency measures are certainly impressive:

- reduced fuel bills for everyone,
- benefits to the national balance of trade through reduced imports,
- creation of new jobs in the local energy efficiency industry,
- preservation of fossil fuel reserves,
- alleviation of air pollution and global warming.[11]

The potential for making demand-side measures effective in the commercial, government and domestic sectors is already well established. Particularly in European cities, insulation programmes for existing buildings and efficient energy use in new buildings and in lighting and transport systems are becoming commonplace. Impressive results have been achieved in medium-size cities such as Freiburg, Bologna and Leicester, but also in larger ones such as Glasgow, Vienna, Copenhagen, Helsinki and Stockholm. They all share substantial programmes for retrofitting existing residential and commercial buildings with better insulation and more efficient boilers, often using *performance contracting* as a cost-effective tool for achieving significant results.[12]

This process is also used in Australia:

Energy Performance Contracting is a smart, affordable and increasingly common way to make building improvements that save energy and money. Any large building or group of buildings is an ideal candidate for performance contracting, including council, state and federal sites, schools, hospitals, commercial office buildings and light industrial facilities.[13]

In the UK, national planning regulations have already significantly improved the energy efficiency of homes, but much more can be done. Two out of three low-income homes still lack even the most basic insulation. Eight million families cannot afford the warmth they need in the winter months. Cold-related illnesses costs the National Health Service over £1 billion a year.[14] In 2002, only one in twelve domestic properties in Britain actually has the level of energy efficiency currently required by law.[15]

COMBINED HEAT AND POWER

It is clear that significant energy conservation can be achieved by a combination of *efficient energy use* and by more efficient *energy supply systems*. In this context the electricity supply to cities is a crucial variable. Most cities are supplied by power stations located a long distance away, fired by coal or gas, with electricity being transferred via high-voltage power lines. Coal stations typically are only 35 per cent efficient. Modern gas-fired stations are slightly better, at 40–50 per cent efficiency.[16]

In contrast, combined heat and power (CHP) stations, located in or close to cities, are typically around 80 per cent efficient. They provide heat, chilled water and electricity to urban buildings and factories. Instead of wasting heat from combustion, they capture and distribute it through district heating systems. They can be fuelled by a wide variety of sources: gas, coal, oil, waste, wood chips or even geothermal.

CHP systems are now commonplace in many European cities. Helsinki has taken their development further than most. Waste heat from local coal-fired power stations is used to heat over 90 per cent of its buildings and homes. The system's very high energy efficiency was achieved because Helsinki's compact land use patterns made district heating a viable option. (The compactness of the city also made the development of a highly effective public transport system economically viable.)

Energy systems that have not been privatised are making particularly rapid advances. In some cities, such as Vienna and Stockholm, energy supply is still operated by their 'city works', which also run their water, transport and waste management systems. The synergies between these services allow a variety of useful interactions. 'It appears that the largest improvements in power distribution and consumption are realised by cities with a municipality-owned electricity company, such as Toronto and Amsterdam.'[17]

In the UK small-scale CHP systems are becoming popular. They are being installed in some office blocks, schools, hospitals and hotels, improving their energy efficiency considerably. In the UK and the Netherlands, CHP schemes have also been set up to heat greenhouses, utilising both hot water and carbon dioxide from waste gases to enhance crop growth for year-round cultivation.[18] This sort of scheme makes a lot of sense for implementing cost-effective and energy-efficient urban agriculture schemes in colder countries (see also Chapter 12).

THE POTENTIAL OF SOLAR HEAT

Every day more than 6,000 times the energy used by all of humanity reaches the earth's surface in the form of solar radiation.[19] We need to learn to utilise this energy, not just for plant growth but also for producing electricity, using the many new technologies now available. In the near future, enormous reductions in fossil fuel use can be achieved by the use of solar energy systems, which are particularly suited to cities with their large roof areas. Solar heat can meet a substantial proportion of a building's requirements.

Solar hot water panels are a mature technology that has been gradually developed and improved all over the world. Investing in a solar water heater is the largest contribution most households can make to the use of renewable energy.

The greatest barrier to widespread uptake of solar power is lack of adequate knowledge. Changing this is a challenge for governments, city authorities, householders and builders. In many countries, the home building industry

SOLAR INTENSITY IN VARIOUS CITIES

City	Output kw per hour/m²/year
Los Angeles	233
Adelaide	210
Athens	183
Melbourne	182
Rome	191
New York	169
Tokyo	149
Berlin	121
London	111

tends to install cheap and short-life conventional water heaters without regard for either life cycle or environmental costs. It is critical for government mandates to change this situation fundamentally.

In 2000, the city of Barcelona introduced a mandatory 'solar ordinance'. All new housing there has to install solar hot water systems. The law also applies to offices, restaurants and public buildings if they have substantial hot water consumption. Old buildings also have to be fitted with solar hot water systems as they are refurbished.[20] Around the Mediterranean the use of solar hot water systems has become commonplace. In some 'blue sky' countries, such as Israel, solar hot water systems are mandatory for residential use and most homes now have such systems. Greece has developed a very large solar hot water system industry. Technologies developed there also include solar absorption chillers that convert the energy in hot water from solar collectors into 'coolth' to be used for air conditioning.

But solar hot water systems are not exclusive to hot, sunny countries. During the 1990s, the solar hot water market in Europe as a whole grew by 11.7 per cent a year. And still the potential of this clean technology is hardly realised. The solar thermal industry estimates that 1.4 billion square metres of solar thermal collectors could be installed in the EU, 100 times more than the capacity of the roughly 14 million square metres installed by 2000.[21] In sunny countries it is a highly cost-effective measure with a payback, typically, of only a two or three years.[22] In cloudier countries such as Germany and Britain, paybacks are longer, but still less than 10 years. In rainy London, the Solar for London initiative has significantly increased the uptake of the technology. In Austria with its relatively cloudy climate, solar hot water systems have been widely adopted. As solar hot water systems become commonplace, their production and installation costs invariably come down with the economies of scale.

In Australia, the solar hot water industry has grown by about 30 per cent per annum in recent years. One Australian company has estimated that its solar hot water systems can reduce the carbon dioxide output of a typical house by the equivalent of that annually discharged by a small car.[23] In addition to hot water systems, solar space heating systems are also being developed in South Australia. These are cheap to run, environmentally friendly, and designed to be tucked away inside the roof of the home or office. The UniSA Solar Space Heating System comprises an air-based solar collector that is integrated with the roofing. It captures and stores the sun's heat in the roof space during the day and releases it in the evening when the heat is needed in the house.[24]

SOLAR ELECTRICITY

The two most common sources of renewable electricity are wind power and solar power. Both do not occur continuously—the sun does not shine at night and the wind does not blow every day—but in many locations they are highly complementary. In 2003, solar electricity was about eight times more expensive than conventional energy in northern countries, but it is expected to become cost competitive as early as 2010 as the technology develops and the market grows.

The solar cells on the market today can convert up to 18 per cent of the solar energy that shines on them into electricity, but this is likely to increase further. Major development programmes in Japan, China, India, the USA and the European Union aim to stimulate photovoltaic technology and its market growth. The technical potential for the generation of electricity from building integrated solar systems, in particular, is very large indeed, even in northerly regions like the UK. Of course, not all buildings will be suitable for the installation of a solar roof or facade, and adoption will be even more rapid in countries with the highest sunshine levels.

In the past, photovoltaic cells were used primarily to power buildings directly and to store surplus electricity in batteries for later use as required. Today, photovoltaic systems tend to operate in tandem with the grid, exporting electricity from buildings when it is not needed and buying it in when required, by use of an inverter.

Japan has been a leader in photovoltaic technology and has an ever-growing number of solar housing estates. The idea is to turn each house from a net energy consumer into a mini-power station. By 2001, there were over 50,000 solar-powered homes in Japan. One large-scale development in Osaka is showing the way. The solar electric panels used there have a dual function, acting as roofing material and solar electric panels at the same time. Any surplus electricity not used in the house can be sold back to the power company. For the average Japanese home that can mean a return of as much as US$50 a month.

According to Chris Flavin, president of the Worldwatch Institute, Washington, this development, supported by Japanese government grants, is a significant pointer to the future:

The many solar systems that now exist in Japan have benefited
from government policies to encourage individual householders to

Solar PV panel
Solar energy is a key technology for powering our cities in the coming decades. The swift transformation from fossil fuel dependence to renewable energy is crucial for sustainable urban development.

put these systems on their rooftops. This is a policy that would
work very well throughout much of the rest of the world. We could
easily create a wind and solar power market that is perhaps
twenty times as large as it is today. And that would encourage
further investment and further market growth.[25]

In German cities solar photovoltaic panels are becoming even more commonplace, despite the country's relatively cloudy skies. In 2000, the German government introduced important so-called feed-in legislation that fixed both subsidies and favourable tariffs for owners of photovoltaic roof receivers. Owners of such installations are paid about 50 cents per kilowatt hour for selling their electricity to the grid, which is about four times the price paid to conventional electricity generators. The policy has led to a massive growth in demand for solar photovoltaic technology across the country.

The preferential tariffs for the owners of residential and community photo-voltaic systems recognise the environmental and social benefits of solar-generated electricity over pool-supplied power, and provides a return sufficient to encourage widespread investment in photovoltaic technology. The cost of this higher tariff is distributed across the whole electricity market. While photovoltaic power will only increase gradually, the higher electricity price paid to owners of these installations is hardly noticed in the overall price of electricity. In any case, the law requires the tariff paid for solar electricity to be reduced by 5 per cent a year.

The aim of the first German Renewables Act, which was passed in 2000, was to install a total of 1000 megawatts of photovoltaic capacity. In 2001 and 2002, it resulted in 80 megawatts of installations. As a result, German companies have now taken globally significant positions in the solar industry. The German solar market reached 0.75 billion euros in 2000 and is expected to reach 3.5 billion euros by 2010. Over 3,000 jobs in production, distribution and installation had been generated by 2000 and this figure is expected to at least quadruple by 2010. The legislation sparked a boom in the entire renewables sector in Germany, which now has an estimated annual turnover of eight billion euros.[26]

In 2003, follow-up legislation was announced. Its aim is to increase the share of all renewable energy in electricity production from 6.3 per cent in 2000 to 12.5 per cent in 2010 and to at least 20 per cent in 2020. This target is in line with the EU policy of increasing the share of renewable energy from

6 to 12 per cent. The great success of the German legislation has been widely acknowledged and similar schemes have now been introduced in other EU countries such as Austria, Spain, France and the Czech Republic.

South Australia is also expected to follow suit. In 2003, solar photovoltaic electricity was about four times more expensive than 'conventional' electricity—around 70 cents per kilowatt hour as compared with 18 cents per kilowatt hour. German-style feed-in legislation here would reduce the payback period for photovoltaic systems to an average of 10 years, massively stimulating demand for them and greatly increasing the numbers of businesses and jobs in this sector.

In the US, too, various cities have substantial solar energy initiatives. Sacramento, California has a particularly dynamic solar programme. By 2002, its Utility Corporation had installed eight megawatts of solar electricity generating capacity. The Los Angeles Department of Water and Power has a vigorous programme for helping householders to switch to green, renewable energy. While people are charged slightly higher prices than conventional sources, they are being encouraged to use electricity more efficiently at the same time.[27]

Freiburg in southern Germany, a city of some 200,000 people, has long been known as a flagship example of sustainable urban development, particularly for its clever public transport system and its proliferation of cycle lanes. It has twice as many bicycles as cars. It was also one of the first cities in Europe to develop experimental solar buildings and its population has responded to the German 'feed-in' legislation with enthusiasm. Because of this, a sizeable solar economy has developed in the city. There are now dozens of renewable energy research institutes, solar energy companies and consultancies, solar engineers and architectural firms that specialise in solar design. By 2003, there were 2,000 square metres of solar cells on Freiburg's roofs and its sports stadium uses solar power to operate its floodlights.

All these examples indicate what is likely to happen in many more cities and regions all over the world in the coming years. By 2010, it seems likely that architects will routinely incorporate solar technology when designing a new building or refurbishing an existing one. In the meantime, to get experience with the technology, governments and urban authorities should vigorously encourage the installation of photovoltaic modules in our cities, enhancing the capacity to install solar systems. Every city should have buildings to test the potential of photovoltaic and develop the local know-how. Even in relatively cloudy cities such as London, every roof or facade is a clean-fuel power station waiting to come into use.

MODERN WIND POWER

Wind power is a form of solar energy in that wind currents are driven by the heat of the sun. At the start of the new millennium, wind power was the world's fastest growing energy industry, with an annual growth at over 22 per cent. To be economic wind turbines must be located in windy, open terrain and because of that they are also highly visible. This has led to vigorous campaigns against wind farm development, but better design and careful visualisation studies before siting is decided can improve the visual impact of wind farms dramatically. Improvements in the technology have also made them much quieter than they used to be.

For electricity supply to cities, wind farms are being located primarily in peri-urban areas, but the potential of urban wind turbine development is also being explored. A growing number of European cities are now implementing active measures to power themselves by wind energy technologies. In 2002 Copenhagen, for instance, supplied 20 per cent of its electricity from wind turbines, located both on-shore and off-shore. In California, in places such as the Altamont Pass, hundreds of small and large wind turbines produce electricity for cities such as Los Angeles and Desert Springs.

The Danish government in the 1980s and 1990s became a pioneer in supporting wind energy development. This resulted in a dramatic reduction in the cost of wind-generated electricity. In Denmark, employment in the wind industry is now larger than in the fishing industry. In 2002, Danish wind turbine companies supplied 3,600 megawatts of new generating capacity, equivalent to five medium-sized nuclear power station blocks. By 2003, more than 100,000 families owned shares in one or more of the country's 6,500 wind turbines. Some 85 per cent of the wind power capacity in Denmark is owned by private individuals or wind cooperatives and in 2003, wind energy supplied 21 per cent of Danish electricity consumption. According to government plans, 50 per cent of Denmark's electricity supply is expected to come from wind by 2030.[28] To meet this ambitious target, wind farm developers are now putting ever larger wind turbines into the Baltic Sea. The German government, too, has ambitious targets for wind power. It is aiming for a wind energy capacity of 20,000–25,000 megawatts by 2030, much of it from off-shore wind farms.

By 2003, Britain had built its the first off-shore wind turbines and expects to have 20 per cent of its electricity to be supplied by renewable energy systems by 2020. Countries with long windy coastlines, such as the UK, can reap

Wind farm in South Australia
Windpower is a sustainable source of energy for cites. Most wind turbines will be located on the outskirts of cities, or off-shore in the sea.

great advantages from developing large-scale, cost-competitive wind power schemes in the coming decades. But it won't stop there. Tidal power is also making rapid progress, particularly in Britain and Norway. There is also a source of energy beneath the waves, whose potential is only just being understood. Ocean energy is the largest untapped resource on the planet and could well provide clean, reliable electricity on a truly giant scale. Several companies are developing turbines to harness the moving water in ocean currents. Electricity generated from tidal currents has the distinction of being highly predictable. Tide tables can be used to project seasonal and daily power outputs, precisely quantifying supplies to on-shore energy grids. Off-shore wind and ocean energy technology, integrated together, are promising to become an abundant resource worldwide.[29]

Initially the emphasis will be on electricity transmission, but as more wind farms are built, they could start using hydrolysis to produce hydrogen to power fuel cell systems for vehicles and buildings, particularly for coastal cities. Says David Elliot, co-director of the Energy and Environment Unit at the UK's Open University:

> In the longer term there could be a shift from electricity transmission to hydrogen transmission. Gas distribution is much more efficient than electricity transmission, and the gas could be stored whereas electricity cannot be easily stored . . . Ultimately there could be giant hydrogen gas grids around the world and hydrogen could also be tanked around, in cryogenic liquid form, in ships.[30]

FUEL CELL TECHNOLOGY

Fuel cells, powered by hydrogen, natural gas or methanol, are rapidly coming of age. They work by converting the gas into electricity by an electrochemical process without combustion. Like photovoltaic cells, fuel cells have taken a long time to become commercially viable. But now their development is accelerating as the world searches for practical ways to produce cleaner energy. Many billions of dollars have been invested in the technology in recent years and several companies are making great strides towards making fuel cells competitive. Large-scale commercial production of fuel cells is likely to be occurring by around 2010.

Hydrogen is an energy carrier rather than an energy source. Its production by hydrolysis, using wind power or photovoltaic cells is a particularly compelling option. The Arizona Public Service utility is experimenting with a solar-based hydrogen-generating system that looks like a space telescope. The sun's radiation is collected in multiple solar dishes that power a hydrogen converter. The hydrogen it produces from water can be stored in tanks and distributed to consumers in the same way as natural gas. This is still an experimental technology, but it could well be the shape of tomorrow's power stations and a prototype for clean, urban energy supplies.

A growing number of cities are introducing fuel cell-powered buses as a first step towards more widespread adoption of fuel cell technology. Two major advantages in city transport are that fuel engines don't burn any fuel when stationary and that the only 'waste gas' coming out of their exhaust pipes is steam. The Greater London Authority has created the London Fuel Cell Partnership in 2002 and, as in other cities, fuel cell-powered buses are now operating experimentally.

More and more countries (and cities) want to get away from fossil fuel dependence and the pollution associated with combustion technology. The concept of a future hydrogen economy based on fuel cell technology is now being taken very seriously, with Iceland taking the lead. Like the internal combustion engine, fuel cell technology is extremely versatile and suitable not only for powering buses, cars, trucks and boats, but also for use in stationary applications. Interestingly, fuel cell systems are as economical on a small as on a large scale. Urban hydrogen pipelines, fuelled locally or connected to national or international grids and supplying fuel cell generators for homes, offices and factories, are beginning to look entirely feasible.

ECONOMIC BENEFITS

Environmentalists emphasise that the future health of the planet will depend on the large-scale introduction of renewable energy. Clean, alternative energy sources exist, but getting policy makers to accept them will mean major changes to long-held habits, and convincing politicians and companies that they make economic sense.

It is plausible that even large cities, whose genesis depended on the routine use of fossil fuels in the first place, will be able to switch to renewable energy in the coming decades. Regulating the energy industry to improve generating efficiency, reduce discharge of waste gases and adopt renewables will profoundly reduce the environmental impact of urban energy systems, while providing many new local jobs.

Evidence from Germany, Austria, the Netherlands and Scandinavia indicates the tremendous potential economic and social potential of new business and employment opportunities from sustainable energy. A great deal can be done to accelerate change by creating new policy frameworks and by creative approaches to consumer information. Obstacles in terms of cost, supply, installation know-how, planning and public awareness can be overcome by creating a supportive economic climate for the sector, bringing together key partners, attracting inward investment and securing local—and export—markets to accelerate the sustainable energy revolution in our cities. Such policies can often be implemented without significant government financial support or other additional costs to society. Figures compiled in Australia[31] indicate the great potential of creating local jobs from renewable energy.

A SUSTAINABLE, LOCAL ENERGY FUTURE

There is overwhelming evidence that increased energy efficiency, combined heat and power and new, sustainable energy systems can be utilised in our

BMW hydrogen cars
The hydrogen economy is widely talked about as the successor to the hydrocarbon economy.
Vehicles as well as buildings are likely be powered by hydrogen in the decades to come.

DIRECT EMPLOYMENT IN ENERGY PER MILLION AUSTRALIAN DOLLARS INVESTED

Technology	Jobs per A$ million invested
Oil shale	0.5
Solar electric	3.5
Energy efficiency	35–50

DIRECT EMPLOYMENT PER MEGAWATT HOUR

Technology	Jobs per million megawatt hours per year produced
Oil shale	46.3
Coal mining and power generation	116
Solar thermal electricity	35–50
Wind	542
Energy efficiency	400–860

cities to mitigate climate change. But the introduction rate of these new technologies is still much too slow to offset annual global increases in energy demand due to urban and economic growth. To reduce emissions significantly requires a rapid phasing in of sustainable energy systems, but major obstacles to their large-scale introduction have yet to be overcome.

Robert Watson, former director of the Intergovernmental Panel on Climate Change, says this:

> While we have subsidies on fossil fuels, it is difficult for renewable energies to penetrate the marketplace. There's an unfair competition. But, if the price of fossil fuel energy were to increase, the average consumer would have much more reason to conserve energy, to have more fuel-efficient cars, more fuel efficient houses. So we need to look at both the policy framework and the technology framework. We need simultaneously to change government policies and energy technologies. On the policy side, we need to eliminate fossil fuel subsidies and to internalise the social and environmental cost of air pollution. We also have to

invest in research and development for new energy technologies and bring them on stream. A strong commitment to new research and development both by governments and private industries is crucial.[32]

In 30 years' time solar installations, wind power and fuel cell technology could provide most of the energy required to run our cities. Wind farms will operate mainly on their periphery—on farms, in estuaries and off-shore. Solar hot water and photovoltaic systems will be an integral part of people's homes and of municipal buildings. We could run both our cars and our homes on renewably powered fuel cell systems. But making all this happen will depend on the strength of public opinion in each country and city. Governments and local authorities need to be persuaded to switch subsidies that prop up fossil fuel and nuclear power to renewable energy instead.

Rather than use energy without regard for its consequences, we could recover the traditional notion that energy should be treated as something to be valued and used to meet our needs in ways that respect the realities of the natural world. A sustainable energy system suitable for the 21st century could help to reestablish the crucial connections between energy, human well-being and the local environment, and could create many new local jobs.

CHAPTER 10

Towards
Zero Waste

From 1950 to 2000, the world's economic activities increased fifteenfold. The growth of consumer societies all over the world has seen a large increase in solid waste produced per head, and the waste mix has also become ever more complex. Entirely new ways were found to use the earth's resources and to combine atoms and molecules into materials that don't occur in nature—such as halogenated hydrocarbons, used in making plastics. Over the last 50 years, we have taken for granted that our wastes are deposited in holes in the ground. However, many of the materials in our wastes are taken from nature but can't be reabsorbed by it.

There is a growing consensus that waste should be regarded as a valuable resource in disguise. The concept of 'waste' should be substituted by the concept of 'resource'. To dump it is a waste of money and a failure to design sustainable products and processes. The purpose of this chapter, then, is to look at new options for dealing with urban waste.

The credo of never-ending economic growth demands that each of us makes an individual contribution to consumption. The logic of this is vividly summarised by US marketing consultant Victor Lebow, who introduced the concept of 'forced consumption' in an article in 1955:

> *Our enormously productive economy . . . demands that we make*
> *consumption our way of life, that we convert the buying and use of*

*goods into rituals, that we seek our spiritual satisfaction, our ego
satisfactions, in consumption . . . We need things consumed, burned
up, worn out, replaced, and discarded at an ever increasing rate.*[1]

Today's 'garbologists' can see a vast difference between what was discarded
in the past and what is dumped today. In pre-19th-century dumps they dig
up objects such as horseshoes, enamelled saucepans, pottery fragments and
leather straps. In today's dumps they find a huge variety of items—televi-
sions, computers, transistor radios, plastic bags and containers, disposable
nappies, mattresses, magazines, building materials, bottles and canisters
containing various, often toxic liquids.

Hopefully future garbologists will see a dramatic reduction in landfilling
in the years to come. It is no longer an option for cities simply to dump their
wastes. Not only does it take up more and more valuable land space, it also
causes discharges of chemicals and pesticides into soil and groundwater, and
of carbon dioxide and methane into the atmosphere. This ultimately damages
plant, animal as well as human health.

Mucking waste dump
London's Mucking waste dump, like New York's Fresh Kills, will soon be full up. Recycling will
soon become the only viable option for urban waste management.

In the case of London, every year some 14 million tonnes of non-biodegradable solid waste are dumped in holes in the ground. Mucking in Essex, on the banks of the River Thames, used to be a gravel pit from which building materials were extracted. Today it receives the rubbish of some two million Londoners. Household, commercial and industrial waste is taken here by barge from central London and *co-disposed* in clay-lined pits. The compacted rubbish is then sealed with a top layer of clay, covered with soil and seeded with grass. Inside the dump, methane gas from the rotting waste is intercepted in plastic pipes and then used to run a small power station supplying electricity to some 30,000 people.[2] London has developed an impressive new waste strategy, with a strong emphasis on reuse and recycling, but it remains to be seen when and how it is implemented.[3]

NEW YORK—WHERE WILL ALL THE WASTE GO?

The Fresh Kills landfill in New York City, with its 12 million people and high standard of living, vividly demonstrates the waste disposal problems of large cities. First opened as a temporary facility in 1947, on the western shore of Staten Island, Fresh Kills was New York City's dump for 53 years, receiving some four million tonnes of domestic and municipal waste a year. At 2,100 acres, it is nearly three times the size of Central Park. It was the world's largest landfill and one of the few man-made structures that can be seen by the human eye from space. In the late 1990s, the piles of trash topped the Statue of Liberty by 25 feet, but in the coming years it will shrink dramatically, in some places by as much as 100 feet.

After accepting two billion tonnes of garbage, New York City's Department of Sanitation (DOS) closed Fresh Kills in 2001 in the face of lawsuits over the air pollution and fearing vast clean-up costs. There were very good reasons for its closure. Its unpleasant odours wafted into residential neighbourhoods on both sides of the Arthur Kill, which separates Staten Island from New Jersey.

Fresh Kills was briefly reopened in 2001 after the September 11th attacks on the World Trade Center towers: 18 hours after their collapse, Fresh Kills received the first load of debris from Ground Zero. Over the next ten months, some 9,000 tonnes a day were deposited and carefully sifted for clues and human remains. More than 65,000 personal items were recovered. Medical examiners tried to match up some of the 19,712 body parts recovered and the remains of some 2,000 victims identified.[4] Since then, Fresh Kills has shut down again.

In addition to its odours, a further reason for the closure was the fact that, unlike modern waste dumps, it is unlined and still leaches hundreds of pounds of toxic chemicals and heavy metals into the Hudson River each day. Under the City's closure programme, the DOS will continue to maintain and monitor the site for at least 30 years. Covering and sealing the unlined garbage mountain will take five years. Intricate maintenance and monitoring systems are being installed to control the gases and leachate emanating from the decaying trash. Yet ironically, despite its bad reputation, Fresh Kills harbours a diverse coastal wetland ecosystem.

Each day, New York City produces some 36,000 tonnes of solid waste. The DOS is responsible for about 13,000 tonnes generated by residents, public agencies and non-profit corporations and this was hauled out to Fresh Kills for 53 years. Private waste disposal companies handle the commercial waste, generated by companies, builders and restaurants. There are no other vacant sites in New York that could take Fresh Kills' place and the city has been forced to ship its garbage elsewhere. Court battles, criminal investigations, administrative haggling and charges of corruption have held up the construction of a huge new waste transfer site in Linden, New Jersey. Even if the plant is built, the cost of disposing of the city's garbage will rise, a major concern in this time of multibillion-dollar budget deficits.

Replacing Fresh Kills comes at a high price. Since it closed, New York City has contracted with four private companies to truck residential garbage to private waste transfer stations in Brooklyn and Queens, and then on to landfills and out-of-state incinerators. But while it cost the city $43 to ship a tonne of garbage to Fresh Kills, it costs between $60 to $100 to ship the same tonne out of New York State. As a result, the city's sanitation budget has more than doubled, from $500 million to some $1.1 billion. That is a lot of money for a city in a continuous financial crisis.

Meanwhile, in New Jersey many people are unhappy with being lumbered with New York City's trash and all the problems associated with potential groundwater contamination and rotting waste. In Elizabeth, New Jersey, local people set up roadblocks to stop incoming garbage trucks. They also want to protect themselves against the illegal dumping of toxic waste. Say local residents:

New York finds an easy way to get rid of their problem. And if
they can, they'll dump it on somebody else's doorstep. 140 trucks

a day is an astronomical amount of trucks for the city of Elizabeth
to deal with. It is time that New York City solved its own
problems, not at our expense.[5]

As such resistance grows, New York—and other large cities running out of landfill space—needs to consider alternative waste disposal options.

Environmentalists stress that there are better ways. They want the city to dramatically improve its waste management and reduction programmes. Despite a law that required New York to recycle 25 per cent of its recyclable material by 1994, the city still hovers around the 20 per cent mark, about half the rate for Philadelphia and far worse than Los Angeles and Chicago. Moreover, this figure includes 33 per cent of waste plastic, glass and aluminium and 5 per cent of waste paper that is collected for recycling but is contaminated and cannot be safely recycled.

A visit to any office building in Manhattan confirms the pathetic rate at which New York recycles paper. 'The city does not follow state laws on recycling', says Timothy Logan, chairman of the New York City Waste Prevention Coalition. 'There is no enforcement on the commercial side.'[6]

INCINERATING IT

Until recently, incineration was widely employed as a convenient waste disposal option in many countries. It certainly has the advantage of reducing waste to a small percentage of its original volume, with energy recovery as an added bonus. But incineration has been falling out of favour. The release of dioxins and other poisonous substances into the environment has given incinerator smokestacks a bad name. Despite pollution control techniques having advanced considerably by the use of a variety of new incineration methods and combustion temperature control systems, the problem of waste gases refuses to go away.

A major reason for the problem with incinerators is that materials are being burned that should not be burned. Modern waste contains large amounts of plastics from toys, computers and packaging that are manufactured using toxic chemicals, including heavy metals. Incineration releases these into the environment—if not in the flue gases then in the ash.

Ash is the second major issue. The story of the waste barge *Khian Sea*, which circled the world with a hold full of incinerator ash in 1988, has become something of a 20th-century myth. It left Philadelphia on an epic voyage to dispose of its cargo of 14,000 tonnes of ash. Its owners did not appreciate that global communications might spread the news of its arrival wherever it appeared. The Bahamas, the Dominican Republic, Honduras, Bermuda, Guinea Bissau and the Netherlands Antilles all refused to take the cargo. Finally, when the *Khian Sea* got to Haiti, that country's dictator Baby Doc Duvalier allowed 4,000 tonnes of the ash to be dumped onto a beach at Gonaives as 'fertiliser'. But after a public outcry the import permit was cancelled and most of the ash was returned to the ship. When Greenpeace scientists tested the 'fertiliser' still remaining on the beach, they found that it contained toxins such as arsenic, cadmium, lead and dioxin. But no one would clean up the beach. Eventually the remaining 13,000 tonnes of toxic ash was dumped into the Indian Ocean.[7]

In developed countries, resistance against waste incineration has grown rapidly in recent years. For instance in Japan, where incinerators are widely used, the discovery of dioxin contamination across the country gave rise to a strong protest movement and hundreds of incinerators have been closed down in recent years. In Britain, environmental groups have successfully prevented the construction of new incinerators in and around London and in other urban areas.

In most cities with incinerators, people have their own particular horror stories to tell. In 2000, a scandal erupted in Newcastle over dioxin-laden ash from the Byker incinerator being spread on the footpaths of community gardens. Local people were told to keep children under the age of two away and not to eat any food grown there. The UK government's Environment Agency failed to uncover the problem for six years, but has since prosecuted Newcastle City Council and the incinerator plant operator.[8]

In the last few years, other objections to incinerators have been voiced all over the world. Recent research shows that they compare badly with recycling in terms of energy conservation. Because of the high energy content of many manufactured products that end up in the rubbish, recycling paper, plastics, rubber and textiles is three to six times more energy efficient than incineration. These are very significant figures given that energy and resource efficiency is regarded as critical for future urban sustainability.[9] Many European cities are increasingly deciding against investing in new incinerator capacity, and they are opting for a combination of recycling and composting instead, with minimal incineration of residual wastes.

As the incinerator industry ran out of markets in the developed countries, it turned to the developing world offering to reduce its growing waste mountains. Some First World governments did not hesitate to support incinerator projects with soft loans, even if incinerators were criticised as unsafe in their country of manufacture.[10] However, protests have since prevented the construction of many incinerators in developing countries, too.

We clearly need to take a fesh look at waste—how it is generated in the first place and how it is managed. In an urbanising world, in which cities use the bulk of the world's resources and discharge most wastes, conventional *linear* waste disposal, in which mixed wastes are dumped in holes in the ground or incinerated, is not a sustainable option. New *circular* systems need to take their place.

REDUCE, REUSE, RECYCLE

So is large-scale recycling a viable alternative to dumping and incineration? It has sometimes been said that recycling is a red herring because of the difficulty of matching the supply of recycled materials with a sustained demand for them. But concern grows about the integrity of the environments on which cities ultimately depend, *reuse and recycling* are becoming the rule rather than the exception in many parts of the world. While not all waste materials can be recycled, much can be done to move in this direction.

Deliberately constructing 'chains of use' that mimic natural ecosystems will be an important step forward for both industrial and urban ecology. It is becoming widely accepted that in our resource use we should mimic natural ecosystems in which all waste is reused as the basis for new growth. In our economies we should create such *chains of use* or *eco-cycles* for waste materials in a deliberate step towards creating sustainable industries and cities.

Right across Europe and the USA, recycling has increased substantially every year. There is a growing consensus that waste segregation, reuse and recycling can have substantial economic benefits, even in developed countries. Cities across Europe have installed waste recycling plants and many new composting plants have been constructed.

In some British cities such as Bath and Leicester, where recycling has advanced a great deal, the benefits for people and the local environment have become evident. The UK landfill tax, introduced in 1996, has increased recycling throughout the UK. New legislation in 2003 aimed to increase household waste recycling to 30 per cent by 2010. This figure is already being exceeded across Europe where 50 to 60 per cent recycling is becoming the norm, and some US regions are not far behind.

Recycling in Curitiba
All over the world cities are having to take recycling seriously as they run out of landfill space.
Crisis becomes opportunity as many new jobs are generated from urban 'zero waste' systems.

In Europe, successful waste management and recycling schemes have greatly reduced the volume of garbage being landfilled or incinerated. European cities are implementing ambitious programmes for developing zero waste eco-cycles, minimising the 'leakage' of wastes and toxic substances into the environment. An important aspect of this is to find ways of helping companies to develop and use appropriate technologies for advanced non-polluting production processes. The issue is not only to recycle as much as possible, but also to avoid waste being generated in the first place and to create closed-loop 'eco-economies' through enabling legislation.

The city of Gothenburg, for instance, has developed an ambitious programme for developing eco-cycles, minimising the release of toxic substances into the local environment by helping companies with the development and the use of appropriate technologies for advanced non-polluting production processes.[11]

ECOPROFIT

The Austrian city of Graz has developed an innovative approach to pollution prevention by vigorous collaboration with local companies. ECOPROFIT benefits local environments while helping companies to profit from upgrading their production and waste management systems. It is an on-going initiative that gives small- and mid-sized enterprises consultative and financial support for integrated environmental management and cleaner production methods. The measures are targeted at the waste and energy sectors, as well as at organisational restructuring.

What was originally called Oekoprofit was started by Austrian scientist Karl Niederl. He envisaged a closed-cycle urban economy similar to the recycling of materials in natural ecosystems. The 'ecological project for integrated environmental technologies' (ECOPROFIT), initiated in 1993, persuaded local companies that it is more cost effective to avoid toxic emissions and wastes than to discharge them into the environment. Information and technical assistance to local companies are coupled with marketing support. Information provision has proved more effective than regulation. Incentives include the promotion of participating companies to the local community as 'ecological market leaders'. Cost savings for individual companies as well as the city arise out of companies' greater production efficiency. The reduced pollution benefits business as well as the city authority, which provides services such as drinking water supply, waste management and environmental remediation.

The goal of each project is to identify measures that can lead to the minimisation of waste and emission through increased efficiency using the following principles:

- The producer is responsible for the whole life cycle of a product, including energy consumption and emissions during the use of the product, its reparability and ability to be recycled or disposed of.
- Anything that leaves the production process should be considered as a product or raw material that can eventually be reused in another production process.
- Every product is optimised regarding reparability and recyclability.
- Production is based on renewable sources of energy and substances that, as far as possible, are based on recycled (secondary) materials.
- The producer chooses materials from renewable resources and releases wastes in a way that does not diminish nature.
- The producer reduces energy demand to a level that can be met by renewable energy systems.

The ECOPROFIT model has been successfully transferred from Graz to many other Austrian, German, Hungarian, Bulgarian and Czech cities, and its influence has reached as far as China and the United States.[12]

WASTE AND THE EUROPEAN UNION

It is important to emphasise that the implementation of zero waste policies ultimately goes beyond the scope of most cities. Legislation at national level and agreements between countries can make a tremendous difference.

This can be seen in Europe where, between 1990 and 1995, the amount of waste generated increased by 10 per cent. Each year the European Union produces 3.5 tonnes of solid waste per head, or a total of 1.3 billion tonnes— of which 40 million tonnes is hazardous waste. Add to this total a further 700 million tonnes of agricultural waste. It is clear that treating and disposing of all this material without harming the environment is a huge headache.

But experiences in Europe indicate that carefully targeted market incentives and the right policy signals at national and local level can make recycling economically—as well as environmentally—advantageous. European Union directives now require member states to introduce legislation on waste collection, reuse, recycling and disposal. The EU's approach is based on three principles: waste prevention; recycling and reuse; and improving final disposal and monitoring. It aims to reduce the quantity of waste going to 'final disposal' by 20 per cent from 2000 to 2010 and by 50 per cent by 2050, with special emphasis on cutting hazardous waste. It wants to achieve this through new waste prevention initiatives, better use of resources and encouraging a shift to more sustainable consumption patterns.

If ways can be found to reduce the amount of waste generated in the first place and lessen its hazardousness by reducing the presence of dangerous substances in products, then disposing of it will automatically become simpler. Waste prevention is closely linked with improving manufacturing methods and influencing consumers to demand 'greener' products and less packaging.

However, if waste cannot be prevented, as many of the materials as possible should be recovered, preferably by recycling. The European Commission has defined several specific 'waste streams'—such as packaging waste, end-of-life vehicles, batteries, electrical and electronic waste—for priority attention, aiming to minimise their environmental impact. Only waste that cannot be recycled or reused should be safely incinerated, with landfill as a last resort. EU directives set strict guidelines for landfill management. They ban certain types of waste, such as used tyres, and have set targets for reducing quantities of biodegradable rubbish. One directive sets tough limits on incinerator emissions.[13]

Germany introduced its the pioneering Recycling and Waste Management Act of 1996 as a first, significant step towards establishing a zero waste eco-economy, laying down principles that apply to the whole of economic life. The legislation stipulates that manufacturers become responsible for the entire life cycle of a product, from the moment materials leave the ground to the time products are discarded. The Act gives priority to waste avoidance by requiring the use of low-waste product designs, eco-cycle waste management, and consumer behaviour oriented to the purchase of low-waste and low-pollution products.

As a result of the legislation, companies now have to label all components to ensure easier recycling when products have reached the end of their life. Cars are designed so that they can be taken apart and easily separated into recyclable components when they have reached the end of the last road. Household appliances can be returned to the factory after they have worn out so that their materials can be turned into the next generation of cooker or fridge. The effect of the legislation has been remarkable. Entire production processes have been redesigned to improve recycling of end-of-life waste products.

Car dump
Cars, like all other industrial products, reach the end of the road. All the parts of a product should be labelled for efficient recycling.

WASTE IN THE USA

In the USA, no effective federal plan exists to maximise recycling and minimise waste, even though the federal government took ultimate responsibility for the nation's waste management in the Solid Waste Disposal Act of 1976. The Act requires states to develop and implement plans to maximise recycling and minimise waste, but after 26 years some states have yet to comply and the EPA is not enforcing the Act. Many states point to the lack of a comprehensive federal waste and recycling plan as the reason for their failure to implement their own plans successfully.[14]

RECYCLING AND COMPOSTING IN VIENNA

In recent decades the city of Vienna has seen the amount of household waste it has to deal with increase every year. The city's waste managers knew that this problem would continue to grow, while there was little chance of creating new incineration plants or landfills. An alternative solution had to be found. The logical option was to move into recycling by introducing a new waste management system. A major challenge was to convince the citizens of Vienna that the throwaway society could not continue for both economical and ecological reasons. In 1995, the separate collection of paper, glass, metal, plastics and bio-waste began. By 2002, the city recycled 43 per cent of its domestic wastes.[15]

A further step was to introduce remanufacturing schemes. Would it be possible to create a 'repair society'? Some 100,000 tonnes of mainly untreated electric and electronic scrap are dumped in Austria's waste depots and incineration plants every year. In 1999, the Repair Network Vienna (RUSZ) was created as an association of well-established commercial repair firms. The 23 member companies now repair a wide range of items from umbrellas to hi-fi systems, VCRs or even bathtubs. Initially RUSZ mainly served the urban poor, but gradually ecologically motivated households became customers as well. Since 1999, it has refurbished some 2,000 tonnes of waste.

RUSZ was the first company in Austria to practise not just waste recycling but waste prevention. Prolonging the life of products reduces the demand for new appliances and thus saves resources. It addresses not only waste issues but also problems of structural unemployment. Hundreds of people who could not find conventional jobs due to their limited skills have found employment through RUSZ.[16]

Adelaide waste dump
Landfills contain large amounts of food which make them very attractive to wildlife. But sustainable cities need to compost their organic waste and use it in urban gardening and agriculture.

The city authorities also decided that in addition to product recycling, closed nutrient cycles would be important for creating a sustainable city. Vienna started an ambitious scheme for bio-waste or organic waste composting for both ecological and economic reasons. Studies showed that composting was cheaper than incineration or dumping of organic materials. But attention also had to be paid to social aspects of composting. Only if citizens could be motivated to play an active role could composting be made to work.

In 1988, Vienna was the first large city in Austria to introduce separate collection of bio-waste. All political parties supported the decision. Good cooperation between the various stakeholders was crucial for the project. To ensure success, many activities were established. Information leaflets about bio-waste collection and composting were published and distributed in ten languages and a special information phone line was set up.

The waste disposal fee paid by every citizen of Vienna finances the scheme. The money saved by the project through its synergy effects lowers the overall fees. Today, Vienna has 43,000 containers for bio-waste. In 1997, 87,400 tonnes of bio-waste were collected separately and 34,000 tonnes of compost were produced. Around 20,000 tonnes of this were used as fertiliser in Vienna's urban farming schemes. The rest was given to citizens for their own gardens as a reward for collecting bio-waste.

By 2000, 90,000 tonnes of organic waste was composted, which was more than half of the available organic waste. The overall saving achieved was more than $10,000,000 per year. This profitable use of compost also boosted organic farming in Vienna, which has even made a profit for the Municipal Department of Forestry and Agriculture. The citizens of Vienna are keen to buy bread, potatoes or vegetables produced with compost made from the city's bio-waste. Half the food eaten in Vienna's hospitals is now produced organically, using compost produced by the city.

SOLID WASTE MANAGEMENT IN COPENHAGEN

Denmark, too, has a highly advanced waste management policy. In 1991, a new national waste disposal tax radically changed requirements on enterprises, transporters and waste treatment plants. It allowed Danish municipalities to manage all aspects of waste through regulatory control. Today they regulate all domestic, commercial, construction/demolition and industrial wastes. Copenhagen's Comprehensive Urban Waste Programme, provides for 58 per cent of the city's waste to be recycled, 18 per cent landfilled and 24 per cent incinerated.

The regulations stipulate that polluters must pay for sorting, transporting and treating waste. Waste producers must separate all waste at the source to avoid contamination through mixing. All waste must be separated into combustible and non-combustible waste, optimising the use of landfills and waste-to-energy plants. Hazardous materials must be separated and either recycled or treated at special facilities.

The city pays for the administrative costs and invests in recycling stations from property tax collections. The number of landfills has been cut from 30 to 3 and most of the city's commercial, industrial and demolition waste is now recycled. These changes occurred very quickly: recycling in Copenhagen grew from 17 per cent in 1988 (129,500 tonnes) to 58 per cent (483,500 tonnes) in 1992. Landfilling dropped from 48 per cent (378,000 tonnes) to 11 per cent (87,200 tonnes) in 1992.[17] Some 50,000 tonnes of non-toxic combustible waste, previously deposited in landfills, is incinerated in the city's waste-to-energy plants.

STEPPING UP ORGANIC RECYCLING

Cities all over the world face important decisions on waste management. In Adelaide, the Wingfield landfill site will be full to capacity by December 2004 and the bulk of waste will have to be disposed of 60 kilometres north of the city. This, in turn, will increase the cost of waste disposal to councils from $26.4 million to $37.9 million, due to additional transportation costs to the new site.[18] These increased costs could be beneficially diverted into investment in an Integrated Resource Recovery and Renewable Energy Centre. In fact, initial plans have been drawn up for a facility that would convert up to 190,000 tonnes of waste materials into resources and energy. It would include a transfer station, material recovery facility, recycling centre, green waste transfer, bio-reactor and composting unit, domestic hazardous waste drop-off, transport fuel production unit, water harvesting and reuse facility, landfill gas extraction unit, process heat and electricity unit and an education centre.

The South Australian government is pursuing its own zero waste policy. The draft Zero Waste SA bill 2003 is a very significant piece of legislation. Its principal objective is to 'promote sustainable waste management practices that, as far as possible, eliminate waste or its consignment to landfill; and operate in a consistent and integrated manner throughout the State; and advance the development of resource recovery and recycling industries'.

South Australia can no longer afford to bury its valuable organic resources in landfills. It has a growing horticulture, viticulture and broad acre farming community dependent on productive soils. The state needs as much quality organic matter as possible to improve and sustain its fragile and carbon-depleted soils. In addition to soil quality problems, water restrictions could have a significant effect on the yields and quality of crops in the future. Growers are increasingly looking to organic composts to aid in water conservation, weed suppression and soil conditioning. Demand for organic composts and mulches in South Australia is increasing as growers realise the importance of improving their soils.[19]

WASTE MANAGEMENT IN THE THIRD WORLD

In the case of solid waste management, cities in the North have much to learn from the ingenuity of cities in the South. Cities there usually make highly efficient use of resources, particularly if people are supported in their recycling activities. While wealthy cities have tended to discard products and materials, people in less affluent places repair and reuse again and again. There are a growing number of cities that are actually moving towards zero-waste systems, tackling social and environmental problems simultaneously. However, even Third World cities have much to gain from enhanced recycling by better uses of technology.

In Cairo, for instance, recycling and composting of wastes have been actively encouraged. A community of Coptic Christians called the Zaballeen reuses and recycles much of the city's solid waste. With the support of the city authorities, they were able to acquire recycling and composting equipment. Metals and plastics are remanufactured into new products. Waste paper is reprocessed into new paper and cardboard. Rags are shredded and made into sacks and bed covers. The Zabballeen also practise pig farming in the middle of the city utilising organic waste. This is composted and returned to farmland on the edge of the city as fertiliser. This urban community has achieved a diversion rate of 85 per cent by setting up an intensive separation scheme and establishing personal working relationships with the households that are being served by the garbage collectors. Some 40,000 people are involved in this recycling system.

The Zaballeen Environment and Development Programme has enabled the 10,000-strong community to earn a good income from its activities. Had the waste management of the city been given over to a conventional waste management company, thousands of waste collectors would have been out of work. Now they are in work while Cairo has avoided putting vast waste dumps on the edge of the city.[20]

Near the Zaballeen community, 150 small factories are hidden away in Cairo's narrow streets. They produce small wheels for trolleys, beds and fridges at competitive prices, using metal waste from a local air-conditioning factory and saving on tonnes of new steel. Glass blowers in the same community use glass waste bought from Cairo's rubbish collectors. They make glass lampshades for the mosques and drinking glasses for local shops and the tourist market.

Manila, capital city of the Philippines, has an infamous waste dump called Smoky Mountain. On this great mountain of garbage live thousands of people in unbelievable squalor in one-room huts made of cardbord, tin or bamboo surrounded by heaps of trash. Children play in pools of polluted water. Many families have lived like this for several generations, somehow accepting their lot in life. People scavenge to collect tin, plastic, glass or anything they can sell for a few pesos. But a meagre livelihood can be accompanied by tragedy. In the rush to get to the rubbish first, people are sometimes bulldozed and buried in the garbage alive.

To the credit of the Manila city government, cholera and other diseases linked to exposure to waste, which were rife among the waste pickers, have been brought under control. Classes are offered for people to learn skills to improve their lot. Ironically, high-rise apartments have been built over older parts of the dump, but the people were afraid to live there because of the waste gases emitted. Despite the fact that Manila is full of squatters, the buildings stand empty.

ZERO WASTE AND INDUSTRIAL ECOLOGY

'Zero waste' is a new slogan for a worldwide movement. *Environmentally*, it implies the recycling of waste materials for cleaner production processes. *Economically*, it implies increased cost savings, profitability and competitiveness through minimising wastes and toxins. Zero waste strategies are seen by its advocates as providing improved profitability, competitiveness and environmental performance through the development and implementation of practices that lead to the reduction and elimination of waste and toxics. In countries as far afield as New Zealand, Australia, Denmark, the USA and Canada, cities and citizen groups are working towards achieving zero waste objectives. Says author Robin Murray:

> *Waste has suddenly become an issue too important to be left to*
> *the waste industry. It is seen no longer as simply a sectoral matter*
> *... There has been a shift from the concentration on pollution*
> *control to a broader policy of 'Zero Waste'.*[21]

In New Zealand, the Zero Waste Network has existed since 1999. It regards strong community involvement as crucial in the implementation of its aims. As a loose affiliation of stakeholders, it is aiming for the complete redesign of the country's production, consumption and waste management system. Half of New Zealand's local authorities have adopted zero waste targets, most aiming to reach them by 2015.[22]

In Australia, Canberra, Melbourne and Newcastle have adopted similar zero waste targets.[23] In Sydney, the first facility for highly mechanised zero waste recycling is currently being built.[24]

Zero waste strategies are also being adopted by businesses all over the world—driven by legislation as well as voluntary action. Zero waste is being incorporated into the business practices of companies including Sony, Mitsubishi, IBM, DuPont and Toyota. In the United States, several major companies are moving towards zero waste strategies:

- Interface Inc., Atlanta, Georgia eliminated over $165,000 in waste a year by designing new 'industrial ecology' methods for making carpets.
- Xerox Corp., Rochester, New York, had savings of $45,000 in 1998 by minimising waste, emissions and energy consumption and by maximising recycling.
- Hewlett Packard, Roseville, California saved $870,000 in 1998 by reducing its waste by 95 per cent.
- Epson, Portland, Oregon saved $300,000 in 2000 by moving towards zero waste.[25]

Zero waste systems are also being advocated by the authors William McDonough and Michael Braungart. In their book *Cradle to Cradle*, they propose taking nature as a model for a new paradigm of production. They envisage an eco-revolution in the way we create products and utilise materials. Their main emphasis is on designing materials and products that can be perpetually reused and point out that we need to learn from nature, which is highly productive and effective in the way it makes all things. Following their own philosophy, they have designed a wide range of new products from carpeting to corporate campuses.[26]

The challenge of creating cradle-to-cradle zero waste systems in our cities is an enormous one. While a good start has been made in many places and concepts are being turned into practice, so much more will need to be done to turn a sustainable zero waste society into reality.

CHAPTER 11

Using Water Efficiently

Looking down from space, the earth is covered with veins and arteries, a vast web of rivers and streams channelling water across the planet, down from mountains and hills, across river valleys and plains, and out towards the world's oceans. Although there is a vast number of rivers and streams, running water accounts for only a small proportion of the water found on earth.

We are mainly made out of water and we can't survive without it. Most human settlements throughout history were built near springs, streams, rivers and lakes, from which people could draw water with relative ease. Water consumption per person in modern cities is greater than ever before and, because local water supplies are often inadequate, water has to be piped in from further and further away. With the world population projected to increase to nine billion by 2050, and with growing affluence and urbanisation all over the world, demand for water will grow steeply in the coming years and decades, unless efficient water use becomes the norm. Without a major change in attitudes, one-third of the world's population could face acute shortages by 2025, which will become increasingly difficult to tackle. Efficient use of water and reuse of waste water is thus one of the great challenges of the 21st century.

Conflicts over water are becoming a major cause of tension *between* and *within* countries. Water is a finite resource, and humans and other living species cannot draw on an ever expanding supply. Only 3 per cent of all

Girl pouring water over herself
Pure, fresh water should not be a luxury but a key element in the life of all cities.

water is fresh, while the remaining 97 per cent is salt water. Of that 3 per cent fresh water, only 0.3 per cent is found in rivers and lakes while the rest is stored in glaciers and ice caps. If the available fresh water were spread evenly, it would be sufficient for all conceivable human needs. But because much of it is either in the wrong place or of poor quality, there is growing concern about the availability of adequate water and the cost of supplying it.

Water conflicts are developing between countries in many parts of the world, often because of the water and food needs of large cities. Conflict areas include:

- Israel, Palestine and Syria over the Jordan and other local rivers,
- Turkey, Iraq and Syria over the waters of the Euphrates and Tigris,
- Egypt, Sudan and Ethiopia over the waters of the Nile,
- Chad, Niger, Nigeria and Cameroon over the waters of Lake Chad,
- Egypt and Libya over Libya's policy of mining Sahara groundwater,
- Botswana and Namibia over the waters of the Okavango delta,
- Botswana, Namibia and Angola over the Cuito River,
- Senegal and Mauritania over dams on the Senegal River,
- the USA and Mexico over the waters of the Colorado and Rio Grande,
- Laos, Cambodia and Vietnam over the Mekong River,
- India and Bangladesh over the waters of the Ganges.

There are also conflicts within countries over water resources, between rural and urban communities, and between indigenous groups and modern society. Increasing conflicts are currently developing in:

- India over major dams such as the Narmada and Tehri complexes,
- China over the Three Gorges Dam complex,
- South Africa over the dams on the Lesotho River,
- the USA over distribution of water supplies from the Colorado River.

In addition, in more and more countries there are conflicts about water privatisation and its effects on the price of water charged in urban areas. Privatisation of water systems is becoming the norm all over the world, but this is often causing deep resentment. The primary product of private water companies is profits rather than water. As profit-maximising enterprises they resent regulation as inhibiting that primary task, and yet regulation is crucial both for making the market work for consumer benefit and for environmental sustainability.[1]

As cities grow all over the world, they are forced to compete with agriculture and industry for limited water supplies. Worldwide, a third of humanity, mostly in cities, does not have access to clean water. In many cities in developing countries, water quality is appalling and waste water treatment non-existent. People in the poorest communities are often forced to obtain water from polluted streams, rivers or wells, or to buy it from vendors at exorbitant prices.

GROWING DEMANDS FOR WATER

Urban growth has inevitably required technical solutions to match increased local water demand with increased supply. Today we consume far more water per capita than in the past. UK citizens use some 400 litres and Americans as much as 600 litres a day. We no longer use water just for drinking and in bathrooms and toilets, but also in food and industrial production. For instance, it takes 125,000 litres of water to produce one car and 1,000 tonnes of water to produce one tonne of grain.

Says Lester Brown, President of the Earth Policy Institute:

> As world water demand has tripled over the last half-century, it has exceeded the sustainable yield of aquifers in scores of countries, leading to falling water tables. In effect, governments satisfy the growing demand for food by overpumping groundwater, a measure that virtually assures a drop in food production when the aquifer is depleted. Knowingly or not, governments are creating a 'food bubble' economy.[2]

At present no less than 70 per cent of the world's fresh water is used for growing food, and as much as 95 per cent in parts of the US, North Africa and Asia. In the next 20 years increased food demand due to population growth and growing affluence could mean that agriculture alone would need up to 20 per cent more water than at present. Yet several countries are already overpumping their aquifers. India, with a population of over one billion people, is overdrawing aquifers in Haryana, Gujarat, Rajasthan, Andhra Pradesh, Tamil Nadu and Punjab, the country's breadbasket. Under the Punjab, water tables are falling by up to one metre per year and aquifer depletion there could reduce India's grain harvest by one-fifth. In parts of Tamil Nadu water tables have already run dry.

Industrial development also requires prodigious amounts of water. China alone is expected to increase its industrial water use by some 600 per cent in the next 20 years. In parts of China, water tables are dropping by around 1.5 metres a year and 400 of its 600 northern cities face acute shortages. He Quincheng, head of Beijing's Geological Environmental Monitoring Institute, notes that the deep aquifer under the North China Plain is seriously depleted and the region is losing its last water reserve: 'Anecdotal evidence suggests that deep wells drilled around Beijing now have to reach 1,000 metres to tap fresh water, adding dramatically to the cost of supply.'[3]

Another increasingly acute problem is water contamination. London doesn't use much water from its own water table but pumps most of it in from the rivers Thames and Lea, because the polluting activities of generations of Londoners have made local groundwater very costly to clean to adequate standards. With industrial development and modern farming proliferating all over the world, pesticides, nitrates, petrochemicals, fluorides, heavy metals and mining wastes tend to seep into groundwater supplies, posing serious health hazards. Cleaning water from highly polluted aquifers is an exceedingly difficult and expensive business.[4]

To bring even good-quality water up to drinking-quality standards it needs to go through various treatment processes. It has to be percolated through sand and charcoal filter beds. Chlorination, which has disinfected water since the late 19th century, continues to be widely used, but it gives water an unpleasant taste and can be harmful to health. Increasingly, ultraviolet light is used to sterilise water, as a less intrusive method of killing harmful bacteria and viruses. Concern about water quality has driven people all over the world not to drink tap water but to go for bottled water instead. However, this is often more expensive than the petrol we put in our cars. Despite the fact that it does not make sense economically or environmentally, use of bottled water is growing every year and vast quantities are trucked into cities over huge distances and at great energy cost.

CITIES AND DAMS

The ruins of the great aqueducts of ancient Rome and its satellite cities across the empire can still be admired today, and so can ancient sewage systems such as Rome's famous Cloaca Maxima, which is still used. Yet these are small compared with the water management systems underpinning modern cities.

Throughout the 20th century many cities were built all over the world despite a lack of adequate local water supplies. Los Angeles is an interesting case in point. Its own Los Angeles River is small and seasonal and as settlers streamed to LA, water diversions and groundwater pumping began to deplete its supply. Cropland and livestock cultivation expanded, while native trees and wet meadows vanished. Los Angeles expanded from 100,000 to 7 million people in the 20th century and this massive growth could not have occurred without substantial new water supplies.

The diversion of the Owens River to Los Angeles in 1913 is a famous example of urban water 'theft', by which William Mulholland and other civic leaders deprived the farmers of the Owens River Valley of irrigation water for their crops and diverted it to Los Angeles instead. The Owens River Aqueduct was the most difficult engineering project undertaken in America up to that time. By building it across mountain and desert, the water turned LA into a vast desert oasis. The Owens River still accounts for 60–70 per cent of Los Angeles's water supply, though the winter snow falls in the Eastern Sierra are somewhat unpredictable, which means that the city's water supply from the Owens River can be as high as 84 per cent in wet years and as low as 16 per cent in dry years.[5]

Even more water was needed to assure a steady supply to the growing city. The Colorado River, nicknamed Red Bull because of the colour of its silt, used to flow uninterrupted along 1,450 miles (2,320 kilometres) from the Rocky Mountains to the Gulf of California. The Hoover Dam was built in the 1930s depression to supply water and electricity to desert cities such as Phoenix, San Diego, Las Vegas and, of course, Los Angeles. The distance from the dam to Los Angeles is 266 miles.

When the Hoover Dam was built it was the highest and most expensive water project ever undertaken, housing the world's largest power plant: 56 per cent goes to Southern California, 19 per cent to Arizona and 25 per cent to Nevada. Five more large dams have since been built on the Colorado River and these days it rarely reaches the sea. In 1941, the first water from the newly completed Colorado River Aqueduct was delivered to Los Angeles. The silt that it used to carry to Colorado built up into a huge delta in the Gulf, but now it is deposited in the dam reservoirs instead and will eventually render them useless. Will the cities die as the dams that feed them become silted up?[6]

The Aswan High Dam in Egypt, commissioned by President Nasser, is a prime example of a modern, large dam. Egypt's greatest construction project since the pyramids was started in 1960 and completed in 1965. It controls the Nile's annual floods, stores water, and then produces large amounts of electricity, particularly to light up Cairo. But four million tonnes of Ethiopia's soil, or silt, carried by the Blue Nile every year are now accumulating in the reservoir. This used to fertilise Egypt's farms, but some of the dam's electricity supply is now used to produce mineral fertiliser. However, the loss of the silt is a major problem in the Nile delta, where the river banks are becoming badly eroded. And because salt water from the Mediterranean is seeping into the delta's groundwater, farmers there had to abandon large areas of land that have become salinised. Because the silt no longer reaches the sea, the fisheries in the southeastern Mediterranean environment have collapsed, though the Aswan reservoir itself has become a thriving fishery in its own right.[7]

In the last 50 years, thousands of large dams have been built all over the world, the tallest being over 300 metres high. Many large, modern cities could not exist without them. Huge water engineering projects go together with large cities—to feed them with irrigated crops and to supply them with water and electricity.

Today the eyes of the world are on vast projects such as the Three Gorges Dam on China's Yangtze River. Also called the 'long river', the Yangtze rises in western Qinghai province and flows 3,720 miles (5,990 kilometres) to the East China Sea. This dam is also being built primarily to benefit large cities and irrigation schemes at the expense of smaller local communities. Construction began in 1994. When completed in around 2014, it will be the largest hydroelectric dam in the world, stretching nearly a mile across and towering 575 feet above the world's third longest river. Its reservoir will reach over 350 miles upstream and displace nearly 1.9 million people. The official budget is over $24 billion, but the cost is likely to rise to three times that amount.[8]

In India, the combined effects of the growth of populations, cities and the economy are greatly increasing water demand. The Narmada and Tehri dams have become notorious for flooding fertile river valleys in the foothills of the Himalayas and depriving hundreds of thousands of local people of land to grow crops, forcing them to migrate to squatter settlements on the outskirts of large cities instead. In India alone, thousands of new dams have dislocated tens of millions of village people and farmers, many of whom have ended up on useless land or in squatter settlements on the edge of large cities.

The Tehri Dam is planned to be the world's fifth highest, 260 metres high and with a reservoir extending to some 45 square kilometres. It is being constructed in the Bhagirathi and Bhilangana valley, tributaries of the Ganges.

Mumbai water pipe

Access to cheap, clean water is a major issue in many cities. This pipeline in Mumbai, passing through the shantytown of Mahim, carries drinking water to more prosperous districts of the city. The people here have to make do with polluted water from ditches, or buy expensive water from street vendors.

When finished, its waters will submerge one town and nearly 100 villages. Nevertheless, the Tehri Dam is not expected to have a life span of more than 40 years. Its waters are intended for irrigating cropland in Uttar Pradesh, which is already well endowed with water. A substantial proportion of Tehri's water will be piped to Delhi, an ever-growing megacity. Yet its average per capita consumption is already 250 litres a day, compared to 10 litres a day for the villagers of the Tehri region.[9]

Large water projects such as the Three Gorges and Tehri Dams are often part-funded by banks in financial centres such as London and New York. It is widely recognised that their short-term economic and water supply benefits are often outweighed by medium-term dangers such as earthquakes, spontaneous collapse and siltation, which can leave devastated landscapes and communities in their wake. A key issue for cities today is whether their people can make more efficient use of water, forgoing the need for expensive and often unsustainable large dam projects. Can water efficiency, rainwater harvesting and waste water recycling reduce external water dependence? Could the role of ever-larger dams be taken by a combination of water conservation measures and smaller scale water development projects? The evidence shows that new thinking is urgently needed.

EFFICIENT USE OF WATER

Large cities usually control large water catchment areas, but this can sometimes be environmentally beneficial. In the 1980s New York City, a city located in a more water-rich area than LA, faced acute water shortages. But instead of expanding supply by the construction of dams, it decided to turn to water demand management to avoid shortfalls. At the same time, the city's water supply districts in New York State have been carefully conserved rather than developed.

In 1986, the city authorities decided to install water meters as a first significant measure for limiting water use. More than 600,000 meters were installed at a cost of $350 million. This enabled the city to monitor its water use by employing pricing as a carefully targeted water management strategy. In 1991, New York City also launched a pilot water conservation programme to stem rising demand. It offered a range of services, such as free leak detection, low-flow showerheads and water-efficient toilet systems. Since 1993, a large-scale water conservation programme has conducted leak detection across the city. By 1995, NYC's average demand had dropped from 1,400 to 1,300 million gallons a day, equalling the safe yield of its water catchments. More recently, further substantial savings have resulted from replacing one-third of the city's 7 gallons-per-flush toilets with 1.6 gallon-per-flush units.[10]

If one of the world's major cities can use water management as a deliberate policy tool, why can't other cities do the same?

NEW WASTE WATER TECHNOLOGIES

As we saw in Chapter 4, in the 19th century rapidly growing cities such as London had a huge problem of polluted water to deal with, as water came to be routinely used as a carrier of liquid waste. In 1855, Dr John Snow was the first to prove that London's public fresh water supplies were contaminated with sewage, causing disease and death. Ever since then the main brief of sewage engineers has been to prevent exposure of people to contaminated water.

Where many people live together and much economic activity takes place, a lot of waste water is generated. Not surprisingly, waste water treatment has made tremendous advances over the last 150 years, yet is one of the very problematic issues in the quest for creating sustainable urban systems. The out-of-sight, out-of-mind solution that was adopted in 19th-century London has been replicated all over the world. The main brief for sewage engineers has been to reduce people's exposure to effluents and to flush the latter out of harm's way.

A few years ago I flew over the city of Rio de Janeiro and saw an extraordinary image: the vast sewage plume of that city, oozing out into the sea. The daily discharges of the Iguacu and Estrela Rivers into Rio's Guanabara Bay include 465 tonnes of organic matter, only 68 tonnes of which receive adequate treatment, and 9.5 tonnes of oil. The waters that drain into the sea are often anoxic; that is, they contain no oxygen at all.[11]

The Rio example illustrates a point made elsewhere in the book: if we wish to create a sustainable world we cannot continue flushing nutrients from the farmland that feeds cities into the sea and polluting coastal waters in the process. A substantial proportion of the artificial fertilisers now used on the world's farms also end up polluting rivers and coastal waters. This one-way traffic of nutrients causes havoc to coastal waters across the planet. Vast quantities of sewage are still flushed away into rivers and coastal waters downstream from population centres. Coastal waters are enriched with human sewage and toxic effluents, as well as the run-off of mineral fertiliser

Rio sewage plume
This is the sewage plume of the city of Rio de Janeiro. Not only are local beaches and coastal waters being polluted, but the nutrients contained in the sewage are being flushed into the sea, never to be returned to the land.

and pesticides applied to the farmland feeding cities. Yet nutrients taken from farms in the form of crops ultimately need to be returned to the land, not flushed into the oceans.

Sewage systems are designed as waste water treatment and disposal systems, but rarely as recycling systems. Sewage treatment is primarily concerned with two issues: removing sludge and objects from waste water, and reducing the discharge of dirty water into the aquatic environment. Conventional waste water treatment is in two or sometimes three stages. After waste water arrives at a treatment works, it is first screened to remove debris. In the primary settlement process that follows, water is stored in retention tanks. Sludge is extracted throughout this process and flushed into separate holding tanks. Secondary or biological treatment comes next. Here bacteria are cultured in the oxygen-enriched waste water, to feed on the nutrients and organic matter it contains. The waste water is then transferred into a final settlement tank, before being flushed into rivers or the sea. In some cases the waste water is treated further, in an expensive tertiary process, in which it is disinfected with ultraviolet light and in which nitrates and phosphates can be stripped out.

Beckton sewage works, London
Sewage technology has made great progress, but today the emphasis should be on sewage recycling rather than sewage treatment.

In the 1990s, the European Union issued a directive to stop all sewage disposal in the sea. As a result water companies, including London's Thames Water, were forced to make expensive investments in new waste water treatment. Thames Water could no longer dump sewage sludge into the Thames estuary and decided to burn it instead. In 2002, it completed two incinerators at Crossness and Beckton sewage works for dealing with the sludge of some four million Londoners. This is a questionable decision, because the phosphates contained in sludge will need to be recovered when the remaining phosphate deposits in North Africa, Florida and Russia, currently used in farm fertiliser, run out in a few decades. But on a positive note, Thames Water has done an impressive job in cleaning the Thames. It is now a clean and 'liveable' urban river and has come a long way since the 'great stink' 150 years ago.

The quest for urban sustainability will certainly require us to rethink the criteria by which we design sewage systems. Instead of building treatment and disposal systems, we need to construct facilities in which nitrates, potash and phosphates contained in sewage can be extracted and used as fertiliser on farms, orchards and market gardens once again. The good news is that people all over the world are working on various recycling systems.

In Bristol, Wessex Water has developed an interesting new technology. It turns the annual sewage output of 600,000 people into 10,000 tonnes of Biogran Natural pellets, a soil conditioner and fertiliser. In a large rotating drum that is heated by burning methane from a sewage farm, the sludge is dehydrated and gradually turned into bone-dry pellets. They are mainly used to revitalise brownfield sites such as the coal slag heaps around former mining towns such as Merthyr Tydfil in southeast Wales. Farmers also use it to put organic matter and nutrients back into depleted farmland. However, because the pellets contain trace quantities of heavy metals, they have not as yet gained acceptance on certified organic farms.[12]

A variety of innovative waste water systems have been developed in recent years. Membrane systems are now available to separate sewage from any contaminants and from dangerous germs such as cryptosporidium, assuring that sewage can be recycled into water safe for drinking. The various new technologies can be used in combination with each other.

THE ECO-MACHINE

In 1981, a revolutionary new waste water treatment technology made its debut, called living or eco-machines. Its inventor, Dr John Todd, sees waste water as a resource rather than a cost. Taking natural water treatment systems

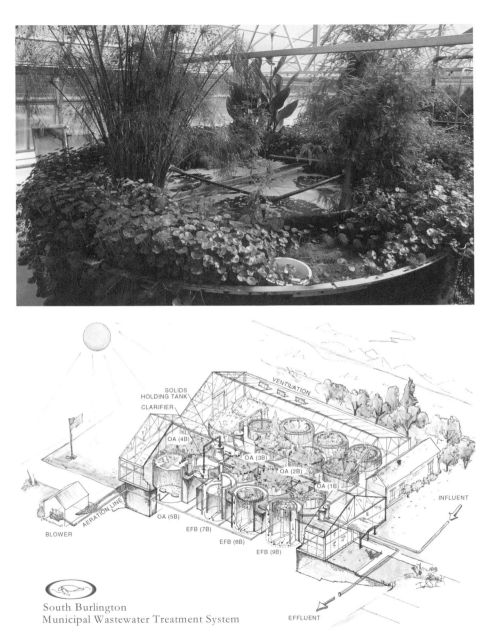

South Burlington
Municipal Wastewater Treatment System

Eco-Machine waste water treatment
This system is a perfect synergy between ecology and technology. This facility in South
Burlington, Vermont, is made up of a series of tanks that contain both plants and micro-fauna
which digest sewage and convert it into fresh water.

such as reed beds as an inspiration, Todd pioneered a new kind of ecological systems design that has become a world leader in the field of ecological water purification. His company, Ocean Arks, has disseminated the concept of the eco-machine all over the world. In 1999, *Time* magazine acknowledged Todd as a 'Hero for the Planet'.

This is the way the system works: raw sewage and air are pumped into a series of linked giant tanks in which some 200 species of plants are suspended in wire mesh containers. While the plants soak up nutrients contained in the sewage, countless bacteria and microbes break down pollutants. As the sewage proceeds from tank to tank, becoming progressively cleaner, fish and snails join in the feast. What comes out of the last tank is sparkling water, clean enough for irrigation, toilet flushing or car washing. The plants in the tanks are harvested and are an abundant source of organic matter to be used as garden compost. Todd's machines cost about half as much to install as traditional sewage treatment plants made of concrete tanks and a maze of pipes. They don't smell, are nice to look at and are educational at the same time. In a school near Toronto where Todd installed a small facility, 'kids flush the toilet and then run around the corner to see what happens', he says.[13]

Todd and his company Ocean Arks have installed dozens of these machines in cities, factories and food-processing plants. Other companies are now selling similar technologies and as a result they are becoming increasingly mainstream.[14] One example of Todd's work is his municipal sewage treatment plant in South Burlington, Vermont. Here a series of tanks containing living organisms set up in a greenhouse treat the sewage of some 1,600 residences and turn it into clean water. The sewage in the plant is treated to a level of cleanliness surpassing the US federal Environmental Protection Agency requirements.

Are there any problems with eco-machine technology? It does take up more space than conventional sewage technology. However, there is no good reason why eco-machines could not be installed throughout our cities, doubling up as sewage treatment systems, small-scale parks and facilities for environmental education.

WATER USE AND WASTE WATER RECYCLING IN ADELAIDE

Adelaide is located in one of the driest regions of the world's driest continent, yet water flows in abundance at the turn of the tap. Each person living there uses about 500 litres a day. In most years, 60 per cent of this water comes from the nearby Mount Lofty range, but there is also a 60 kilometre pipeline from the Murray River. In wet years, 40 per cent of Adelaide's 200 million tonnes of water comes through this pipeline, though in dry years this can increase to 90 per cent. There is ever-growing concern about the viability of continued large-scale abstraction of water from the Murray by a total of three million people. The Murray–Darling basin covers over a million square kilometres of southeastern Australia and encompasses much of the country's best farming and grazing land. In the light of other water needs, it is clearly of the essence for irrigation water to be used as efficiently as possible. Like the Colorado River in the United States, the Murray now rarely reaches the sea. The quality of its water has been declining because of inadequate recharge and tainted run-off from farmland. The problem of rising salt levels in the river and on the adjoining land will take many decades to solve. The overuse of water from the river could soon affect the sustainability of the very activities that crucially depend on the water: farming, industry, urban water supplies, tourism and recreation are all threatened by the continued decline in the health of the Murray.[15]

Because of continuing problems of water supply, the government of South Australia has taken major initiatives on efficient use of water. In 2003, it imposed a $30 'Save the Murray' levy to deal with the overuse of the river water. Despite being a financial cost, this has enjoyed very high public acceptance. In 2004, the government passed legislation obliging all households to install a water tank to capture rainwater.

Adelaide generates almost 100 billion litres of waste water a year, while 110 billion litres of stormwater drain into the Gulf of St Vincent. Both these resources are increasingly being put to productive use. The city's groundwater could also be used more actively. In metropolitan Adelaide, high-quality groundwater from a deep aquifer beneath the city is being tapped by the soft-drink and beer industries. Many local recreation and sports fields rely on pumped water to stay green. In addition, reclaimed water has started to be 'banked' in aquifers to be recovered for later use in irrigation via a technology known as aquifer storage and recovery.[16]

The city of Salisbury in metropolitan Adelaide has developed a substantial network of 36 wetlands covering some 250 hectares, reducing local flood risks while also providing wildlife habitats. Stormwater, which was seen as a problem in the past, is now being harnessed and utilised, enhancing economic development as well as environmental sustainability. By recycling stormwater through wetlands, the discharge of polluted water into the sea is also minimised.

Salisbury wetlands
Cities such as Adelaide, located in low rainfall regions, need to store as much of their stormwater as possible. The wetlands reduce flood risks, become wildlife habitats and store water for use in the dry season, both above and below ground.

In another interesting scheme in the McLaren Vale south of Adelaide, a major wine-producing area, negotiations for efficient water use by irrigators were successfully conducted. The growers there used groundwater for irrigating grapevines. As water shortages loomed, they agreed to reduce their use of groundwater to sustainable yields, a reduction up to 50 per cent of existing licences. As the growers understood that these reductions were necessary for ensuring their long-term livelihood, no compensation for the reduced allocations had to be offered. At the same time, treated waste water was made available for grapevine irrigation, assuring the best possible uses of limited water supplies.[17]

A growing proportion of water is first used in households and then made available for irrigating urban farms. In Adelaide's northern district of Virginia, 7,000 hectares of vegetables and fruit are irrigated with treated waste water, 30 billion litres of 'class A' reclaimed water are provided via a waste water pipeline, and a further 18 billion litres of irrigation water are pumped from the underlying aquifer every year. Where water supplies are limited, waste water irrigation is an appropriate technology, although high quality standards have to be assured. The water has to be purified before use and, wherever possible, applied via underground piping systems, limiting direct human contact.[18]

THE EAST CALCUTTA WETLANDS

Across the world, wetlands are widely used as nutrient sinks and to filter impurities from water as part of sewage treatment. In many Indian cities such wetlands used to be an important source of water supply and were well looked after. However, as modern sewage systems were installed, many such wetlands have been neglected over the years, causing flooding and water-logging in urban areas.

Not so in Calcutta. It does not have a conventional sewage treatment system. Its 11 million people's daily output of 680 million litres of waste water is treated in the East Calcutta wetlands, an 'integrated wetlands system' consisting of a collection of both natural and artificial ponds.

A series of canals channel the city's waste water into the wetlands. The waste water flows into shallow collection ponds for up to ten days. During this time, light penetrates the water and reacts with the sewage to create an environment rich in algae and plankton, which is ideal for fish to feed and grow on. Maintenance of the ponds is minimal, but in order for small fish to thrive the water needs to be churned up and snails, which also thrive on the algae, need to be picked out of the ponds. Water hyacinths are used to stop the banks from eroding. By the time the water leaves the wetlands, it is almost drinkable and can be used for irrigating farmland.

The limited amounts of industrial sewage that find their way into the ponds are also dealt with by the water hyacinths, which have been found to be highly effective at removing pollutants. They need to be harvested at regular intervals, to reduce the turbidity of the effluent entering the maturation ponds and to increase sunlight penetration. The water hyacinths are harvested, dried and used in compost. Duckweed is also harvested and used as a cattle and chicken feed.

The ponds are a flood cushion for the city, a natural treatment system for Calcutta's waste water, and also a system for harnessing the nutrients available in waste water by fishing and farming. The intricate patchwork of canals, fish ponds, rice paddies and vegetable plots, which covers 8,000 hectares, is an extraordinary ecosystem in its own right. The algae in the waste water ponds are eaten by fish such as carp and tilapia and transformed into edible protein. The rest becomes compost for growing vegetables. Thus the East Calcutta wetlands are a cost-effective and sustainable sewage treatment facility and also provides a living for 20,000 people.

Some 20 tonnes of fish and 150 tonnes of vegetables are produced every day. The fish farmers sell most of the fish and earn a gross per capita income of about US$3 per day, more than three times the minimum daily agricultural wage in India. The fish contain fewer pathogens than most other fish available in the markets and are perfectly safe to eat. While pisciculture is the mainstay of wetlands, the rice, fruit trees, vegetables and flowers grown on the banks of the canals further help to ensure the system's economic as well as ecological sustainability. The biggest menace is from thieves, so groups of men have to guard the ponds and the fields at night.

In many cities in developing countries, wetlands or natural depressions accumulate waste water and become health risks for humans. The integrated wetland system provides a low-cost, ecologically balanced and community-linked sanitation option for cities with ample sunshine. It is a sustainable treatment and resource recovery system that can be used to remove contaminants and nutrients from water with remarkable efficiency. It does not require fossil fuel energy—it is a biological reactor powered by the sun. And by utilising nutrients and organic material in the sewage, it also enhances the economic base of local people through fish farming, horticulture and animal husbandry.

Dr Dhrubajyoti Ghosh is the executive engineer for the Calcutta Metropolitan Water and Sanitation Authority. He says:

> This system could be replicated in other countries where there is sun and poverty. It is much cheaper than other technologies for treating sewage and recycling waste. If I have failed in one thing it is this: not enough people know about it or are benefiting from it. Now I am happy to give any advice free of charge. This is the best system of its kind in the world and could help millions of people. Such projects can be completed within 18 months compared to 5 years for conventional sewage treatment systems. But a lot of money is to be made by engineers and foreign companies selling sewage systems to the Third World.[19]

PROBLEMS IN BANGLADESH

All over the world many millions of wells have been drilled in recent years to supply towns and villages, and in some places they have provided great improvements in local living conditions. Nevertheless, in others they have brought major problems.

In Bangladesh, tens of millions of people are being poisoned by drinking well water laced with arsenic, usually without knowing it. In the last 30 years, hundreds of thousands of deep tube wells were dug throughout Bangladesh and experts encouraged people to drink well water because it was free of the bacteria that caused water-borne diseases such as diarrhoea and other intestinal problems. But the people of Bangladesh have exchanged water-borne diseases for arsenicosis. It was only in 1993 that many of the 'clean' wells were discovered to contain dangerous quantities of the poison. Arsenicosis can cause cancers of the bladder, kidney, lung and skin, diseased blood vessels, and also diabetes, high blood pressure and reproductive disorders. Arsenic-contaminated water is not restricted to developing countries. Other countries such as the USA, Australia, Argentina, Brazil, Chile, Hungary, Mexico, Taiwan, Thailand and Vietnam also have problems with this poison.

WATERPROOFING OUR CITIES

It is crucial for people worldwide to understand that water, as well as waste water, is a valuable resource that needs to be handled imaginatively and frugally. 'Waterproofing' our cities requires the involvement just not of specialists, but of everyone.

Cities are dependent on healthy ecosystems to supply their water. The water cycle starts in the clouds and, as water flows down mountains via streams, rivers, lakes and wetlands, it ends up in water pipes and sewage systems. As pressure on the world's water supplies grows, and as competition between various uses increases, water conflicts are looming, with the water poor asserting their interests against the water rich.

In this context, public debates about the balance between urban, agricultural and commercial uses of water, and their relative social, economic and environmental benefits, are becoming very important. Only a well-informed public can address the issues through democratic debate. Solutions dependent on burning ever more fossil fuels to operate conventional sewage systems, to desalinate water, to transport water across the world in giant plastic bags, or to tow icebergs to water-poor locations, won't solve the world's water problems. However, by studying the complex water cycle we can make a start at mimicking natural systems and using water in our cities in sustainable ways.

CHAPTER 12

Relearning
Urban Agriculture

This chapter explores the potential of cities for supplying a significant proportion of the food they consume from their own territory or their immediate hinterland. Urban agriculture is conducted within cities, or on their peripheries. In many cities in developed countries supplying food locally would currently not be considered as a realistic option, but elsewhere it is seen as an integral part of the urban economy.

Over the last 50 years agriculture has become ever more capital intensive. The energy technologies that have made cities of millions of people possible have also helped create energy- and technology-dependent food systems, and urban food supplies originate in an increasingly global hinterland. London, for instance, has a surface area of some 160,000 hectares, but it currently requires over 50 times its own area, or around 8.4 million hectares, to supply it with food. Much of that farmland, of course, is not located in Britain itself, but across Europe and in places as far away as the USA, Canada, Brazil, Thailand or New Zealand.[1]

People are being designed out of the farming system. In the UK, for instance, only 1.5 per cent of the population still works the land. Rural landscapes across the world no longer exist in their own right but are mainly for supplying food demands from distant cities, via food distribution centres located near airports, ports or motorways. Food is shipped, trucked or flown in 'just in time' from somewhere, anywhere, never mind where. In the United

States food typically travels between 1,500 and 2,500 miles from farm to plate, as much as 25 per cent further than it did in 1980.[2] One British case study shows how the ingredients of a typical Sunday lunch for four people, consisting of chicken, potatoes, carrots, mangetout beans and Brussels sprouts, would have travelled over 24,000 miles to reach a dinner table, consuming 52 megajoules of energy.[3]

It is not only the energy input into our food system that should concern us, but also its environmental impacts. The largest land surfaces required for feeding cities in developed countries are for meeting their demand for meat with animal feeds such as soya beans, manioc and maize. As outlined in Chapter 5, increased meat consumption has become a major cause of deforestation in rainforest regions in Brazil, Thailand, Malaysia and Indonesia. Now increased meat consumption in countries such as China is causing the conversion of rainforest and savannah into farmland in places such as Mato Grosso on the southern edge of the Amazon.

As cities get richer, people get used to buying food from the supermarket rather than growing it locally. Leading busy urban lives, few people have the time to ascertain how the food they eat has been produced. A rich variety of food is simply taken for granted and the sustainability of its supply is not much of a concern. If cod from the North Sea runs out, pollack from Alaska is served up instead. If the soil on Australian farms erodes, we can eat bread made from grain produced in Argentina or Canada. Yet sooner rather than later we will hit the limits of global food supplies. We urgently need to examine how sustainable our food systems are, and whether we should supply more of our food from close by.

HISTORY REVISITED

Urban agriculture can be traced to the world's earliest civilisations. The Sumerians, Aztecs, Mayans and Incas all produced food within their cities, which were usually located on good-quality land with access water. Urban and peri-urban farming was the norm before long-distance food transport became an option. As Chapter 3 describes, in medieval cities in Europe crops used to be grown within their walls as well in their immediate hinterland. Ancient Rome was an exception, relying on vast quantities of grain being shipped in from North Africa.

An interesting example of urban farming at the beginning of the 20th century is given by horticulturalists who cultivated land on the outskirts of

Paris. According to Peter Kropotkin, they grew between three and six crops a year. He quotes one grower, M. Ponce, who produced 250,000 pounds of vegetables on a little more than one hectare with seven other workers. Using ingenious techniques for increasing soil and air temperatures during the colder months, some 5,000 growers, working about 900 hectares of land, supplied the vegetable needs of around two million Parisians and even shipped some of their crops all the way to London. To make the soil as productive as possible, they applied 30 centimetres of horse manure to their vegetable beds every year. When growers had to relocate, they would dig up the highly productive topsoil they had created and take it with them to their new plot.[4]

London, like Paris, had its own local supplies of fruit and vegetables. Heathrow in west London was a major centre of market gardening until right after the Second World War. Its light, sandy soil is very suitable for vegetable growing.

Today, of course, Heathrow has become a rather different sort of place—largely concreted over with runways, roads, hangars and flight terminals. Ironically, it is still a major food supplier: meat, fish, fruit and vegetables are flown in from thousands or even tens of thousands of miles away. This global harvest offers Londoners unparalleled culinary variety, courtesy of cheap, untaxed aviation fuels costing a mere 18 pence a litre. In fact, far more energy goes into the food we eat than it actually contains. By the time food has been produced, transported and processed in this way, it will have consumed disproportionate amounts of energy. Flying tiger prawns in from South America, or mangoes or mangetouts from Africa, requires hundreds of times more energy than the calories they actually contain. This reliance on a food system based on cheap fossil fuels is highly unsustainable.

PROSPECTS FOR URBAN FARMING

Not all cities today are so import dependent. For instance, Florence is still surrounded by orange and olive groves, vineyards and wheat fields, which meet a large proportion of its food requirements. Many cities in Italy, France and Germany still have a very strong relationship to their immediate hinter-land, with 'peri-urban' agriculture very much in evidence. Local food production for urban markets continues to be practised in many places. In recent years researchers, politicians and urban planners, particularly in developing countries, have increasingly acknowledged its significance. Urban agriculture is being more and more seen as contributing to food security, improved nutrition, poverty alleviation and local economic development. In thousands of cities around the world people are quietly getting on with growing crops. According to the United Nations Development Programme, some 800 million people, or nearly 8 per cent of the world's population, are now engaged in urban agriculture worldwide, with the majority in and around Asian cities. Some 200 million of these are commercial producers, with three-quarters of these working the land full time.

The following examples give a glimpse of the remarkable scale of urban agriculture:

Singapore is fully self-reliant in meat and produces 25 per cent of its vegetable needs.

Bamako, Mali, is self-sufficient in vegetables and produces half or more of the chickens it consumes.

Dar-es-Salaam, one of the world's fastest growing large cities, now has 67 per cent of families engaged in farming compared with 18 per cent in 1967.

65 per cent of Moscow families are involved in food production compared with 20 per cent in 1970.

For those who believe that urban food growing is practised only in poor countries here are examples to the contrary: there are 80,000 community gardeners on municipal land in Berlin with a waiting list of 16,000.

The 1980 US census found that urban metropolitan areas produced 30 per cent of the dollar value of US agricultural production. By 1990, this figure had increased to 40 per cent.[5]

Urban farmers grow plants and herbs and raise animals for food. They also produce tree seedlings, ornamental plants and flowers. To be competitive in the context of a globalising food system, they must be highly innovative and adaptable, establishing close contacts with consumers and utilising low-cost inputs easily available in cities, such as sewage, compost and manure.

Urban cultivation is not only beneficial as regards food supply, but can also benefit urban biodiversity. The urban environment is often richer in fauna and flora than rural farmland, particularly in private gardens, because cities usually have a greater variety of trees and flowers than intensively farmed land with large fields and a limited crop diversity. This diversity can be deliberately encouraged by urban planning policy. Organic cultivation in cities can also increase the capacity of soils to absorb water and reduce run-off floods after rainstorms.[6]

Over the last several years I have had the opportunity to experience urban agriculture in different parts of the world. It has become apparent to me that urban cultivation is making a crucial contribution to the food security of billions of people, through commercial production as well as subsistence cultivation. The potential for food self-reliance from small spaces is remarkable. The author John Jeavons claims that a family of four typically needs a garden of only 1,000 square feet with a six-month growing season to feed itself, with two-thirds of that space taken up by grains.[7]

CHINA'S URBAN VILLAGES: A STRATEGY FOR PROTECTING FARMLAND

The Chinese government aims to protect most of the country's farmland by the twin strategy of amalgamating villages and merging farms. Widely scattered villages are being consolidated into a few large 'urban villages' that are intended to improve rural living standards, and to make the delivery of services to people easier and more convenient. Jiangsu Province alone is consolidating its over 280,000 villages into over 50,000 larger settlements, expecting to gain some 200,000 hectares of farmland in the process.[8]

As the Chinese government sees it, millions of farmers have been living on very small patches of land that are just about sufficient for families to survive on, but too small for modern agricultural production. It claims that the productivity of farming has significantly increased wherever rapid increase in the use of small tractors and trucks has occurred. But the mechanisation and modernisation of farming has created a huge excess labour force. The national application rate for chemical fertilisers increased from 58.9 kilograms per hectare in 1978 to 213.3 kilograms per hectare in 1993. During the same period average grain yields rose from about 2.5 tonnes per hectare to some 4.1 tonnes per hectare. In 1994 it was estimated that China had a huge surplus of agricultural workers and that by 2000 some 300 million farmers will not be needed in agriculture, equivalent to the entire population of the USA.

Until recently, highly intensive urban cropping systems made many cities in China self-sufficient in food from land areas administered by them. This policy was pursued systematically by Mao Tse Tung and has been modified only to a limited extent since the changes introduced by Dang Tsiao Ping. Despite China's rapid industrial development, food production is being purposefully maintained on peri-urban farmland. In Tianjin, 20 per cent of people work in farming, in Shanghai 15 per cent and in Beijing 12 per cent, compared with about 45 per cent who work in industry.[9]

Shanghai is China's most important industrial, commercial and financial centre, a metropolis of some 15 million people. The total land area administered by its authorities extends to 634,050 hectares. About 58 per cent of this land is occupied by the city itself, while 42 per cent, mainly on the periphery, is devoted to intensive agriculture. On 12,700 hectares of peri-urban land, 1.3 million tonnes of vegetables are produced per year, or 4,000 tonnes per day, supplying around 60 per cent of the city's vegetable needs.

Hydroponic (soil-less) vegetable cultivation in greenhouses is strongly supported by the city authorities. But traditional raised-bed cultivation is still predominant, with polythene tunnels much in evidence. The traditional practice of using night-soil as fertiliser continues to be widely practised. Growers use large earthenware jars to store the night-soil, which is diluted with water and then ladled onto the crops. However, the apartment blocks now springing up all over China's cities have flush toilets, making the collection and use of night-soil as fertiliser much more difficult.

> Shanghai has entered the fast lane of urbanisation, but the city
> administration has also realised that that the city will not be able
> to develop without a reliable local food supply. The city
> authorities are aiming for a considerable level of agricultural
> production within the city to assure a stable food supply for the
> urban population.[10]

Some 800,000 people work on the city's own peri-urban farmland, producing vegetables, fruit, milk, eggs, chicken, pork, carp and catfish meat.[12] A further two million work the land in the rural areas to the south of the city, with a greater emphasis on growing wheat and rice. The city's policy is to produce some at least a million tonnes of grain locally, assuring a high degree of self-sufficiency.

Some of the growers on the land in and around Shanghai are older local people who continue a lifelong farming practice, but many farmers are migrants from rural areas doing jobs in which the people of Shanghai are becoming less keen to engage.

In Beijing, I found much the same approach to urban farming as in Shanghai. The city authorities administer large areas of farmland. However, because the winter months are much colder there, farmers use ingenious methods to cope, maintaining cultivation with very little dependence on

Shanghai
Shanghai is one of the world's fastest growing cities, yet half the 630,000 ha administered by
the city authorities has been set aside for urban agriculture.

artificial heat, despite the icy weather that prevails for several months. To
keep the heat in their polythene greenhouses at night, they cover them with
several layers of bamboo mats.

The growth of Beijing to a city of around 11 million people has swallowed
some arable land in recent years, reducing its area from 408,000 to 300,500
hectares between 1991 and 2001. On the other hand, the area under orchards
has gone up substantially during this period, from 50,000 to 85,000 hectares.
This is because they require less water and fertiliser, making them a highly
sustainable system of cultivation.[12]

Throughout China, city authorities are required by the central government
to ensure the production of substantial amounts of food from the urban areas
they administer. It appears as though this policy is here to stay despite rapid
urbanisation. The Chinese authorities are keenly aware of the importance of
including agriculture in planning their new cities. A vigorous stand has been
taken against excessive urban sprawl, by designating 80 per cent of China's
arable land as 'fundamental farmland'. To build on this land, four different
authorities have to give their approval—local, county, and provincial govern-

ments, as well as the State Council. Illegal development on protected farmland is no less than a capital offence.[13]

In Japan, too, urban agriculture is still much in evidence. In Tokyo and the surrounding prefectures some 12,500 acres are arable land. Nearly 4 per cent of Greater Tokyo's labour force, over 670,000 people, is involved in agricultural work of some sort. From the air, a patchwork of rice paddies looks like it is sewn together by thick bands of roads. Similar patterns of peri-urban faming can be observed throughout Asia, in industrially developed countries such as South Korea and Taiwan, as well as in developing countries such as Cambodia, Laos and Vietnam.[14]

CUBA'S GREAT EXPERIMENT

In recent years Cuba has become a world-beating laboratory for the development of organic urban agriculture. It demonstrates how a major crisis can be turned into an opportunity through deliberate policy. Following the collapse of the Soviet Union in 1989, food security in Havana and other cities became a major concern. Cuba had lost its main sugar market and 85 per cent of its export earnings, and the US trade embargo caused further economic hardship. When food shortages due to the lack of fuel for tractors and lorries caused serious food supply problems, the government decided to encourage people to practise agriculture within cities. Soon gardens sprouted up everywhere—housing estates, schools, community centres, hospitals and factories.

Cuba's urban agriculture programme aims to provide each person with at least 300 grams of fresh vegetables per day, a figure considered by the FAO as appropriate for maintaining good health. Among the most popular crops are tomatoes, sweetcorn, lettuce, onions, cabbage and carrots. Urban food growing is a source of employment for many people and provides fresh produce with zero transportation costs. By 2002, more than 35,000 hectares of urban land were being used for the intensive production of fruits, vegetables and spices. Some 117,000 people work in the urban gardens, which produce over half the vegetables grown in Cuba.

It was Cubans of Chinese origin who were a major inspiration behind the urban agriculture revolution, persuading Cubans whose diet did not include copious amounts of vegetables that they should change the way they ate. With cookery classes conducted at the urban farms, Chinese-style cooking seems to be catching on. In Havana, vegetarian restaurants are doing good business, and people from all walks of life have come to expound the health benefits of fresh, organic, locally grown food.

Farming in Hanava
Havana, Cuba, has a proliferation of both orchards and vegetable plots. It has become a place of pilgrimage for people interested in urban agriculture. Much of the city's fruit and vegetable supplies are grown within the city.

Havana has become a world leader in urban agriculture, as food production was decentralised from large mechanised state farms to urban cultivation systems. With some three million people, nearly 20 per cent of Cuba's population, Havana is the largest city in the Caribbean. Today more than 50 per cent of its fresh produce is grown within the city limits, using organic compost and simple but effective irrigation systems. The workers in many state enterprises grow their own food. The government has also helped hundreds of thousands of people to set up vegetable gardens, and to plant fruit trees and raise chickens and rabbits.

Urban farming has evolved into three main forms—state-owned research gardens (*organicponicos*), private gardens (*huertos privados*) and popular gardens (*huertos populares*). Organic crops are mainly grown on raised vegetable beds, which make very efficient use of whatever plot of land is available. The main source of compost is bagasse trucked in from Cuba's sugar cane fields. Ironically, the sugar cane is grown with artificial fertilisers, but the bagasse is composted and effectively becomes an organic growing medium. Cuba's urban agriculture programme provides good-quality seeds, and advice on composting, crop rotation, earthworms and dealing with bacterial and fungal diseases without relying on chemical pesticides.[15]

In recent years, Cuba's 200 biotechnology centres have opened up a significant new export market by offering advice on successful organic cultivation methods in other countries such as Jamaica and Venezuela. In Caracas, Cuban-style vegetable gardens can now be found amid busy inner-city streets. Inspired by what he saw in Cuba, President Hugo Chavez ordered intensive urban farming schemes across Venezuela's cities in a bid to enhance food self-sufficiency.[16]

URBAN AGRICULTURE IN POORER COUNTRIES

Since pre-colonial days, urban farming has been an important activity in African cities. In the hot climate the problem of food storage encouraged local food production. Urban farming profoundly influenced the morphology of cities such as Accra and Kumasi in Ghana, which were surrounded by a zone of intensive farming. Kampala, in Uganda, was also described as a city set in an immense garden. But since colonial times farming has often been regarded as inappropriate for modern cities. Kenyan authorities have viewed urban cultivation as a blight on the landscape, yet two-thirds of urban Kenyans are farmers. In Zambia in the 1970s and 1980s, harsh repression of urban cultivation was justified on the grounds that urban farming facilitated the breeding of malaria-carrying mosquitoes.

Because the growing of food in and around cities makes a valuable contribution to both food security and poverty alleviation, a large proportion of urban land in African cities continues to be cultivated. In Kampala, urban farmers produce about 30 per cent of the people's needs for meat and eggs. In Accra, Ghana, 3 per cent of the city's labour force is engaged in urban farming and fishing, and urban farmers supply 90 per cent of vegetables. Dung generated by livestock farming is the main source of fertiliser for vegetable growing. In Dar-es-Salaam, Tanzania, crop production takes up 34,000 hectares, or 23 per cent of the metropolitan area, and 90 per cent of the vegetables sold are grown within the city limits. In Harare, Zimbabwe, land under cultivation nearly doubled to 9,000 hectares from 1900 to 1993, representing some 20 per cent of the city's total area.[17]

Vast areas of cropland and grazing land in Africa are being lost through degradation. On the southern edge of the Sahara alone, some 250,000 square miles of once-productive land have become desert over the past 50 years. Declining rural conditions, as in the example of Nouakchott, Mauritania in Chapter 5, often drives urbanisation in Africa. But everywhere one can see urban farming.

Egypt, a desert country with only a small strip of irrigated land along the Nile, has very little land available for farming. In fact, over half its grain supplies are actually imported, mostly from the USA. Over 95 per cent of Egypt's population live on just 5 per cent of its land, on farms as well as in its cities. Cairo is another large city that is seeking to balance urban and rural activities. Its 13 million people live in one of the most densely populated cities in the world, 32,000 people per square mile. Over centuries Cairo has grown haphazardly and people and workshops, markets and mosques live cheek by jowl.

During the last 30 years, millions of people have moved from farming villages into the city, looking for new opportunities. They have brought their traditions with them and created a rich culture of urban farming, to supplement their families' food supplies. On the edge of the city there are many small farms, with donkeys and oxen providing manure to keep the fields fertile and provide transport. The crops cultivated there are usually marketed in Cairo the same day they are picked.

While fruit and vegetables are available relatively cheaply from the countryside, animal products are not. Perhaps not surprisingly, no less than 80,000 head of livestock are kept within the city itself. Around 20 per cent of families keep chickens, ducks, pigeons, goats, sheep, and even cows on top of the flat roofs of their houses. For poorer people this is a way of dealing with the high prices of animal proteins and also a hobby. The milk, meat and eggs that people can produce at home are better and cheaper than those in the market. While many city officials in Cairo frown on urban farming, the million or more people who keep animals profoundly disagree, and many attempts to stop their animal husbandry have failed.[18]

In South Africa, it was strictly forbidden during apartheid to grow crops in and around cities, because that meant people were there to stay, which was outlawed at the time. But in recent years a dramatic growth in urban agriculture has occurred.

The South African community group Abalimi Bezekhaya—'planters of the home'—is transforming the sandy Cape Flats outside Capetown into a productive green environment, slowly turning an apartheid landscape into a settlement area with a local resource base and a green environment. Khayelitsha and Nyanga townships, home to over a million black and coloured people, are tough places to live. Abalimi Bezekhaya was set up to facilitate urban food gardens in these places, where residents had little access to fresh vegetables. Two non-profit community garden centres were established to supply low-cost manure, seeds, seedlings, tools and pest control remedies as well as comprehensive environmental education. By 1991, over 7,000 people utilised the centres' resources and sales were growing at 80 per cent per annum. By 2002, the centres provided agricultural resources to up to 5,000 subsistence farmers each year. The organic vegetables from the Cape Flats are sold in markets across Capetown.[19]

All over the world urban farming is in ascendance. In Lima, Peru, a city of eight million people, shanty towns sprawl across barren desert land. Yet their inhabitants produce everything from sweet potatoes and artichokes to chicken, fish and pork. Many of these urban farmers are recent immigrants from the Andes mountains, where agriculture has been a way of life for thousands of years. Their skills have been put to good use, providing much needed food and income to poor neighbourhoods.[20]

In Mexico City, where some 18 million people live on about 100,000 hectares, the rural background of many of the city's inhabitants has assured vigorous urban agriculture and the food self-reliance of large numbers of people within one of the largest urban concentrations of the world. Local milk supply is an interesting feature and 1.7 million inhabitants rely on urban dairy farmers for their milk and cheese. Here in many small dairy businesses, Holstein cows from the mechanised stables on the outskirts of the city are milked by hand, with their owners selling the milk to the public. Most of the fodder for the cows comes from wastes generated by the city's large fruit and vegetable distribution centres.[21]

In Siberia urban farming is thriving, too, despite its cold climate. On the outskirts of cities such as Irkutsk, on the shores of Lake Baikal, I have seen people grow an amazing variety of vegetables, both for private consumption and for sale in the city's markets. Producers, who usually live in tower blocks in the city, grow vegetables and fruit in their private dacha gardens. They extend the very short growing season by providing tomatoes, cucumbers and even melons in well-insulated greenhouses.

Urban farming in Siberia
Even in the cool summer climate in Siberia vegetable gardens thrive and most people grow their own soft fruit and vegetables on the edge of cities.

URBAN FARMING IN THE USA

Anybody who thinks that urban farming is only a phenomenon of poorer countries should have a look around parts of New York City. In the Bronx, one can find an astonishing range of vegetable gardens that sprang up in the 1980s, primarily in areas where drug-related gang warfare had resulted in houses being burned down and left abandoned. With the help of staff from New York Botanical Gardens, local people have turned dozens of vacant lots into thriving vegetable gardens. Many grow crops for the sake of their children, wanting them to learn about growing vegetables and keeping chickens and rabbits. All over the world this is a very important aspect of urban agriculture.

In deindustrialising cities such as Pittsburgh and Detroit, thousands of acres of land have been given over to food growing by unemployed workers. In California, too, urban farming is widely practised. In San Francisco, a highly effective urban farming scheme has been set up for prisoners inside jail. In a six-year programme, prisoners in one of the county jails work on a ten-acre garden within the prison grounds and learn to become gardeners. Former inmates who have moved back into the community then get the opportunity to work as gardeners for a wage.[22] In the university city of Davis, some enlightened developers decided to build a 'permaculture' suburb in the 1980s. They surrounded the new solar-powered and heated houses with vegetable plots and orchards. There is even a vineyard that produces wine right in the middle of Davis.

The revival of urban and peri-urban commercial agriculture in the USA is remarkable because one would not expect it in such an affluent country. The 1990, US census found that urban metropolitan areas produced 40 per cent of the dollar value of US agricultural production, up from 30 per cent in 1980.[23] Clever marketing, as well as consumers' desire to know where their food comes from, has a lot to do with it.

The rapid increase in the numbers of farmers' markets speaks for itself. By 2002, some 2,000 new farmers' markets were operating in US cities, often specialising in organic produce and allowing growers to market their produce to local customers. They have proved that growing crops for local consumption can be both lucrative and environmentally beneficial.

In some places, urban fringe cultivation has been developed as community-supported agriculture: in such schemes participants purchase a share in any produce in advance and have a say in what crops are grown. Participants have the right to visit the farm and help with the cultivation and harvesting of crops. Vegetable box schemes, providing customers with a selection of vegetables in season, also enjoy growing popularity. The distribution is often subcontracted to local traders.

URBAN FARMING IN THE UK

In the UK, there has been considerable pressure on urban farming. In Nazeing in Essex, on the outskirts of London, one can see how things have changed. Like Heathrow, Nazeing used to be a major centre for vegetable growing, in

Food growing in the Bronx
In the Bronx in New York derelict land has been given over to local people to grow crops for their own consumption and enjoyment.

a landscape covered in greenhouses. But today few growers can compete with cheap, imported vegetables and many had to abandon their plots. Those that are left produce only one crop, cucumbers. They grow these hydroponically, in greenhouses that look like operating theatres, with the plants surrounded by white sheets of plastic. Most of the growers are not British by origin, but are the offspring of Italian prisoners of war. After the war, they gradually took over the greenhouses, because in the winter months they can keep on supplying supermarkets by trucking over lorryloads of cucumbers from southern Italy.

In some cities, such as Bristol, attempts have recently been made to set up new organic market garden schemes. At Leigh Court outside the city, an abandoned market garden has been revived and a successful organic vegetable box scheme set up. But things are not easy. It is difficult to compete with imported vegetables and two-thirds of the organic vegetables that are consumed in Britain are actually trucked in from elsewhere, accumulating lots of energy consumption and food miles in the process. Nevertheless, we are seeing significant initial steps to try to revive urban fringe agriculture in cities across

Farmers' market
Urban farmers' markets are thriving in rich as well as poorer countries. By direct sales, farmers cut out middlemen and customers get fresh food.

the UK. Like in the USA, there has also been a rapid increase in the number of farmers' markets, to about 300 in 2002.

Many people continue to associate urban cultivation with times of desperate need. But there are still hundreds of thousands of people cultivating allotments, or community gardens, across the UK. Traditionally retired men used to cultivate allotments, but increasingly younger middle-class people want to grow some of the vegetables for their families and have taken over empty plots. At a time when work sharing is becoming the norm for large numbers of urban people, additional opportunities to create livelihoods or leisure activities for themselves are regarded as important. Urban food growing is certainly one of the options.

Allotment holders have a variety of motives: some people mainly want to supply food for their families and achieve greater self-determination. Others want to get closer to nature and relieve stress. Others want to contribute to making British cities more sustainable and reduce dependence on farmland across the world.

URBAN FARMING AND PLANNING POLICY

Planners and urban administrators are often not keen on urban food production. They tend to think of it as a messy business for which there is no room in modern cities. But there is a growing consensus that urban agriculture is important for many people, in rich and poor cities, and should have government support at national as well as municipal level. Urban farming is now widely seen as an important source of food and income generation, and as something that should be supported by adequate institutional frameworks.

Opposition to urban agriculture has also come from public health authorities because of concern about the use of polluted water for irrigating crops and soil contamination by industry and transport. However, research has shown that there are ways of dealing with contamination. While land polluted by heavy metals, such as cadmium and lead, does require special precautions by growers, this problem can be tackled in various ways. Growers are encouraged to maintain a high soil pH with addition of plenty of lime to help immobilise heavy metals. Also, it is useful to add plenty of compost to the soil and to plant crops using the 'deep bed method'—creating vegetable beds in wooden or brick frames on top of the soil surface.

Creating nutrient-rich soil is not usually a problem in cities because, by definition, they are places where plant nutrients accumulate in great abundance. There is no need to use chemical fertilisers. A great variety of organic materials can be composted and incorporated into garden soil—kitchen wastes, old newspapers, the leaves of city trees, and even human and animal faeces. The issue of waste water irrigation in urban agriculture has already been discussed in Chapter 11.

In times of crisis, such as war or recession, growing food has always been essential to the survival of city people. Today, many cities that have experienced industrial decline and derelict land should be made available for food growing. In a period of economic globalisation, substantial unemployment is endemic in many cities, forcing large numbers of people to adopt new survival strategies, including spending some of their time on growing food. The provision of land for urban agriculture is certainly becoming a significant planning policy option. In Britain, city farm projects have already been established on derelict land in some 20 cities. In Germany, derelict land in former coal mining cities such as Essen has been set aside for urban agriculture projects.

Rather than competing with rural agriculture, urban and rural agriculture should be seen as complementing each other. Urban farming usually focuses on products that require closeness to urban markets, such as perishable vegetables, fresh milk, flowers and ornamental plants, and poultry. In both rich and poor cities demand for local produce is on the increase. Urban farming contributes to both the liveability and the sustainability of cities, and planners should recognise that it is important to set aside land for such purposes, both within cities and as an integral part of urban greenbelts.

CHAPTER 13

Building
EcoPolis

The voyage of discovery is not in seeking new landscapes but in having new eyes. (Marcel Proust)

The world is no longer divided by the ideologies of 'left' and 'right,' but by those who accept ecological limits and those who don't. (Wolfgang Sachs, 2003)

It is in the cities of the 21st century that human destiny will be played out and the future of the biosphere will be determined. For many years, people all over the world have been trying to think of ways in which modern cities can be made truly sustainable. The fact is that urbanisation is an immensely powerful phenomenon and it would be an illusion to think that the large cities that have sprung up all over the world will somehow go away, even if we wanted them to. Huge investments have been made in infrastructure, housing, public and commercial buildings and these are increasing further every day. The vast urban clusters that are emerging as a result are now a fact of life. It is crucial, therefore, to try to convert our cities into sustainable habitats in which we can truly enjoy our lives.

Many of the world's major environmental—and indeed social and economic—problems will only be solved through finding innovative ways of redesigning and managing our cities. But this requires us profoundly to change the value systems embedded in our urban and our national cultures. Only a deep cultural transformation—feeding through into new personal attitudes, political engagement, economic practices and uses of technology—can ensure that we take the necessary steps.

People in premier cities like London, Los Angeles and New York are setting the dominant patterns of contemporary culture that ripple around the planet. They have imposed a new, seemingly self-confident order on the world that has everything to do with human endeavour and pride. But they have tended to forget that for their physical existence, and for the very air they breathe, they depend on the integrity and health of the natural world—from their local hinterland to the living earth as a whole.

Peter Huber, who writes for *City Journal* and the *Wall Street Journal* in New York, is aware of the concerns of environmental groups about the impact of urban production and consumption, but he ultimately dismisses them somewhat triumphantly. He says in an article called 'How Cities Green the Planet':

> *Think of the skyscraper as America's great green gift to the planet.*
> *It packs more people onto less land, which leaves more wilderness*
> *undisturbed in other places, where the people aren't.*[1]

This perspective may contain a grain of truth. Compact cities do indeed save areas of wilderness from direct human occupation because they confine large numbers of people in relatively small spaces. And large cities do have some potential to maximise human benefit with minimal environmental impact. But Huber then goes on to say that places like Manhattan are good for the planet because they no longer primarily rely on farms and forests for their key supplies, and that the primary feedstock of modern cities is subterranean resources, developed by urban finance and science:

> *There was abroad, at one time, the notion that cities grew*
> *parasitically off the countryside, that all economic wealth derived*
> *from the land, and that the city grew rich only by expropriating*
> *the bounty of honest folk who tilled the soil. If this were ever true,*
> *it's no longer true today. The industrial revolution severed half the*
> *links between wealth and land; the information revolution has*
> *severed most of the rest. Wealth now springs from the third*
> *dimension, beneath the surface, and from the fourth, the*
> *boundless caverns of the mind. The city, its capital, and its*
> *knowledge are the fonts of those kinds of wealth.*[2]

Huber's triumphalism gets in the way of sober analysis. One of his key arguments concerns the carbon dioxide discharged by cities. Huber says the reafforestation that has been occurring across the USA is sufficient to reabsorb the collective carbon dioxide output of cities, including New York, and is sufficient to counter climate change. This is simply incorrect. In 2002, the USA as a whole discharged 1.63 billion tonnes of carbon dioxide into the atmosphere and under a business-as-usual scenario, this will rise to 2.1 billion tonnes by 2020.[3] US cities (including New York) produce at least 80 per cent of this carbon dioxide. To absorb it would require a forested area more than twice the entire land surface of the United States. The ecological footprint of the US as a whole is nearly three times its surface area.[4] By 2100, Huber's supposedly sustainable New York may well have the rising waters of the Hudson River lapping at the foundations of the very skyscrapers that he considers to be a great green gift to the planet.

Creating sustainable cities requires us to think quite differently. If we wish to live in cities, including New York, we need fundamentally to transform the way they use resources, and to turn concepts of sustainability into a practical reality. It remains to be seen whether gas-guzzling megacities of millions of people can undergo a process of ecological redesign. This will certainly require vigorous and determined efforts. According to a detailed study by four major US Research Institutes:

> By 2010, U.S. emissions of carbon dioxide . . . could be cut to 10 per cent below 1990 levels while national energy costs are reduced by $530 per household annually and nearly 800,000 additional jobs are created.[5]

Voluntary measures will not sufficiently reduce greenhouse gases and there is an urgent need for a mandatory climate change policy to address carbon emissions.[6]

WHAT SIZE CITIES?

Many people have deplored the emergence of ever-larger cities all over the world. Living in cities with many millions of people, we have departed from a close attachment to nature. Can a world of megacities be viable in the long term—environmentally, socially or economically? Can large cities reconfigure themselves into sustainable eco-technical systems? In a sustainable world, is there a limit to the size of cities? How much urbanisation is enough?

Large cities certainly have much to offer in terms of social interaction, cultural diversity and economic opportunities. But the fact is that two-thirds of urban residents live in cities of half a million people or less, although even these are still much larger than most cities in previous human history.

Can we find ways to encourage the resurgence of smaller cities? At the 1976 Habitat Conference, the UN's first major conference on cities, a major concern was to try to prevent large-scale urbanisation worldwide. At that time images were proliferating in television programmes and magazine articles of appalling living conditions for vast numbers of people. It was becoming apparent that in many places urban growth was occurring haphazardly and without adequate planning. As I sought to show in Chapter 5, urbanisation can increase people's living standards, but it can also pose major health threats, particularly for the hundreds of millions of people who live in slums and squatter camps without inadequate infrastructures and with high concentrations of pollutants and disease.

Cities all over the world need to reemerge as centres of a sustainable civilisation, as places of creativity, health, beauty and conviviality and above all else of sedentary living. To be viable in the long term, they need great public spaces and buildings, with good and affordable housing and adequate facilities for community living.

CULTURE AND SUSTAINABILITY

Thought has created the unstable world in which we now live—manifested in megatechnology, megacities, global power structures and vast environmental impacts. Today thought also generates new ideas for creating liveable and sustainable cities.

A key issue we need to address is how the tremendous creativity of urban people can be applied to the imperative of sustainable development. Premier cities like London, New York and Los Angeles are global hubs of human creativity, as expressed in their large and diverse range of cultural activities. Their very cultural success tends to make them see themselves as centres of the universe: with their music and film industries, broadcasting and publishing houses, cultural institutions, universities, advertising and design companies, and financial and commercial enterprises. They need to be challenged to actively summon their creativity to support rather than undermine sustainable production and consumption.

Disney Concert Hall, Los Angeles
Frank Gehry's Disney Concert Hall has given a new cultural focus to downtown LA. How can such powerful expressions of artistic creativity be harnessed to the imperative of sustainable urban development?

The success of the cultural industries in large cities is now being copied in smaller ones. Creativity and culture have come to feature strongly in the toolkit of urban regeneration. Music venues, theatres, museums and universities are widely seen as a new economic base for cities. Universities attract fee-paying students, often from abroad, and cities with vibrant cultures attract crowds of visitors. The concept of the creative and knowledge-based city has been tested across Europe and America, and has certainly contributed to the revival of many places, including Bilbao, Liverpool, Newcastle, Glasgow, Chattanooga and Pittsburgh.

It is worth being cautious, however, about thinking that cultural revival will always be a sufficient condition for urban regeneration. Cities go in and out of fashion. Tourist-based regeneration, in particular, can suffer as visitors make different choices and decide to go elsewhere instead. The cultural dynamism of cities should certainly be directed towards creating master-pieces of human creativity. But a calmer, more serene, more self-reliant vision of cities may be needed now, one that helps them fulfil their potential as places where the human spirit can flower.

Cultural vibrancy should be seen as a key component of sustainable urban development, ensuring that cities realise their full potential as centres of creativity, education and communication. If cultural regeneration is linked to sustainable urban development, many different social sectors can become involved. Politicians, developers, architects, civil engineers, designers, journalists, writers, teachers, film makers and youth groups are all needed to make a difference. It is particularly important to encourage the media to do imaginative reporting on the challenges and benefits of sustainability, and the potential for the ecological redesign of cities.

BEST PRACTICE AND PARTICIPATION

To make informed decisions, people need a good knowledge base. For this purpose the collection and dissemination of best practices are crucial, giving people information about projects that have made cities into better places. Ever since the publication of Agenda 21 at the Rio Earth Summit in 1992, cities have been at the centre of a growing global effort to create a healthy, more equitable and environmentally sustainable world. The 1996, Habitat II Conference in Istanbul made much of the fact that while cities are places where problems can proliferate, city people also want to improve their situation wherever possible.

The UN Habitat Best Practices and Local Leadership programme was a flagship initiative of the Istanbul conference. Since 1996, it has collected thousands of examples from around the world, which can be accessed on the Internet, and it has maintained direct contacts with urban groups worldwide, reaching even the poorest communities. The programme allows cities to link into these activities and to utilise local expertise in sustainability as a transferable, worldwide resource.[7] The International Council for Local Environment Initiatives (ICLEI) has also compiled a substantial body of material on best practices that is being disseminated through its own very substantial global network.[8]

Best practice initiatives cover issues such as:

- poverty reduction and job creation,
- crime prevention and social justice,
- access to shelter and land,
- development of urban agriculture,

- improved production/consumption cycles,
- gender and social diversity,
- infrastructure, water and energy supply,
- enterprise and economic development,
- innovative use of technology,
- waste recycling and reuse,
- environmental protection and restoration,
- improved transport and communication,
- participatory governance and planning,
- self-help development techniques,
- women's banks and local money systems.

In a global process many organisations and websites are now dealing with good practices for turning cities into sustainable and liveable places, as well as policies and implementation processes. With an ever-growing number of people becoming urban dwellers, an exciting mutual learning process has been initiated. All over the world people are forming alliances to improve their local environment, to improve housing and living conditions and to reduce environmental impacts.[9]

Sustainability is no longer of interest only to 'greenies'. More and more people are becoming aware of their stake in a sustainable world and of the fact that our lifestyles today will profoundly affect the chances of coming generations to shape their *own* future. In this context, it is crucial to extend popular participation in decision making to restore people's confidence in local democracy. Neighbourhood forums, action planning and consensus building should be widely practised, because under appropriate circum-stances these processes lead to better decisions and easier, more cost-effective implementation. With the help of modern communications technologies, wider citizen involvement can be incorporated in strategic decision making. Says Charles Landry of the UK consultancy COMEDIA:

> *All new forms of democratic involvement of people in decisions about their city's future depend upon radical notions of debate, conversation and communication. This means that people and the potential of 'human capital' have to be recognised as major assets for city futures.*[10]

For this purpose people need the chance to meet across social sectors in order for a critical mass of committed individuals to emerge, and this applies

Curitiba Environment University
Curitiba's open air Environment University brings together young and old to learn about their city and to help shape its future.

particularly to young people. Curitiba set up a 'University of the Environment' where people, young and old, can learn about sustainability in an atmosphere of creativity and fun. All cities would greatly benefit from such centres where people learn together in a purposeful and dynamic way.

THE DIGITAL ECOCITY

Cities have always been centres of communication and electronic systems have dramatically enhanced that role. If, as author Manuel Castells suggests, the new economy is organised around global networks of capital, management and information, will other voices get a chance to be heard? Can communication emanating from cities reflect the sustainability imperative?

Making sure that cities create and maintain stable relationships with the world around them is a new task for everybody—financiers, business people, city politicians, administrators and people at large. New tools are required to help us make appropriate decisions. The global power of

COM A RECICLAGEM CURITIBA SALVOU

4072180

ÁRVORES
SE TODAS AS CIDADES DO BRASIL
SEGUISSEM ESTE EXEMPLO:

81493686

LIXO QUE NÃO É LIXO
50 Kg DE PAPEL
= 1 ÁRVORE
CURITIBA
PREFEITURA MUNICIPAL

Ecofeedback
In some cities, such as Curitiba, public displays indicate how many trees have been saved by timber and paper recycling by citizens.

our cities needs to be matched with early warning systems enabling us to respond to undesirable developments as they occur. One such tool is *eco-feedback*—which allows us to account to ourselves for our impacts on the planet and ways to ameliorate them.

Eco-feedback is a system of information feedback that helps individuals subtly change their behaviour patterns in accordance with their own experiences. The concept was first developed by an organisation called the Global Action Plan (GAP) to help householders regularly monitor their use of energy and water and their output of waste. GAP members work together in groups in which people learn to save money by making better choices and by reducing the environmental impacts of their lifestyles.

In Curitiba, eco-feedback is used by the city authorities in public displays that indicate how paper and timber recycling reduces the city's impacts on forests, and encourages people's personal involvement in recycling schemes. Such displays could also be used, for instance, to indicate when air pollution has reached dangerous levels. This would be particularly effective if accompanied by incentives from local authorities to reduce the need for car travel. Eco-feedback displays could also help improve communication between cities regarding sustainability initiatives, perhaps in conjunction with urban intranets.

SUSTAINABLE CONSUMPTION: JAPAN'S SEIKATSU CLUB

At times of relative affluence and of growing environmental pressure, there always seems to be a reaction from sections of society. This was so in 19th-century Europe and America as the romantic movement emerged, and in the 20th century with the rise of the green movement. The same has occurred in Japan, and a prominent example is the Seikatsu Consumer Club.

Consumer action is crucial for changing attitudes. Japan's Seikatsu Club—or 'livelihood club'—with 12 million members throughout the country is probably the world's most powerful example of successful consumer action. Around 95 per cent of its members are women. They believe that housewives can help create a society that is harmonious with nature by taking action from their homes. The Club refuses to handle products that are detrimental to the health of its members or the environment. In 1989, it received the 'Right Livelihood Award', the alternative Nobel Prize, in recognition of its achievements.

The Club was formed in 1965 to allow its members to buy milk and subsequently other drinks in bulk. Reusing rather than recycling bottles became symptomatic of the Club's concern with the environment. As a result of its efforts, bottle sizes in local bottling plants have now been standardised. This allows for more than eight million bottles to be reused every year. Bottles first used for milk return refilled with fruit juice or soy sauce in a continuous cycle of reuse. This helps to reduce waste, but also makes people aware of the waste disposal problems of modern society.

After the Club's initial focus on milk, some members began to study the quality and safety of the food they were buying in the shops. When products were found wanting, the Seikatsu women petitioned growers and food processors to make improvements. Increasingly they started buying direct from approved producers and so realised their joint purchasing power.

An advance ordering and joint buying system enables Club members to plan their consuming life and provides continuity to producers. The Club is dedicated to the environment, empowerment of women and improvement of workers' conditions. Using environmental ethics that make economic sense, it provides low-cost household goods to high environmental standards. It procures quality food by signing contracts with local farmers. The Club buys the produce in exchange for a guarantee that only organic fertilisers and the fewest possible chemicals will be used. When they cannot find products of adequate quantity or quality, Club members will consider producing them themselves instead.

With the growth in female participation in Japan's labour force, the Seikatsu Club set up women workers' collectives to undertake both distribution and other service enterprises, including health, education, food preparation and child care. It encourages political action and has managed to get over 100 members elected to various municipal councils, aiming to 'change daily life and change the society'. The Club has also established a not-for-profit insurance company for its ever-growing membership.

ECOLOGICAL (RE)DESIGN

Paul Downton of Urban Ecology, Australia, proposes a fundamental change in the way we conceptualise our cities:

> *Cities are the human nest—they are where most of us live. They could reflect the values of life-enhancing, health-giving cultures. If cities are central to the ecological crisis they must became parts of its solution . . . An ecological city is as much about balance between human society as it is about balance between humans and nature. An Ecopolis is . . . a package of concepts, ethics and programs for making cities that are places of ecological restoration.*[11]

Creating truly sustainable, post-fossil fuel cities is perhaps the greatest task of the coming decades. It is also a particular challenge for the architectural and engineering companies that design and build our cities. Can they stimulate the development of solar buildings by developing their own initiatives? The London engineering company Battle McCarthy has developed a comprehensive ecological design philosophy for building construction. It summarises this as follows:

> *The primary goal of engineering is to maximise benefits in the efficient use of materials, energy and skills . . . Engineering has a tendency to resist and exclude natural forces, creating an isolated envelope where energy-intensive machinery is required to maintain the internal environment. Yet engineering is dominated by natural phenomena: gravity and wind forces, temperature and humidity, light and sound, air quality and movement, vibration and reverberation.*

The building structure and envelope should be used not to resist, but to filter, channel and deflect critical natural forces, to create an internal environment geared towards the building's function, to provide light, heating, cooling, sound modulation and fresh air for the comfort of the occupants. The functions of structure and skin then merge, allowing the building to become an integrated mechanism that combines comfort and structural stability . . . acting as moderators between humans and the environment.[12]

SUSTAINABLE GOA: CITIES AS SELF-RELIANT SYSTEMS

In India the environmentalist Aromar Revi and his architect colleague Sanjay Prakash have identified the need for a new urbanism they call 'RUrbanism'. Their aim is to assure that cities are well adapted to local ecosystems and their potential to supply resources on a sustainable basis. In a plan for the ecological redesign of the city of Panjim in Goa, they make the following points:

'RUrbanism' is the sustainable integration of rural and urban communities. It is a sophisticated new set of design principles and practices governing land use, energy, transportation, governance, and all aspects of economic, ecological, and social development for a major city. It is a new framework for thinking about how to put an existing city onto a pathway toward genuine sustainability— particularly a city in the developing world, but the framework could apply in many other contexts. A new set of principles for sustainable infrastructure design was developed for the static (long-lasting) and dynamic (fast-changing) elements of the city. The design takes living biological systems as its starting point.

The city is reimagined as an organism, with cells, skeletal structures, circulatory systems, and skin as the metaphors and models for the buildings, neighbourhoods, transportation systems, and the meeting points between city and rural or natural spaces. Urban and rural meet each other in many small pockets, where dwellings jut out, and rural land juts in. One can imagine nearly everyone looking out their windows onto rice paddies and vegetable gardens, and beyond to forest and farm land. The boundaries between city and country remain clear; and yet country is much closer to city, and the interdependence between both is plainly visible to all, and indeed experienced daily.[13]

Revi has identified seven organising principles for sustainability:

- The basic human needs of all people should be satisfied and they should be provided with an equal opportunity to realise their human potential.
- Material needs should be met materially and non-material needs non-materially.
- Renewable resources should not be used faster than their regeneration rates.
- Non-renewable resources should not be used faster than their substitution rates by renewable resources.
- Pollution and waste should not be produced faster than the rate of absorption, recycling or transformation.
- The precautionary principle should be applied where the 'response' time is potentially less than the 'respite' time.

Similar ideas have been developed in Britain by the Bioregional Development Group, which, together with the Peabody Trust and the architect Bill Dunster, created the Beddington Zero Energy Development in South London, already described in Chapter 8. Pooran Desai and Sue Riddlestone, in their book *Bioregional Solutions*, described the importance of creating sustainable, bioregional economies in and around our cities, which make sustainable use of local resources by adding value in a series of production processes that also create new, local jobs. In conjunction with the World Wide Fund for Nature they have come up with the concept of One-Planet Living, reducing the ecological footprint of people living in Europe by two-thirds. Their approach combines the creation of highly energy- and resource-efficient buildings with a lifestyle that is, above all else, concerned with resilience and sustainability.

BUILDING ECOPOLIS

I would like to conclude this book with a practical vision of a truly liveable and sustainable city. EcoPolis is a term that is used by various organisations around the world. I employ it here as a generic term for the sustainable cities of the future. Imagine the following scenario, which summarises many of the ingredients of a sustainable, large modern city.

EcoPolis is a city that has gone through two decades of transformation. By 2020, it has made tremendous progress in ecological redesign. Its people have applied a purposeful global perspective informed by great cultural energy and ethnic diversity to their local situation. It is a place where people from many parts of the world inspire each other with their own unique stories, their creative imagination and their determination to foster tolerance and respect.

At the start of the new millennium the creation of a new elected, strategic authority, which enshrined the rights of the public to participate actively in decision making, has proved to be of enormous consequence. Public apathy has given way to a lively popular culture. Reluctant, passive acceptance has given way to active participation in urban life. In EcoPolis, playfulness is greatly encouraged and there has been a renaissance of the arts and cultural creativity. Comedians on various TV and radio channels have their own shows that make fun of the 'good old days' of graffiti, smog, traffic jams and sewage in the river.

EcoPolis draws on the best available knowledge on sustainable urban development from around the world. It is an active member of various national and international city organisations that share databases on urban best practice regarding transport, energy and recycling technology, health care, education, housing and strategies for sustainable business. With its partner cities around the world, it both disseminates and acquires knowledge on implementing a sustainable future.

Zero-energy buildings of all kinds have become the norm rather than the exception, greatly reducing the city's overall energy consumption without forgoing high living standards. Long debates about architectural styles have led to the pursuit of aesthetically pleasing architecture that also creates optimal living and working conditions. Architectural practices and civil engineering companies in EcoPolis now derive substantial revenues from exporting their know-how around the world.

Regeneration and sustainable development

A participatory culture helped EcoPolis become a city aiming to work towards great environmental quality, enhanced by the creation of many new small parks and the planting of many more trees. Imagine a city that has rediscovered its local roots, its bioregion, with its river as its main artery. After decades of being neglected and ignored, the city's river and canal network have been reincorporated into its life as transport routes and as water parks for easy access by its people. At weekends they are full of boats, with many anglers sitting on their banks.

Strategic spatial planning acquired a major new impetus due to the policies of the strategic authority. In preparing its Sustainability Plan, the people of EcoPolis have greatly benefited from drawing on the rich variety of expertise present in the city. The city's EcoPlan helped ensure that many empty brownfield sites were filled with new housing, parks, urban farms, employment and cultural centres, with substantial social and employment benefits. The plan also has also made sure that EcoPolis, despite continuing population growth, does not spill over into the greenbelt around the city.

EcoPolis in 2020 has become a city very different from the hyper-modern chrome and plastic urban visions that predominated after the Second World War. It has come to see its role not in being flashy, but in pioneering the liveable and sustainable city. The many new buildings constructed in the last 20 years were increasingly inspired by the vision of sustainable design. Incentives from central government have strongly encouraged developers to create new buildings, including tall buildings, that are constructed to the highest ecological and energy efficiency standards. And with much of the inherited building stock undergoing regular renovation, ecological upgrading of the existing stock has also become the norm.

A city that was the product of fossil fuel technology is well on its way to being powered largely by renewable energy. Much-improved building insulation standards have ensured that an ever-increasing number of buildings minimise the need for heating even on the coldest winter days. Individual buildings have dramatically reduced their need for external energy supplies by using photovoltaic cells on their walls and roofs, with the electricity grid often used only as a back-up. Groups of buildings share fuel cell-operated combined heat and power systems.

The economy

What has sustainability meant for urban businesses? Businesses in EcoPolis, like everywhere else, certainly have the desire to continue. Each wants to be sustainable in its own right, in its own particular way within its own market segment. In EcoPolis the new emphasis on sustainable development has rekindled the entrepreneurial spirit. It has become both a market and a production centre for environmental technology. New manufacturing plants for green technologies have sprung up in many places, particularly on brownfield sites. Photovoltaic modules, fuel cell systems and a wide range of eco-friendly building materials are now being made in new production centres on the outskirts of the city and employ large numbers of people. The expertise gained in this field has helped greatly to increase EcoPolis's share of manufacturing, exporting both products and know-how.

The financial services sector has also gone through a great transformation. There is a major new emphasis on funding new local business rather than forever scouring the world for investment opportunities. EcoPolis has purposefully developed its know-how in ethical investment and become a leader in financing and supporting sustainable development elsewhere. It now acts as a key broker for expertise and investment in all aspects of sustainable management. Carbon trading and reforestation projects, in particular, have increasingly taken over from financing environmentally destructive logging and mining.

EcoPolis has also created 'affordable business premises' for thousands of new small- and medium-size companies. This development was enhanced by the widely held view that the city should have the benefit of a diverse economy, offering opportunities for the many varied skills present in its population, not merely a monolithic emphasis on finance, insurance and other services.

Many entrepreneurs in EcoPolis have started new ethical or green businesses. These have proved to be profitable as well as socially and environmentally responsible. The new emphasis on fair trade by many companies guarantees a fair price to growers and producers for their goods and products. Organic farmers and food processors have greatly gained in market share.

There is now a green or ethical choice in most business sectors, changing the way in which business is done, including social and environmental concerns in the whole investment process. EcoPolis's businesses have grasped a historic opportunity to implement their own measures for sustainable development. They have become aware of their responsibility to help reduce the ecological footprint of their city.

Transport

The air is cleaner for a number of reasons: there have been major developments in sustainable transport technology, with clean, fuel cell-powered vehicles now predominant on the streets. When stationary, they don't burn fuel or utilise battery power. The optimal integration between private and public transport systems has become a central feature of transport policy. There is also a new emphasis on local living and local employment opportunities, and walking and cycling have returned across the city as significant modes of personal transport.

Traffic has greatly benefited from strategic planning measures and it is now much easier to get around the city. Road pricing in the city centre has contributed to major improvements in travel patterns, with more and more people choosing to use public transport and shared taxis. New cost-effective, fuel cell-powered shared taxis, with semi-fixed routes across the city, have been greatly welcomed. Cyclists can use dedicated bike lanes, the number of which has grown, and new pedestrian zones within EcoPolis have contributed to local development.

Waste management

EcoPolis has also transformed its waste system. While it used to dump most solid waste in landfill sites, it has now adopted a zero waste system. From being a world leader in waste dumping it has turned into a leader in reuse, recycling and remanufacturing, creating tens of thousands of 'green-collar' jobs in the process. Much of this is organised on a local scale, in conjunction with community employment schemes. A wide range of new industries have sprung up adding value to waste. Discarded glass bottles are turned into new flooring materials, and plastic waste is made into park benches or even into fibres for the fashion industry. And virtually all bio-waste is now composted.

Local revival

With greater emphasis on local production for local need, EcoPolis has also created new local trading centres. Many covered malls have been created, with a great diversity of workshops and community shops accessible under one roof. These also contain voting booths in which people can contribute to democratic decision making on key issues affecting their city. Whenever decisions directly affect the future of young people, they too are invited to register their vote and voice their views.

EcoPolis is a city of gardens and people cherish their colourful flower and wildlife gardens. Now there are also more fruit trees and vegetables are grown again, both within the city and on its periphery. Urban farming, neglected for many years, has been revived. New market gardens on the edge of the city have been complemented by dozens of farmers' markets. Community gardens have gained new popularity, with shared greenhouses and cafés as part of the scene. The revival of community gardening has also occurred because the city's air is cleaner than before and people feel safer about growing crops, for their own use and even for sale.

A sense of community has regained a central role in EcoPolis. Community and neighbourhood are reasserting themselves because they provide crucial frameworks for social belonging. However, this is complemented by inter-national networking facilitated by global communication systems.

Notting Hill Carnival
Dancing in the street, such as is this city carnival, can make an enormous contribution to the enjoyment of urban living, though not everybody may want to join in.

Ken Yeang eco-tower
The Malaysian architect Ken Yeang is a pioneer in 'bio-climatic' architecture. His tall buildings are full of greenery to reduce the need for air conditioning and to create a pleasant environment within the building.

FINALE

If we get things right in the coming years and decades, cities will become the beacons of a culture of sustainability. They will be energy and resource efficient, people friendly, ethnically diverse and culturally rich. In large northern cities enhanced sustainability will contribute significantly to employment. In cities in the south, significant investment in infrastructure will make make a vast difference to health and living conditions.

The greatest energy of cities should flow *inwards*, to create masterpieces of human creativity, not *outwards*, to draw in ever more products from ever more distant places. The future of cities crucially depends on utilising the rich knowledge of their people, and that includes environmental knowledge. Cities ultimately are what their people are. If we decide to create sustainable cities, we need to create a cultural context for them. In the end, only a profound change of attitudes, a spiritual and ethical change, can bring the deeper transformations required.

Creating urban lifestyles that are both comfortable and sustainable is desirable as well as perfectly feasible. In this book I have tried to assemble the evidence that we can create a revolution in urban problem solving—for the benefit of city people themselves as well as to reduce their impacts on the world. A wide variety of innovative approaches to urban planning and resource management are available to us, and to implement them we need vigorous new partnerships between all sectors of society—national governments, local authorities, community groups, NGOs and the private sector.

In cities all over the world a significant start has been made—let us realise the full potential of these opportunities.

Notes

CHAPTER 1

1. WWF, *Living Planet Report*, Gland, 2002.
2. Strong, Maurice, Address to the American Planning Association, Toronto, 9 April 1995.
3. United Nations, *World Urbanisation Prospects*, New York, 1999.
4. UN Habitat, *An Urbanizing World, Global Report on Human Settlements*, Oxford University Press, Oxford, 1996.
5. Girardet, Herbert, *Creating Sustainable Cities*, Schumacher Briefing 2, Green Books, 1999; O'Meara, Molly, 'Reinventing Cities', Worldwatch Paper 147, Worldwatch Institute, Washington, 1999.
6. Hallberg, Milton C., *Economic Trends in US Agriculture and World Food Systems since World War II*, Iowa State University Press, 2001.
7. Constanza, Robert, *et al.*, 'The Value of the World's Ecosystem Services and Natural Capital', *Nature*, 387: 253–60, 1997.
8. Agenda 21 text, www.un.org/esa/sustdev/documents/agenda21/english/agenda21toc.htm.
9. Aalborg Charter, www.iclei.org/europe/ECHARTER.HTM.
10. Istanbul Declaration, www.unhabitat.org/unchs/english/hagenda/ist-dec.htm.
11. Local Government Declaration to the World Summit on Sustainable Development, www.iclei.org/rioplusten/declaration_eng.pdf.
12. United Nations, *World Urbanisation Prospects*, New York, 1999.

13. Worldwatch Institute, Washington, www.worldwatch.org/press/news/2000/03/25/.
14. Cering, Doje, China's Minister of Civil Affairs, 14–8-2000, http://english.peopledaily.com.cn.
15. Basu, Sujay, 'Report on India's Energy Scene', www.helio-international.org/Helio/anglais/reports/india.html.
16. Joplin, John and Girardet, Herbert, *Creating a Sustainable London*, Sustainable London Trust, London, 1997.
17. Gorelick, Steven, Small is Beautiful, Big is Subsidised, ISEC, Week, Dartington, 1998.
18. International Panel on Climate Change (IPCC), 'Climate Change 2001, Synthesis Report', www.ipcc.ch/pub/SYRspm.pdf.
19. Watson, Robert, Interview for the *People's Planet* TV series.
20. Climate Biz, The Business Resource for Climate Management, www.climatebiz.com/sections/news_detail.cfm?NewsID=26271.
21. Weizsaecker, Ernst von, and Lovins, Amory, *Factor Four*, Earthscan Publications, London, 1997.
22. UN Habitat Best Practices website, www.bestpractices.org.
23. Critchfield, Richard, *Villages*, Anchor Press, Doubleday, New York, 1981.

CHAPTER 2

1. Mumford, Louis, *The City in History*, Pelican Books, London, 1966.
2. Sahlins, Marshall, *Stone Age Economics*, Aldine de Gruyter, 1972.
3. Flannery, Tim, *The Future Eaters*, Grove Press, New York, 1994.
4. Clottes, Jean, Conservateur General, 'Palaelithic Art in France', French Ministry of Culture, www.bradshawfoundation.com/clottes; Sieveking, Anne, *The Cave Artists*, Thames and Hudson, London, 1979; Clottes, Jean (ed.), *Return to Chauvet Cave: Excavating the Birthplace of Art*, Thames and Hudson, London, 2003.
5. Devore, Irven and Lee, Richard, *Man the Hunter*, Aldine, Chicago, 1968.
6. Hanotte, Bradley *et al.*, 'African Pastoralism, Genetic Imprints of Origins and Migrations', *Science*, 296, 2002.
7. Russell, Peter, www.peterussell.com/SP/Atlantis.html.
8. History of Jericho, www.jericho-city.org/history.html.
9. Joshua, 6.
10. Mellaart, James, *Catal-Huyuk, A Neolithic Town in Anatolia*, McGraw-Hill, New York, 1967.
11. Catal Huyuk website: http://catal.arch.cam.ac.uk.
12. Sumer's legacy, http://members.bellatlantic.net/~vze33gpz/sumer-faq.html.

13. www.dainst.org/index_2895_de.html.

14. www.wsu.edu/~dee/MESO/GILG.HTM.

15. Gilgamesh Epic, translation by Robert Temple, 1991.

16. Gilgamesh summary, http://www.wsu.edu:8080/~dee/MESO/GILG.HTM.

17. Whitehouse, Ruth, *The First Cities*, Phaidon, Oxford, 1977.

18. Woolley, C. Leonard, *Excavations at Ur*, Apollo Editions, New York, 1965.

19. McClung Museum, University of Tennessee, http://mcclungmuseum.utk.edu/specex/ur/ur-flood.htm.

20. Kramer, Samuel Noah, *The Sumerians*, Chicago University Press, Chicago, 1963; Ponting, Clive, *A Green History of the World*, Penguin Books, London, 1991.

21. Seymour, John and Girardet, Herbert, *Far From Paradise*, BBC Publications, London, 1986.

22. Brown, Lester, interview for the *People's Planet* TV series.

23. Gomme, A.W., *The Population of Athens in the Fifth and Fourth Centuries B.C.*, Basil Blackwell, Oxford, 1933.

24. From Plato, *Critias*, translated by Benjamin Jowett, Internet Classics, http://classics.mit.edu/Plato/critias.html.

CHAPTER 3

1. Hodge, A.T., *Roman Aqueducts and Water Supply*, Duckworth, London, 1992.

2. Frontinus, Sextus Julius, 'The Aqueducts of Rome', www.ku.edu/history/index/europe/ancient_rome/E/Roman/Texts/Frontinus/De_Aquis/text*.html.

3. Pliny the Elder, *Natural History*, Loeb Classical Library, Harvard University Press, Cambridge and London, 1989.

4. Perlin, John, *A Forest Journey: The Role of Wood in the Development of Civilization*, Harvard University Press, Cambridge and London, 1991.

5. De Vries, B. and Goudsblom, J. (eds), *Mappa Mundi: Humans and Their Habitats in a Long-Term Socio-Ecological Perspective*, Amsterdam University Press, Amsterdam, 2002.

6. Chevalier, Raymond, *Sciences et Techniques à Rome*, Presses Universitaires de France, Paris, 1993.

7. Auguet, R., *Cruelty and Civilization: The Roman Games*, Routledge, London, 1994.

8. Raven, Susan, *Rome in Africa*, Longman, London, 1984.

9. Carter, V.D. and Dale, T., *Topsoil and Civilisation*, University of Oklahoma Press, Norman, 1974.

10. Huntington, Ellsworth, *Civilization and Climate*, Yale University Press, New Haven, 1921.

11. Grant, Lindy and Bates, David (eds), *Abbot Suger of St-Denis: Church and State in Early Twelfth-century France*, Longman, London, 1998.
12. Perlin, John, *A Forest Journey: The Role of Wood in the Development of Civilization*, Harvard University Press, Cambridge and London, 1991.
13. Gimple, Jean, *Medieval Technology*, Victor Gollancz, London, 1976.
14. Thuenen, Johann Heinrich von, *The Isolated State*, Loyola University Press, Chicago, 1960.
15. Thuenen, Johann Heinrich von, http://people.hofstra.edu/geotrans/eng/ch6 en/conc6en/vonthunen.html.
16. Benevolo, Leonardo, *The History of the City*, Scolar Press, London, 1980, pp 292–4.
17. Barbaro, Nicolo, *Diary of the Siege of Constantinople in 1453*, translated by Jones, J.R., Exposition Press, New York, 1969.
18. Perlin, John, *A Forest Journey: The Role of Wood in the Development of Civilization*, Harvard University Press, Cambridge and London, 1991.
19. Galeano, Eduardo, *The Open Veins of Latin America: Five Centuries of the Pillage of a Continent*, Latin America Bureau, 1998.
20. Menzies, Gavin, *1421, The Year China Discovered the World*, Bantam Press, London, 2002.
21. *Japan for Sustainability Newsletter*, Nos. 8 and 9, www.japanfs.org/mail/index.html.

CHAPTER 4

1. Mumford, Lewis, *The City in History*, Secker and Warburg, London, 1961.
2. Bailey, Mark, 'Railway Regulation in the 19th Century', www.mfbailey.co.uk/economics/papers/rail.pdf.
3. Volti, Rudi, 'Steam Engine', *The Encyclopaedia of Science, Technology, and Society,* Facts on File, New York, 1999.
4. Teaching History Online, www.spartacus.schoolnet.co.uk/TEXcotton.htm.
5. Engels, Friedrich, *The Condition of the Working Class in England in 1844*, Swan, Sonnenschein, London, 1892.
6. Miller, Hugh, *The Old Red Sandstone or New Walks in an Old Field*, John Johnstone, Edinburgh, 1841.
7. Mumford, Lewis, *The City in History*, Secker and Warburg, London, 1961.
8. www.spartacus.schoolnet.co.uk/ITBradford.htm.
9. Archives Hub, Edinburgh University Library, www.archiveshub.ac.uk/news/02101803.html.
10. Mumford, Lewis, *The City in History*, Secker and Warburg, London, 1961.
11. Aston University, www.cs.aston.ac.uk/oldbrum/Housing.html.

12. Schofield, Robert, *Lunar Society of Birmingham*, Oxford University Press, Oxford, 1963.
13. Wohl, Anthony, *The Eternal Slum: Housing and Social Policy in Victorian London*, Edward Arnold and McGill-Queens University Press, 1977.
14. Robins, Nick, 'Loot: In Search of the East India Company', www.open-democracy.net/debates/article-7–29–904.jsp.
15. Jevons, William Stanley, *The Coal Question* [1865], Augustus M. Kelley, New York, 1965.
16. Gordon, Robert and Malone, Patrick, *The Texture of Industry, An Archaeological View of the Industrialization of North America*, Oxford University Press, Oxford, 1997.
17. Professor Michael Faraday, letter to editor of *The Times*, 5 July 1855.
18. Liebig, Justus, *Agriculturchemie*, Friedrich Vieweg und Sohn, Braunschweig, 1976, pp 88–92.
19. Hugo, Victor, *Les Misérables*, Jean Valjean, Book II, Chapter 1.
20. www.luise-berlin.de/bms/bmstxt97/9707gesc.htm.
21. Berlin's history, www.berlin-geschichte.de/Historie/.
22. Hahn, Hermann and Langbein, Fritz, *Fünfzig Jahre Berliner Stadtentwässerung 1878–1928*, Verlag Alfred Metzner, Berlin, 1928.
23. www.berliner-rieselfelder.de/Materialien/schlenther-etal-1996.pdf.
24. Hinshaw, John, *Steel and Steelworkers: Race and Class Struggle in Twentieth Century Pittsburgh*, State University of New York Press, Albany, 2002.
25. 'Demographia, City on a Hill', www.demographia.com/db-nyc2000.htm.
26. Goodwin, Jason, *Otis: Giving Rise to the Modern City: A History of the Otis Elevator Company*, Ivan R. Dee, Chicago, 2001.

CHAPTER 5

1. United Nations, *World Urbanisation Prospects*, New York, 1999.
2. United Nations University/Institute of Advanced Studies, 'Urban Ecosystem Analysis, 1993', www.ias.unu.edu/binaries/UNUIAS_UrbanReport2.pdf.
3. World Resources Institute Washington, 'Urban Growth', www.wri.org/wr-98–99/citygrow.htm.
4. United Nations, *World Urbanisation Prospects*, New York, 1999.
5. N'Dow, Wally, in Kirdar, Uener (ed.), *Cities Fit for People*, United Nations Publications, New York, 1997.
6. Ecosmart Concrete, www.ecosmart.ca/enviro_cement.cfm.
7. British Embassy, Beijing, 'Chinese Economy in Brief', information sheet, November 2003.

8. UN Habitat, *An Urbanizing World, Global Report on Human Settlements*, UN Centre for Human Settlements, 1996, p 13.

9. Alexander, Arthur J., 'Japan's Economy in the 20th Century', Japan Economic Institute Report No. 3, 2000, www.jei.org/Archive/JEIR00/0003f.html#premeijii.

10. Swaney, Dennis, Boyce Thompson Institute, Cornell, USA, www.edie.net/gf.cfm?L=left_frame.html&R=http://www.edie.net/news/Archive/5218.cfm.

11. *Japan for Sustainability Newsletter*, No. 2, www.japanfs.org/mail/index.html.

12. www.cepr.org/pubs/EEP/EEP22/inside%20information.htm.

13. www.tdctrade.com/tdcnews/9811/98111701.htm.

14. Castells, Manuel, *The Network Society*, Blackwell, Oxford, 1996.

15. Sassen, Saskia, *Cities in a World Economy*, Pine Forge Press, Thousand Oaks, CA, 2000; Sassen, Saskia, 'Cities in the Global Economy', in Paddison, Ronan (ed.), *Handbook of Urban Studies*, Sage, Thousand Oaks, CA, 2001.

16. Castells, Manuel, *The Network Society*, Blackwell, Oxford, 1996.

17. Heilig, Gerhard, 'Can China Feed Itself?', IIASA, Laxenburg, 1999, www.iiasa.ac.at/Research/LUC/ChinaFood/argu/trends/trend_30.htm.

18. Worldwatch Institute, *The State of the World, 1996*, Earthscan, London, 1997.

19. Trans Century Green Project Plan, http://us.tom.com/english/537.htm; http://svr1-pek.unep.net/soechina/drivf/driv51.htm.

20. Hardoy, Jorge, Mitlin, Diana and Satterthwaite, David, *Environmental Problems in Third World Cities*, Earthscan Publications, London, 1992.

21. McGrnahan, Gordon *et al.*, 'Sustainability, Poverty and Urban Environmental Transitions' in Satterthwaite, David (ed.), *Sustainable Cities*, Earthscan, London, 1999.

22. India Core, 'Investment Needs in Urban India', www.indiacore.com/urban-infra.html.

23. Abiodun, Josephine Olu, 'The Challenges of Growth and Development in Metropolitan Lagos', www.unu.edu/unupress/unupbooks/uu26ue/uu26ue0i.htm.

24. Davis, Mike, *Urban Control: The Ecology of Fear*, Open Magazine Pamphlet Series, 4, Westfield, New Jersey, 1994

25. Sara, Sally, *Letter from Johannesburg*, Australian Broadcasting Corporation, 19 September 2003

26. Louw, Antoinette *et al.*, 'Crime in Johannesburg', Institute for Security Studies, ISS Monograph Series No. 18, February 1998.

27. Knight, Richard, 'Housing in South Africa', http://richardknight.homestead.com/files/sisahousing.htm.

28. Cities Alliance, www.makingcitieswork.org/toolsAndResources/implementation/citiesAlliance.

29. Cities Alliance, www.citiesalliance.org/citiesalliancehomepage.nsf/.

30. Cities Alliance, *Cities Without Slums, Annual Report*, World Bank, Washington, 2002.
31. UNCHS, *Cities in a Globalising World: Global Report on Human Settlements*, Earthscan, London, 2001.

CHAPTER 6

1. Girardet, Herbert, 'Cities as Superorganisms', www.oneworld.org/guides/thecity/superorganisms.
2. Seeley, T.D., 'The Honey Bee Colony as a Superorganism', *American Scientist*, Vol. 77, November–December 1989.
3. Colding, J. *et al.,* 'The Stockholm Urban Assessment', unpublished report.
4. Jacobs, Jane, *Cities and the Wealth of Nations*, Vintage Books, New York, 1985.
5. Castells, Manuel, *The Rise of the Network Society*, Blackwell, Oxford, 1996.
6. Greater London Group, 'London's Size and Diversity', London School of Economics, London, 1996.
7. United Nations, *The Habitat Agenda*, New York, 1996.
8. Wackernagel, Mathis, and Rees, William, *Our Ecological Footprint: Reducing Human Impact on the Earth*, New Society, Gabriola Island, 1996.
9. The International Institute for Sustainable Development, 'Urban and Ecological Footprints', www.gdrc.org/uem/footprints/.
10. Girardet, Herbert, 'Getting London in Shape for 2000', London First, 1996, unpublished report.
11. City Limits London, www.citylimitslondon.com.
12. WWF, 'Living Planet Report 2002, Summary', www.panda.org/downloads/general/LPR2002Summary.pdf.
13. Folke, C. *et al.,* 'Ecosystem Appropriation by Cities', *Ambio Magazine*, 1997.
14. Campanale, Mark, personal communication, London.
15. Worldwatch Institute Washington, *State of the World 1999*, W.W. Norton, New York, 1999.
16. Fearnside, Philip, INPA, Manaus, Brazil, www.inpa.gov.br.
17. 'Feeding 9 billion', *People's Planet* TV series, CNN, Discovery Channel, 2001.
18. Brown, Lester, from an interview for the *People's Planet* TV series, CNN, Discovery Channel, 2001.
19. Steffen, W. *et al.,* *Global Change and the Earth System*, Springer, Berlin, 2003, pp 120 and 243.
20. Kalundborg website, www.symbiosis.dk.
21. Girardet, Herbert, 'Creating a Sustainable Adelaide', www.planning.sa.gov.au/csa/report.pdf.

CHAPTER 7

1. Gadher, Dipesh, *Sunday Times*, London, 26 February 2004.
2. Worldwatch Institute, *Vital Signs*, W.W. Norton, New York, 2002.
3. 'Bangkok to Combat Traffic Congestion', BBC News 21 December 2001, http://news.bbc.co.uk/2/hi/asia-pacific/1723804.stm.
4. 'Delhi's Bold Plan for Traffic Free Streets', BBC News, 14 October 2003, http://news.bbc.co.uk/1/hi/world/south_asia/3155484.stm.
5. Downton, Paul, 'Cities for a Greenhouse World', Urban Ecology Australia, www.urbanecology.org.au/articles/citiesforgreenhouse/index.html.
6. Knoflacher, Hermann, *Zur Harmonie von Verkehr und Stadt*, Boehlau Verlag, Vienna, 1993.
7. Olson, Martha, in *Race, Poverty and the Environment*, Fall 1995.
8. Banister, David, and Pucher, John, 'Can Sustainable Transport Be Made Politically Acceptable?', 83rd TRB Conference, 12 January 2004.
9. Channel News Asia, 23–1-04, www.channelnewsasia.com/stories/afp_asia-pacific/view/67591/1/.html.
10. Alexander's Gas and Oil Connections, www.gasandoil.com/goc/news/nts 32806.htm.
11. China People's Daily, 24 March 2004, http://english.peopledaily.com.cn/200403/24/eng20040324_138304.shtml.
12. Environment and Forecasting Institute in Heidelberg, *Oeko-Bilanz eines Autolebens*, Heidelberg, December 2003.
13. Sprawlcity, www.sprawlcity.org.
14. Environmental News Network, 'Sprawling Solutions', www.enn.com/features/1999/10/102999/sprawl3_5917.asp.
15. Car Cities, www.eoc.csiro.au/lb/lbbook/urban/yb2.htm.
16. Marketing Science Centre, University of Adelaide, 'Effectiveness Testing Report of Proposed Cycling Strategies for Metropolitan Adelaide', 1996.
17. South Australia's Draft Transport Plan, April 2003.
18. City Living, www.adelaidecitycouncil.com/Council/publications/Dev_Info/CITYLIVING.pdf.
19. Gehl, Jan, 'Public Spaces and Public Life', City of Adelaide, 2002.
20. *Federal Bank of Boston Regional Review 2000*, www.bos.frb.org/economic/nerr/rr2000/q1/wass00.htm.
21. Johnson, Elmer, 'Collision Course: Can Cities Avoid a Transportation Pileup?', *American City & County*, March 1994.
22. Federal Reserve Bank of Boston, *Regional Review 2000*, Vol. 10. No. 1 www.bos.frb.org/economic/nerr/rr2000/q1/wass00_1.htm.
23. Mehaffly, Michael, 'Orenco Station, Hillsboro, Oregon', *Terrain.org, Journal for the Built Environment*, Issue 10, www.terrain.org/unsprawl/10/.

24. Lerner, Jaime, interview for the TV series *People's Planet*, CNN and Discovery Channel.

25. Zurich Public Transport Policy, www.epe.be/workbooks/tcui/example6.html.

26. UN Habitat Best Practices Programme, www.bestpractices.org.

27. Gehl, Jan and Gemzoe, Lars, *New City Spaces*, The Danish Architectural Press, Copenhagen, 2000.

28. Knoflacher, Hermann, *Zur Harmonie von Verkehr und Stadt*, Boehlau Verlag, Vienna, 1993.

29. Walkable Communities Inc., Florida.

30. Electric Cars, www.electriccars.com/; Automotive Intelligence News, www. autointell.com/news-2000/May-2000/May-23–00-p5.htm.

CHAPTER 8

1. Olmstead, Fredrick Law, *Basic Principles of Planning*, New York, 1870.

2. Owen, Robert, *A New View of Society* [1816], Macmillan, London, 1973.

3. Robert Owen website, www.robert-owen.com/.

4. Buckingham, James Silk, *National Evils and Practical Remedies with the Plan of a Model Town*, Peter Jackson, Late Fisher, Son, & Co., London, 1849.

5. Bournville Village Trust, www.bvt.org.uk/.

6. Howard, Ebenezer, *Garden Cities of Tomorrow*, Faber and Faber, London, 1902.

7. Hetherington, Peter, 'Rebirth for Decaying 1950s New Town', *The Guardian*, 21 July 2003.

8. Olmstead, Fredrick Law, *Basic Principles of Planning*, Introduction, New York, 1870.

9. Le Corbusier, *The Modulor*, Faber and Faber, London, 1954.

10. Trachtenberg, Marvin, and Hyman, Isabelle, *Architecture: From Prehistory to Post-Modernism*, Prentice-Hall, Englewood Cliffs, NJ, 1986.

11. Tony Milburn, from an interview for the Channel 4 TV series *Deadline*, 2000.

12. Rogers, Richard, 'Introduction' to Gehl, Jan, and Gemzoe, Lars, *New City Spaces*, The Danish Architectural Press, Copenhagen, 2000.

13. Congress of the New Urbanists Charter, http://user.gru.net/domz/charter.htm.

14. Alexander, Christopher, *The Nature of Order*, Book 3, Centre for Environmental Structure, Berkeley, CA, 2003.

15. Odón, Elorza, Mayor of San Sebastián, Northern Spain.

16. Desai, Pooran, and Riddlestone, Sue, *Bioregional Solutions*, Schumacher Briefing 9, Green Books, Dartington, 2002.

17. Enrique Peñalosa, Mayor of Bogotá, http://pps.org/topics/whyneed/newvisions/penalosa_speech_2001.

18. Ecovillages Network, http://gen.ecovillage.org/.
19. *Tao Te Ching*, translated by Peter Merel, www.clas.ufl.edu/users/gthursby/taoism/ttcmerel.htm.
20. Aldinga Arts EcoVillage, South Adelaide, www.aldinga-artsecovillage.com.au/.

CHAPTER 9

1. Heede, R., Rocky Mountain Institute, Snowmass, Colorado, personal communication.
2. Flavin, Chris, 'Reinventing the Energy System', in *State of the World 1999*, W.W. Norton, New York, 1999.
3. Flavin, Chris and Dunn, Seth, *Rising Sun, Gathering Winds—Policies to Stabilise the Climate and Strengthen Economies*, Worldwatch Institute, Washington, 1997.
4. Duerr, Hans-Peter, Global Challengers Network, personal communication.
5. Schumacher, E.F., *This I Believe*, Green Books, Dartington, Devon, 1999.
6. Intergovernmental Panel on Climate Change, www.ipcc.ch/pub/un/syreng/spm.pdf.
7. Department of Trade and Industry, 'Our Energy Future—Creating a Low Carbon Economy', Energy White Paper, DTI London, February 2003.
8. Reuters, 'Planet Ark', 22 January 2001.
9. KPMG, 'Solar PV Electricity Can Be Competitive with Conventional Power in the Short-term', KPMG Business Analysis for Greenpeace, September 1999.
10. International Council For Local Environmental Initiatives, www.iclei.org/co2.
11. Energy Savings Trust, *Meeting the Challenge to Safeguard Our Future*, London, 1992.
12. Girardet, Herbert, *Studies of the Green Sector in Four European Cities*, London Development Agency, 2003.
13. Australasian Energy Performance Contracting Association, www.aepca.asn.au/.
14. National Energy Action, Newcastle, 1997.
15. Energy Savings Trust, *Meeting the Challenge to Safeguard Our Future*, London, 1992.
16. Combined Heat and Power Association, London, 1998.
17. Nijkamp, Peter and Perrels, Adriaan, *Sustainable Cities in Europe*, Earthscan, London, 1994.
18. *Grower Magazine*, London, 21 March 1996.
19. Flavin, Chris, *Power Surge: Guide to the Coming Energy Revolution*, W.W. Norton & Co., New York, 1994.

20. Barcelona Ordinance, An Application of Solar Thermal Systems into Buildings, www.uniseo.org/wordpdf/barcelona.pdf.
21. The Solarserver, Forum for Solar Energy, www.solarserver.de/index-e.html.
22. Beasley Industries, Adelaide, www.beasley.com.au.
23. The Solarserver, Forum for Solar Energy, www.solarserver.de/index-e.html.
24. Saman, Wasim, University of South Australia, personal communication.
25. Flavin, Chris, President, World Watch Institute, interview for the *People's Planet* TV series.
26. Fast Solar Energy Facts, Solar Energy Germany, www.solarbuzz.com/Fast FactsGermany.htm.
27. Los Angeles Department of Water and Power, www.ladwp.com/ladwp/home page.jsp.
28. Danish Wind Industry Association, www.windpower.org/en/faqs.htm.
29. Blue Energy, Canada, www.bluenergy.com.
30. Elliot, David, *A Solar World: Climate Change and the Green Energy Revolution*, Schumacher Briefing 10, Green Books, Dartington, Devon, 2003.
31. Greenpeace, www.greenpeace.org.au/climate/archive/nonewoil/jobsbrief.html.
32. From an interview for the *People's Planet* TV series.

CHAPTER 10

1. Lebow, Victor, *Journal of Retailing*, Spring, 1955.
2. London Western Riverside Authority, Annual Report, 1991–2.
3. London Waste Management Strategy, www.london.gov.uk/mayor/strategies/waste/index.jsp.
4. *Time*, 'Remains of the Day', www.time.com/time/covers/1101020909/land fill/5.html.
5. From the documentary series *People's Planet*, CNN, 2000.
6. *Gotham Gazette*, 'Garbage after Fresh Kills', www.gothamgazette.com/iotw/garbage.
7. *CounterPunch*, 20 September 1992.
8. Friends of the Earth, UK, Press Release, 5 January 2001.
9. Worldwatch Paper 121, Washington, 1994.
10. Tangri, Neil, *Waste Incineration: A Dying Industry Technology*, www.no-burn.org/resources/summary/English.pdf.
11. ICLEI, *The Local Agenda 21 Planning Guide*, Toronto, 1996.
12. EcoProfit, Graz, www.graz.at/umwelt/down/oeKOPROFIT97.pdf.
13. European Commission, 'Waste Policy', http://europa.eu.int/comm/environment/waste/index.htm.
14. Zero Waste America, Philadelphia, Personal communication.

15. Dr Gerhard Gilnreiner, Vienna, personal communication.

16. Repair and Service Centre RUSZ, Schanzstrasse 20–22, A-1150 Vienna, Austria.

17. Copenhagen Environmental Protection Agency, Flaesketorvet 68, Koben-haven V.

18. Metropolitan Adelaide Waste Plan.

19. Jeffries, Lachlan, Jeffries Group, Adelaide, Personal communication.

20. The Mega-Cities Project, *Environmental Justice, Promising Solutions at the Intersection of Environment and Poverty*, New York, 1994.

21. Murray, Robin, *Zero Waste*, Greenpeace, London, 2002.

22. Zero Waste, New Zealand, www.zerowaste.co.nz/.

23. 'No Waste by 2010', Canberra, www.nowaste.act.gov.au/.

24. Global Renewables, Sydney, www.energydirectory.com.au/companies/grl.htm.

25. Zero Waste Alliance, USA, www.zerowaste.org/#what.

26. McDonough, William and Braungart, Michael, *Cradle to Cradle: Remaking the Way We Make Things*, North Point Press, New York, 2002.

CHAPTER 11

1. Barlow, Maude and Clarke, Tony, *Blue Gold: The Fight to Stop the Corporate Theft of the World's Water*, W.W. Norton, New York, 2002.

2. Brown, Lester, 'Water is Fuelling a Food Bubble', www.peopleandplanet.net/doc.php?id=1901.

3. Barlow, Maude and Clarke, Tony, *Blue Gold: The Fight to Stop the Corporate Theft of the World's Water*, W.W. Norton, New York, 2002.

4. Vidal, John, 'Blue Gold: Earth's Liquid Asset', *The Guardian*, 22 August 2002.

5. *Mono Lake Newsletter*, www.monolake.org/newsletter/00spring/9.htm.

6. Sunset Cities, www.sunsetcities.com/hoover-dam.html.

7. Schall, Dan, 'Aswan High Dam, Construction, Effect on Egyptian Life and Agriculture, and Environmental Impacts', www.ems.psu.edu/academic/cause2001/schall.doc.

8. International Rivers Network, www.irn.org/programs/threeg/index.shtml.

9. Kishwar, Madhu, 'The Controversial Tehri Dam in the Himalayas', http://free.freespeech.org/manushi/tehri/tehri.html

10. Platt, Rutherford *et al.*, 'A Full Clean Glass?', *Environment*, June 2000.

11. Kreimer, A. *et al.*, 'Rio de Janeiro: In Search of Sustainability', World Bank Paper 195, *Towards a Sustainable Urban Environment: The Rio de Janeiro Study*, World Bank, Washington, 1993.

12. Wessex Water, www.biogrannatural.co.uk/pages/other/links.html.

13. *Time*, 22 March 1999
14. Ocean Arks, www.oceanarks.org.
15. River Murray Forum, Parliament House, Adelaide, 25 February 2003.
16. www.clw.csiro.au/education/groundwater/south_australia.html.
17. Bellette, Kathryn, Adelaide City Council, personal communication.
18. Urban Agriculture Magazine, No. 3, 2001, www.ruaf.org/1–3/30–32.html.
19. Ghosh, Dhrubajyoti, 'Integrated Wetland Systems for Wastewater Treatment and Recycling', RHUDO/USAID, New Delhi.

CHAPTER 12

1. Girardet, Herbert, *Creating Sustainable Cities*, Green Books, Dartington, 1999.
2. Halweil, Brian, 'Home Grown: The Case for Local Food in a Global Market', Worldwatch Paper 163, Worldwatch Institute, Washington, 2002.
3. Sustain, 'London, Eating Oil', www.sustainweb.org/pdf/eatoil_pr.PDF.
4. Kropotkin, Peter, *Field, Factories and Workshops* [1899], George, Allen and Unwin, London, 1974.
5. UNDP, *Urban Agriculture*, New York, 1996.
6. Deelstra, Tjeerd and Girardet, Herbert, 'Urban Agriculture and Sustainable Cities', in Bakker, N. *et al.*, *Growing Cities, Growing Food: Urban Agriculture on the Policy Agenda*, RUAF, 2000.
7. Jeavons, John, *How to Grow More Vegetables than You Ever Thought Possible on Less Land than You Can Imagine*, Ten Speed Press, Berkeley, CA, 1982.
8. US Embassy Beijing, 'China's Farmland Loss Rings Alarm Bells', 1997, www.fas.org/spp/guide/china/earth/landloss.htm.
9. Choi, Songsu, 'Urban Development in China', World Bank, 2001, www.world bank.org/wbi/sdenveconomics/udm/docs/M1S1ChoiSongsuEN&CN.pdf.
10. Yi-Zhong, Cai and Zanghen, Zhang, 'Shanghai: Trends Towards Specialised and Capital-Intensive Urban Agriculture', in Bakker, N. *et al.*, *Growing Cities, Growing Food: Urban Agriculture on the Policy Agenda*, RUAF, 2000.
11. Liu, Evan, Shanghai City Council, personal communication.
12. Wolf, J. *et al.*, 'Urban and peri-urban agriculture in Beijing', *Environment and Urbanization*, Vol. 15, No. 2, 2003.
13. Environmental News Network, 'Sprawling Solutions', www.enn.com/features/1999/10/102999/sprawl3_5917.asp.
14. Ginsburg, Norton and McGee, Terry, *The Extended Metropolis: Settlement Transition in Asia*, University of Hawai'i Press, Honolulu, 1991.
15. Kovaleski, Serge F., 'Cuba Goes Green, Government-Run Vegetable Gardens Sprout in Cities Across Island', *Washington Post*, 26 November 1999, www.cityfarmer.org/CubaGreen.html.

16. Reuters, 'Cuba exports city farming "revolution" to Venezuela', 22 April 2003, www.globalexchange.org/countries/cuba/sustainable/651.html.

17. Research Development Centre, 'Reusing Organic Solid Waste in Urban Farming in African Cities', http://web.idrc.ca/en/ev-33948–201–1DO_TOPIC. html.

18. Gertel, Joerg and Samir, Said, Cairo's Urban Agriculture, www.ruaf.org/ reader/growing_cities/Cairo.PDF.

19. Afrol News 27–2-02, South African urban desert transformed, www.afrol. com/News2002/sa013_cape_flats.htm.

20. City Farmer, www.cityfarmer.org/potatocentre.html.

21. City Farmer, 'Urban Agriculture in Mexico City', www.cityfarmer.org/ mexico.html.

22. The Garden Project, San Francisco, www.saturdaymarket.com/garden.htm.

23. UNDP, *Urban Agriculture*, New York, 1996.

CHAPTER 13

1. City Journal, Winter, 2000, www.city-journal.org/html/10_1_how_cities.html.

2. City Journal, Winter, 2000, www.city-journal.org/html/10_1_how_cities.html.

3. The Carbon Gap, http://aceee.org/press/carbgap.jpg.

4. The Earth Council, 'Ranking the Ecological Footprint of Nations', www. ecouncil.ac.cr/rio/focus/report/english/footprint/ranking.htm.

5. American Wind Energy Association, Energy Innovations: A Prosperous Path to a Clean Environment, www.awea.org/faq/co2econ.html.

6. Environment News Service, 11–7–03, 'U.S. C02 Emissions Will Rise Absent Strong Policy', www.ieta.org/Library_Links/IETAEnvNews/Jul11_Pew.htm.

7. UN Habitat Best Practices and Urban Leadership Programme, www.best pactices.org.

8. ICLEI Case Studies database, www2.iclei.org/iclei/casestud.htm.

9. European Academy of the Urban Environment SURBAN database, www. eaue.de/.

10. Landry, Charles, www.comedia.org.uk/themes-4.htm.

11. Downton, Paul, 'Cities for a Greenhouse World, Urban Ecology Australia', www.urbanecology.org.au/articles/citiesforgreenhouse/index.html.

12. Battle McCarthy, Multidisciplinary Engineering: Capability Statement, London, 2001, www.battlemccarthy.com/.

13. Atkisson, Alan, 'Introducing "RUrbanism": The Goa 2100 Project by Aromar Revi, Rahul Mehrotra, Sanjay Prakash, and G.K. Bhat', unpublished report.

Bibliography

Alexander, Christopher, *The Nature of Order*, Book 3, Centre for Environmental Structure, Berkeley, 2003

Atkisson, Alan, 'Introducing "RUrbanism": The Goa 2100 Project by Aromar Revi, Rahul Mehrotra, Sanjay Prakash, and G.K. Bhat', unpublished report

Auguet, R., *Cruelty and Civilization: the Roman Games*, Routledge, London, 1994

Barbaro, Nicolo, *Diary of the Siege of Constantinople in 1453*, translated by Jones, J.R., Exposition Press, New York, 1969

Barlow, Maude and Clarke, Tony, *Blue Gold: The Fight to Stop the Corporate Theft of the World's Water*, W.W. Norton, New York, 2002

Benevolo, Leonardo, *The History of the City*, Scolar Press, London, 1980

Buckingham, James Silk, *National Evils and Practical Remedies with the Plan of a Model Town*, Peter Jackson, Late Fisher, Son, & Co., London, 1849

Carter, V. D. and Dale, T., *Topsoil and Civilisation*, University of Oklahoma Press, Norman, 1974

Castells, Manuel, *The Network Society*, Blackwell, Oxford, 1996

Chevalier, Raymond, *Sciences et Techniques a Rome*, Presses Univertaires de France, Paris, 1993

Cities Alliance, *Cities Without Slums*, Annual Report, World Bank, Washington, 2002

Colding, J. *et al.*, 'The Stockholm Urban Assessment', unpublished report

Constanza, Robert *et al.*, 'The Value of the World's Ecosystem Services and Natural Capital', *Nature* 387: 253–60, 1997

Critchfield, Richard, *Villages*, Anchor Press, Doubleday, New York, 1981

Davis, Mike, *Urban Control: The Ecology of Fear*, Open Magazine Pamphlet Series, 4, Westfield, New Jersey, 1994

Deelstra, Tjeerd and Girardet, Herbert, 'Urban Agriculture and Sustainable Cities', in Bakker, N. *et al.*, *Growing Cities, Growing Food, Urban Agriculture on the Policy Agenda*, RUAF, 2000

Department of Trade and Industry, *Our Energy Future – Creating a Low Carbon Economy*, Energy White Paper, DTI, London, February 2003

Desai, Pooran and Riddlestone, Sue, *Bioregional Solutions*, Schumacher Briefing 9, Green Books, Dartington, 2002

De Vries, B. and Goudsblom, J. (eds), *Mappa Mundi, Humans and their Habitats in a Long-Term Socio-Ecological Perspectice*, Amsterdam University Press, Amsterdam, 2002

Devore, Irven and Lee, Richard, *Man the Hunter*, Aldine, Chicago, 1968

Elliot, David, *A Solar World, Climate Change and the Green Energy Revolution*, Schumacher Briefing 10, Green Books, Dartington, 2003

Energy Savings Trust, 'Meeting the Challenge to Safeguard Our Future', London, 1992

Engels, Friedrich, *The Condition of the Working Class in England in 1844*, Swan Sonnenschein & Co., London, 1892

Environment and Forecasting Institute in Heidelberg, Oeko-Bilanz eines Autolebens, Heidelberg, 12–2003

Flannery, Tim, *The Future Easters*, Grove Press, New York, 1994

Flavin, Chris, *Reinventing the Energy System, in State of the World 1999*, W.W. Norton, New York, 1999

Flavin, Chris and Dunn, Seth, *Rising Sun, Gathering Winds – Policies to Stabilise the Climate and Strengthen Economies*, Worldwatch Institute, Washington, 1997

Galeano, Eduardo, *The Open Veins of Latin America, Five Centuries of the Pillage of a Continent*, Latin America Bureau, 1998

Gehl, Jan, *Public Spaces and Public Life*, City of Adelaide, 2002

Gehl, Jan and Gemzoe, Lars, *New City Spaces*, The Danish Architectural Press, Copenhagen, 2000

Ginsburg, Norton and McGee, Terry, *The Extended Metropolis: Settlement Transition in Asia*, University of Hawai'i Press, Honolulu, 1991

Girardet, Herbert, 'Getting London in Shape for 2000', London First, 1996, unpublished report

Girardet, Herbert, *Creating Sustainable Cities*, Schumacher Briefing 2, Green Books, Dartington, 1999

Girardet, Herbert, *Studies of the Green Sector in Four European Cities*, London Development Agency, 2003

Gomme, A.W., *The Population of Athens in the Fifth and Fourth Centuries B.C.*, Basuil Blackwell, Oxford, 1933

Goodwin, Jason, *Otis: Giving Rise to the Modern City, A History of the Otis Elevator Company*, Ivan R. Dee Publisher, Chicago, 2001

Gordon, Robert and Malone, Patrick, *The Texture of Industry, An Archaeological View of the Industrialization of North America*, Oxford University Press, Oxford, 1997

Gorelick, Steven, *Small is Beautiful, Big is Subsidised*, ISEC, Week, Dartington, 1998

Grant, Lindy and Bates, David (eds), *Abbot Suger of St-Denis, Church and State in Early Twelfth-century France*, Longman, London, 1998

Hahn, Hermann and Langbein, Fritz, *Fünfzig Jahre Berliner Stadtentwässerung 1878–1928*, Verlag Alfred Metzner, Berlin, 1928

Hallberg, Milton C., *Economic Trend in US Agriculture and World Food Systems since World War II*, Iowa State University Press, Ames, 2001

Halweil, Brian, 'Home Grown: The Case For Local Food In A Global Market', Worldwatch Paper 163, Worldwatch Institute, Washington, 2002

Hardoy, Jorge, Mitlin, Diana and Satterthwaite, David, *Environmental Problems in Third World Cities*, Earthscan Publications, London, 1992

Hodge, A.T., *Roman Aqueducts and Water Supply*, London, Duckworth, 1992

Howard, Ebenezer, *Garden Cities of Tomorrow*, Faber and Faber, London, 1902

Huntington, Ellsworth, *Civilization and Climate,* New Haven, Yale University Press, 1921

Jacobs, Jane, *Cities and the Wealth of Nations*, Vintage Books, New York, 1985

Jeavons, John, *How to Grow More Vegetables: Than You Ever Thought Possible on Less Land than You Can Imagine*, Ten Speed Press, Berkeley, CA, 1982

Jevons, William Stanley, *The Coal Question* [1865], Augustus M. Kelley, New York, 1965

Joplin, John and Girardet, Herbert, *Creating a Sustainable London*, Sustainable London Trust, London, 1997

Knoflacher, Hermann, *Zur Harmonie von Verkehr und Stadt*, Boehlau Verlag, Vienna, 1993

Kropotkin, Peter, *Field, Factories and Workshops* [1899], George, Allen and Unwin, London, 1974

Kramer, Samuel Noah, *The Sumerians*, Chicago University Press, Chicago, 1963

Kreimer, A. *et al.*, 'Rio de Janeiro: In Search of Sustainability', World Bank Paper 195, Towards A Sustainable Urban Environment: The Rio de Janeiro Study, World Bank, Washington, 1993

Louw, Antoinette *et al.*, *Crime in Johannesburg*, Institute for Security Studies, ISS Monograph Series No. 18, February 1998

N'Dow, Wally, in Kirdar, Uener (ed.), *Cities Fit for People*, United Nations Publications, New York, 1997

McDonough, William and Braungart, Michael, *Cradle to Cradle: Remaking the Way We Make Things*, North Point Press, New York, 2002

McGranahan, Gordon *et al.*, Sustainability, Poverty and Urban Environmental Transitions, in Satterthwaite, David (ed.), *Sustainable Cities*, Earthscan Publications, London, 1999

Mardon, Roy and Jopling, John, *Gaian Democracies, Redefining Globalisation and People Power*, Schumacher Briefing 9, Green Books, Dartington, 2003

Mellaart, James, *Catal-Huyuk, A Neolithic Town in Anatolia*, McGraw-Hill, New York, 1967

Menzies, Gavin, *1421, The Year China Discovered the World*, Bantam Press, London, 2002

Meyer, Aubery, *Contraction and Convergence, The Global Solution to Climate Change*, Schumacher Briefing 5, Green Books, Dartington, 2000

Miller, Hugh, *The Old Red Sandstone or New Walks in an Old Field*, John Johnstone, Edinburgh, 1841

Milward, S., *Urban Harvest*, Geographical Publications, London, 1987

Mumford, Louis, *The City in History*, Pelican Books, London, 1966

O'Meara, Molly, 'Reinventing Cities', Worldwatch Paper 147, Worldwatch Institute, Washington, 1999

Owen, Robert, *A New View Of Society* [1816], Macmillan, London, 1973

Perlin, John, *A Forest Journey, The Role of Wood in the Development of Civilization*, Harvard University Press, Cambridge and London, 1991

Platt, Rutherford *et al.*, 'A Full Clean Glas?', *Environment*, June 2000

Pliny the Elder, *Natural History*, Loeb Classical Library, Harvard University Press, Cambridge and London, 1989

Ponting, Clive, *A Green History of the World*, Penguin Books, London, 1991

Raven, Susan, *Rome in Africa*, Longman, London, 1984

Register, Richard, *Ecocities, Building Cities in Balance with Nature*, Berkeley Hill Books, Berkeley, 2002

Richardson, Benjamin Ward, *Hygeia, a City of Health*, London, 1876

Sahlins, Marshall, *Stone Age Economics*, Aldine de Gruyter, Chicago, 1972

Sassen, Saskia, *Cities in a World Economy*, Pine Forge Press, Thousand Oaks, CA, 2000

Sassen, Saskia, *Cities in the Global Economy*, in Handbook of Urban Studies, ed. Paddison, Ronan, Sage Publications, Thousand Oaks, CA, 2001

Scheer, Hermann, *The Solar Economy, Renewable Energy for a Sustainable Global Future*, Earthscan Publications, London, 2002

Schofield, Robert, *Lunar Society of Birmingham*, Oxford University Press, Oxford, 1963

Schumacher, E.F., *This I Believe*, Green Books, Dartington, Devon, 1999

Seymour, John and Girardet, Herbert, *Far From Paradise*, BBC Publications, Lodnon, 1986

Sit, Victor (ed.), *Chinese Cities, The Growth of the Metropolis since 1949*, Oxford University Press, Oxford, 1988

Steffen, W. *et al.*, *Global Change and the Earth System*, Springer, Berlin, 2003

The Mega-Cities Project, Environmental Justice, Promising Solutions At The Intersection of Environment and Poverty, New York, 1994

Thuenen, Johann Heinrich von, *The Isolated State*, Loyola University Press, Chicago, 1960

Trachtenberg, Marvin and Hyman, Isabelle, *Architecture, from Prehistory to Post-Modernism*, Prentice-Hall, Englewood Cliffs, NJ, 1986

UNCHS, *Cities in a Globalising World, Global Report on Human Settlements*, Earthscan Publications, London, 2001

UNDP, Urban Agriculture, New York, 1996

UN Habitat, *An Urbanizing World, Global Report on Human Settlements*, Oxford University Press, Oxford, 1996

UN World Urbanisation Prospects, New York, 1999

Volti, Rudi, *Steam Engine, The Encyclopaedia of Science, Technology, and Society*, Facts on File, New York, 1999

Wackernagel, Mathis and Rees, William, *Our Ecological Footprint*, New Society, Philadelphia, PA, 1996

Worldwatch Institute, *The State of the World, 1996*, Earthscan, London, 1997

Worldwatch Institute Washington, *State of the World 1999*, W.W. Norton, New York, 1999

Worldwatch Institute, *Vital Signs*, W.W. Norton, New York, 2002

Wolf, J. *et al.*, 'Urban and peri-urban agriculture in Beijing', *Environment and Urbanization*, Vol. 15, No. 2, 2003

Weizsaecker, Ernst von and Lovins, Amory, *Factor Four*, Earthscan Publications, London, 1997

Whitehouse, Ruth, *The First Cities*, Phaidon, Oxford, 1977

Wohl, Anthony, *The Eternal Slum: Housing and Social Policy in Victorian London*, Edward Arnold and McGill-Queens University Press, 1977

Woolley, C. Leonard, *Excavations at Ur,* Apollo Editions, New York, 1965

WWF, Living Planet Index, 2002

Yi-Zhong, Cai, and Zanghen, Zhang, *Shanghai: Trends Towards Specialised and Capital–Intensive Urban Agriculture*, in Bakker, N. *et al.*, *Growing Cities, Growing Food, Urban Agriculture on the Policy Agenda*, RUAF, 2000

PHOTOGRAPHIC CREDITS

Index